LITERARY
TRANSCENDENTALISM

STYLE AND VISION IN
THE AMERICAN RENAISSANCE

LAWRENCE BUELL

LITERARY
TRANSCENDENTALISM

Style and Vision in the
American Renaissance

LITERARY
TRANSCENDENTALISM

Style and Vision in the
American Renaissance

LAWRENCE BUELL

Cornell Paperbacks

CORNELL UNIVERSITY PRESS
Ithaca and London

TO MY FAMILY

Acknowledgments

This book owes its existence to a succession of teachers who showed me the possibilities of literary study by example as well as prescription. For support and criticism in my studies of Transcendentalism, I am grateful to James McConkey, G. Ferris Cronkhite, Walter Slatoff, and especially Jonathan Bishop. Equally important has been Arthur Mizener's constant encouragement through the years.

To Oberlin College I am indebted for support (through a leave of absence and two grants-in-aid) to pursue research. The George and Eliza Howard Foundation also supported my research with a generous grant in 1969–1970.

My colleagues Dewey Ganzel, Robert Pierce, and John Olmsted read portions of this manuscript at various stages of its evolution and contributed valuable insights. Richard Brown, in many long conversations, helped my understanding of New England history. I am also indebted to former Oberlin students for suggestions on a number of topics, especially to Suzanne Bernstein, Dan Campbell, and Bruce Nygren. Ms. Bernstein also served as my research assistant in 1971.

The officers of several libraries have given me permission to examine and quote from manuscripts in their possession. Quotations from manuscripts by Emerson, Thoreau, A. Bronson Alcott, and William Ellery Channing II are by permission of the Harvard College Library. The Massachusetts Historical Society has granted permission to quote from manuscripts by

Theodore Parker and Christopher Cranch; the Andover-Harvard Theological Library of the Harvard Divinity School, from Theodore Parker; the Boston Public Library, from Elizabeth Peabody; and the Wellesley College Library, from Jones Very. For permission to quote from manuscripts by Emerson, Alcott, Channing, and Cranch I am indebted also to the Ralph Waldo Emerson Memorial Association, to Mrs. F. Wolsey Pratt, to Mr. Laurence M. Channing, and to Mrs. Emerson Evans, respectively.

Doubleday & Company, Inc., has granted permission to reprint "A Transcendental Conversation" from *The American Transcendentalists,* edited by Perry Miller.

Earlier versions of a few portions of this book appeared in *American Quarterly* (1968, 1972) and in *American Transcendental Quarterly* (1971). I am grateful to the editors for permission to use this material here.

I am grateful also to the staff of the Oberlin College Stenographic Services Department for typing my manuscript.

Finally, I have dedicated this book to my family, to whom I owe much more than any public acknowledgment can tell.

LAWRENCE BUELL

Oberlin, Ohio

Contents

Abbreviations

JA   *The Journals of Bronson Alcott.* Selected and edited by Odell Shepard. Boston: Little, Brown, 1938.

JE   *Journals of Ralph Waldo Emerson.* 10 vols. Edited by Edward Emerson and Waldo Emerson Forbes. Boston: Houghton Mifflin, 1909–1914.

JMN   *The Journals and Miscellaneous Notebooks of Ralph Waldo Emerson.* 8 vols. to date. Cambridge: Harvard University Press, 1960——.

JT   *The Journal of Henry D. Thoreau.* 14 vols. Edited by Bradford Torrey and Francis H. Allen. Boston: Houghton Mifflin, 1906.

Ossoli   *Memoirs of Margaret Fuller Ossoli.* 2 vols. Edited by James Freeman Clarke, Ralph Waldo Emerson, and William H. Channing. Boston: Phillips, Sampson, 1852.

Tr   *The Transcendentalists: An Anthology.* Edited by Perry Miller. Cambridge: Harvard University Press, 1950.

W   *The Complete Works of Ralph Waldo Emerson.* 12 vols. Edited by Edward W. Emerson. Boston: Houghton Mifflin, 1903–1904.

Wa   Henry Thoreau. *Walden.* Edited by J. Lyndon Shanley. Princeton: Princeton University Press, 1971.

Wr   *The Writings of Henry David Thoreau,* vols. I–VI. Boston: Houghton Mifflin, 1906.

LITERARY
TRANSCENDENTALISM

*Style and Vision in the
American Renaissance*

Introduction

The purpose of this book is to survey the literary art and criticism of the American Transcendentalists and to contribute in the process to a better understanding of the relationship between style and vision in all nonfictional literature.

Most of what the Transcendentalists wrote falls into this category of nonfictional literature, presenting a mixture of piety, poetry, and sententiousness that is neither art nor argument but a compound of both. Their criticism shows a similar ambivalence. Largely for this reason, their aesthetic is still imperfectly understood, even though much scholarship has been devoted to various aspects of the movement. It is relatively easy, for example, to picture Emerson as a romanticized descendant of Jonathan Edwards or as a harbinger of America's literary independence; it is harder to explain how his combination of the roles of clergyman and poet distinguishes his work in its own right, because he did not realize either role in a profound or consistent way. Compared to the great European romantics, Emerson seems provincial and inhibited; compared to Edwards, he seems dilettantish, a gourmet of spiritual ideas. The Transcendentalist movement as a whole, by the same token, has appealed to scholars more as a symptom of New England's intellectual flowering —or decay—than for its intrinsic merits as a body of literature or as a system of thought.

From one point of view this consensus is justified: undoubtedly Emerson and his circle *are* more important for historical reasons than for the quality of their achievements in art, philosophy, and theology. As is often pointed out, however, their stature increases when one considers them as "thinkers" or "prophets" rather than in terms of a particular intellectual discipline. One then begins to get caught up in the excitement of their vision; their very lack of discipline begins to seem a source of greatness; and it is the critics of their impure art or shallow theology who begin to seem parochial. Even those readers who are fundamentally unsympathetic to Transcendentalist idealism often come to respect the suggestiveness, rhetorical power, and fineness of discernment in works like Emerson's "Self-Reliance" and Theodore Parker's *Discourse of the Transient and Permanent in Christianity*. Neither is fully satisfying as an exposition of theology or as a work of art, yet one feels that such classifications do not matter, that the two discourses are in any case impressive literary-religious performances.

Criticism needs to find better ways of measuring the qualities of such works, in order to account for the impression of excellence they convey and to explain their impact upon large numbers of readers both then and now. This book attempts such an inquiry. Through a combination of intellectual history, critical explication, and genre study, it undertakes to outline the nature and evolution of the Transcendentalists' characteristic literary aims and approaches, and the ways in which these express the authors' underlying principles or vision.

So far the word "Transcendentalism" has been used in a very general sense; to avoid confusion, it should be defined more precisely, since the term is notoriously vague.[1] "Vagueness" was in-

---

[1] Of the many short overviews of Transcendentalism, perhaps the most satisfactory are Howard Mumford Jones, "Transcendentalism and Emerson," in *Belief and Disbelief in American Literature* (Chicago: University of Chicago Press, 1967), pp. 48–69; and Alexander Kern, "The Rise of Transcendentalism, 1815–1860," in *Transitions in American Literary History*, ed. Harry Hayden Clark (Durham, N.C.: Duke University Press, 1953), pp. 245–315.

deed what "Transcendentalism" chiefly connoted in its first
popular usage in New England. As Le Corbusier has remarked
of the term "abstract" in art criticism, avant-garde movements
always have ridiculous names, because they are baptized by their
enemies; Transcendentalism was no exception. The label was
first applied in disparagement, to suggest outlandishness. The
implication of an organized school of thought with fixed doctrines was misleading: actually, the Transcendentalists had no
specific program or common cause, and their beliefs were often
in a state of flux. Some therefore refused to accept the rubric,
and those who did differed in their interpretations of it. James
Freeman Clarke called himself a Transcendentalist simply because he did "not believe that man's senses tell him all he
knows." [2] For George Ripley the term meant, more specifically,
a belief in "the supremacy of mind over matter" (*Tr*, p. 255).
Christopher Cranch, however, considered Transcendentalism as
nothing more than "that living and always new *spirit* of truth,
which is ever going forth on its conquests into the world" (*Tr*,
p. 301). Jonathan Saxton claimed that "every man is a transcendentalist"; [3] Emerson denied that there was such a thing as a
"pure Transcendentalist" (*W*, I, 338). Small wonder, then, that
at one time or another studies of every major Transcendentalist
have tried to disassociate their hero from the charge of Transcendentalism.[4]

Nevertheless, the term does have an accepted core of meaning,
which can be stated briefly and I think uncontroversially. Further ramifications are possible, and some will be introduced below, but for the moment a short working definition should
suffice.

[2] John Wesley Thomas, *James Freeman Clarke: Apostle of German Culture to America* (Boston: Luce, 1949), p. 131.

[3] "Prophecy—Transcendentalism—Progress," *Dial*, 2 (1841), 87.

[4] For a list of instances, see William R. Hutchison, *The Transcendentalist Ministers: Church Reform in the New England Renaissance* (New
Haven: Yale University Press, 1959), p. 28n. This book is the best available study of the theological and ecclesiastical aspects of Transcendentalism.

Historically, New England Transcendentalism can be viewed as one of many instances of the widespread religious ferment which took place in America during the first half of the nineteenth century.[5] As a self-conscious movement, Transcendentalism served as an expression of radical discontent within American Unitarianism (which, in turn, was a liberal movement within Congregationalism), arising from objections to Unitarian epistemology and the Lockean psychology upon which it was based. Locke held that all human knowledge is derived empirically, through the experience of the senses; the Unitarians, accepting this as a premise, held that God and his laws are apprehended by rational reflection on the natural creation and the revelations of scripture, rather than by direct intuition.[6] To the young Unitarian radicals of the 1820s and 1830s, however, this position was oppressive, for it seemed to cut man off from God. Stimulated by post-Kantian thought, as interpreted chiefly by Goethe, Carlyle, and especially Coleridge, they began about 1830 to contend, with the aid of a distinction adapted from Coleridge, that in addition to his "understanding" or capacity for empirical reasoning man has a higher mental faculty, or "Reason," which enables him to perceive spiritual truth in-

[5] For a general sense of the contemporary religious context of Transcendentalism, see Perry Miller, *The Life of the Mind in America, from the Revolution to the Civil War* (New York: Harcourt, 1965), Book I; Alice Felt Tyler, *Freedom's Ferment* (Minneapolis: University of Minnesota Press, 1944), Parts I and II; William Warren Sweet, *The Story of Religion in America* (New York: Harper, 1930), pp. 258–284; Winthrop Hudson, *Religion in America* (New York: Scribner, 1965), pp. 158–203.

[6] A thorough discussion of the Unitarians' relation to Locke would take into account discrepancies between them and Locke resulting from the fact that the Unitarians received his ideas largely through the medium of his Scottish successors, the so-called Common Sense School. See, for example, Edgeley Woodman Todd, "Philosophical Ideas at Harvard College, 1817–1837," *New England Quarterly*, 16 (1943), 63–90, and especially Daniel Howe, *The Unitarian Conscience: Harvard Moral Philosophy, 1805–1861* (Cambridge: Harvard University Press, 1970), pp. 27–44 and passim.

tuitively.[7] The Unitarians' idea of reason/understanding (they used the two terms interchangeably) was actually more liberal than their critics realized; as we shall see in Chapter 1, Unitarianism can be said to have paved the way for the radicals' position. Nevertheless the distinction made by the latter between two sharply differing mental faculties was a significantly new departure.

The concept of a higher Reason is the heart of what came to be called Transcendentalism. Those who recognized such a faculty sometimes called it by different names, such as "Spirit," "Mind," "Soul," and they also differed in the claims they made for it. For some Transcendentalists it was simply an inner light or conscience; for others is was the voice of God; for still others it was literally God himself immanent in man. Some regarded the informing spirit primarily as an impersonal cosmic force; others continued to think of it in traditional anthropomorphic terms. Ecclesiastically, the Transcendentalists ranged widely in their radicalism: James Freeman Clarke, William H. Furness, and Convers Francis were moderates who eventually became pillars of the Unitarian establishment; Jones Very claimed (briefly) that he was the new Messiah.[8] Though this might seem to have been an unacceptably nebulous situation, in fact the Transcendentalists did not differ among themselves as much as Kant did from some of his German successors.

The vagueness of the principle "uniting" the Transcendentalists seems to pose more of a problem when it comes to deciding who was a Transcendentalist and who was not. As we shall

[7] Precisely what Emerson and other Transcendentalists meant by the intuitive perception of truth is a nice question which is discussed at length in Chapter 2, below. In calling the intuitive faculty by the name of Reason, they were faced from the start with a semantic paradox which they never satisfactorily resolved.

[8] Individual Transcendentalists also differed markedly in their radicalism on specific issues. Thus Alcott insisted more than Emerson on the idea of immanence, but also retained a belief in a personal God, as did Very.

soon see, conservative Unitarians could sound quite transcendental when, in reaction against Calvinism, they praised reason and the moral sentiment. The idea of the authority of spiritual intuition also crops up in many contexts outside the Transcendentalist movement—as is to be expected, since mystical pietism was one of the most dynamic forces in the tradition of American evangelical Protestantism as a whole. Charles G. Finney, Horace Bushnell, Henry Ward Beecher, and John Greenleaf Whittier might all be called Transcendentalists of a sort. But these facts become troublesome only if one insists on placing a transitional figure like Channing either inside or outside the ranks, or on putting Emerson and Alcott in the same category with figures who had no direct connection with the original movement. The problem disappears if we think of Transcendentalism as a state of mind originating in a specific matrix—the reaction against rationalism within Unitarian thought—but emanating outward to stimulate such people as Whitman and Melville, and arising coincidentally in a number of other places besides New England under similar intellectual conditions. Some figures may be regarded as more or less central to the movement, others as more or less peripheral. Among the more important figures during the most vigorous years of the movement (1835–1845) one would certainly want to include Bronson Alcott, Cyrus Bartol, Orestes Brownson, Ellery Channing, W. H. Channing, James F. Clarke, Christopher Cranch, John S. Dwight, R. W. Emerson, Margaret Fuller, Frederick Henry Hedge, Theodore Parker, Elizabeth Peabody, George and Sophia Ripley, Henry Thoreau, and Jones Very. In the next circle of importance would come such ministers as Charles T. Brooks, Convers Francis, William H. Furness, William B. Greene, Sylvester Judd, Samuel Osgood, Samuel Robbins, Caleb Stetson, and Thomas Stone; and such laymen as Caroline Dall, Charles Lane, the young James Russell Lowell, Charles K. Newcomb, Caroline and Ellen Sturgis, Anna and Samuel Ward, and Charles S. Wheeler. As harbingers, one would include William Ellery Channing, James Marsh, and

Sampson Reed; as third-generation keepers of the faith, Moncure Conway, O. B. Frothingham, Thomas Wentworth Higginson, Samuel Johnson, Samuel Longfellow, Franklin B. Sanborn, and David Wasson. Eminent peripheral figures would include George Bancroft, Lydia Child, William Lloyd Garrison, Isaac Hecker, Caleb Sprague Henry, and Walt Whitman. This list could easily be quadrupled by adding the remaining members of Brook Farm and Fruitlands, and other outsiders like Emily Dickinson who imbibed large doses of Emersonianism.

Since this study is not a history of the movement but a description of one aspect of it, it seems less useful to present a complete roster and account of the participants, which has already been done by others, than to extrapolate a general profile. The majority were born and reared in the vicinity of Boston. Almost all reached Transcendentalism by way of Unitarianism before they were thirty years old; more than half were at least trained for the Unitarian ministry; almost all the men attended Harvard. Many were from backgrounds of wealth and gentility, though their immediate families were of widely varying economic status; and virtually all were of old New England stock, typically descending, on both sides, from ancestors who had come to America well before 1700. Almost all supported, with varying degrees of enthusiasm, the great moral reforms of the day—the temperance, antislavery and nonresistance movements —though most were reluctant to engage in organized social action, except in abolitionism during the decade before the Civil War. Finally, most were to some degree involved in the arts, especially literature, though usually as amateurs rather than professionals. At least half wrote significant amounts of poetry; more than half wrote literary criticism; most tried to keep diaries at some period; and almost all, at one time or another, wrote essays, sermons or orations with some pretension to literary merit. This predilection for literary activity seems to have been caused by a variety of factors, both cultural and personal, which are explored in Chapter 1.

Perry Miller once described Transcendentalism as an early instance of the recurring pattern of generational conflict in American society (*Tr*, pp. 12–13). In view of what has happened in America during the twenty years since Miller wrote, his appraisal is most provocative. In its liberal, upper-middle-class origins and in its short-lived but colorful exuberance, marked by insistence upon personal freedom and spiritual reform, the Transcendentalist movement strongly resembles the revolution of sensibility which we have been witnessing among educated young people in our time. Thoreau may not have been the first hippie, but he is justly cited as a precedent for "Consciousness III"; and unjustly neglected aspects of Transcendentalism and related contemporary movements, such as communalism, are now being taken more seriously than they had been for many years. The "relevance" of Transcendentalism is easy to exaggerate but useful to bear in mind, for although very little is said directly about the matter in this book, I believe that the Transcendentalists' style of aesthetics has as much contemporary significance as their style of life.[9]

Because of its special emphases, the present study is of course more selective in its treatment of the Transcendentalist movement than a historical survey would be. The following chapters concentrate, for example, on the period before the Civil War, when Transcendentalism was at its height, almost to the exclusion of the rather attenuated third generation of the movement. Much more is said about Thoreau, Ellery Channing,

[9] For a good example of the use and misuse of the analogy between Transcendentalism and contemporary youth culture, see Herbert London, "American Romantics: Old and New," *Colorado Quarterly*, 18 (1969), 5–20. To compare Whitman with Ginsberg is one thing; to link Theodore Parker with Bob Dylan is another. The term "Consciousness III" was coined by Charles Reich, in *The Greening of America* (New York: Random House, 1970), a book which is written in somewhat the same style as a Transcendentalist essay and has for that reason been received with somewhat the same perplexity.

Very, and Whitman, bcause of their literary importance, than about Ripley, Hedge, and Brownson, who were more significant figures in other ways. I do not imply that literary excellence is to be considered the sole or even the primary interest of the majority of the Transcendentalists, for it certainly was not, nor that the Transcendentalists are important chiefly as writers, rather than as pastors, educators, reformers, or ideologues. On the contrary, writing was for most of them little more than a means of pursuing these commitments. I would argue, however, that the spirit of the Transcendentalist movement is best understood by taking a literary approach toward what the Transcendentalists had to say about the issues which preoccupied them, because their way of looking at those issues is markedly poetic rather than analytical and because they attached great value to creativity and self-expression.

How should we read Transcendentalist literature? Or any nonfictional literature, for that matter? Now that the "new criticism," to quote one of its original advocates, seems to have "reached a point of exhaustion" [10] as an innovative force in the analysis of poetry, drama, and narrative fiction, an increasing number of scholars have begun to realize that large areas of the western literary tradition to which new critical methods are not so easily adaptable have been almost entirely unexplored. In the case of American literature, Howard Mumford Jones has diagnosed the situation well.

Our histories of American literature are deficient in a number of [areas]. They seldom or never, for example, recognize the greatness of American biographical writing. . . . They scarcely know what to do with most nonfictional prose. . . . They do not know what to do with the powerful library of travel literature written by Americans. . . . But I think the greatest deficiency in these manuals is

[10] René Wellek, *Concepts of Criticism*, ed. Stephen G. Nichols, Jr. (New Haven: Yale University Press, 1963), p. 359.

their failure to recognize the existence of that type of writer the French call the moralist. For him American literary criticism has small space.[11]

Unfortunately it is much easier to agree with Jones's critique than to answer his call. W. K. Wimsatt, in his reaction to Boswell's *Journals,* no doubt speaks for many readers: "This true drama refuses to be measured completely by the norms of the fictional." But "having said that," he adds, "we return to the categories—because these are all we can pretend to expound or criticize." [12] The same idea runs through the recent and timely critical reappraisals of Victorian prose: that the way to understand nonfiction is to treat it as if it were fictive. As the editors of one important symposium point out, the general consensus of the contributors is that

the correct critical attitude toward an object viewed aesthetically must then be formal rather than ethical or practical, although it may well be concerned with the ethical and practical questions which are the substance of the aesthetic object. So viewed, the object will seem to be flawed insofar as the writer's vision lacks formal coherence. (One of the traditional and, we believe, generally valid assumptions of critics is that the failure of formal coherence implies the inadequacy of the vision itself.) It is not a question of whether the writer finds the best form for the expression of his vision, for this implies a distinction between the vision and the materials he uses to give it expression.[13]

As this passage suggests, criticism still finds it hard to resist moving from a concern with form to a philosophical formalism,

[11] *History and the Contemporary* (Madison: University of Wisconsin Press, 1964), pp. 135–136.

[12] William Wimsatt, *Hateful Contraries: Studies in Literature and Criticism* (Lexington: University of Kentucky Press, 1965), p. 168.

[13] George Levine and William Madden, eds., *The Art of Victorian Prose* (New York: Oxford University Press, 1968), pp. xii–xiii. For an effective rejoinder, see Patrick J. McCarthy, "Reading Victorian Prose: Arnold's 'Culture and Its Enemies,'" *University of Toronto Quarterly,* 40 (1971), 119–135.

from a concern with expression to a disregard for the demands of the author's vision. Such an attitude cannot help but impose on literary history a hierarchy of values according to which the more fictive genres seem by definition "better" than, say, the autobiography or the sermon, and the distinctive literary purposes of the latter are undervalued or, at worst, even considered stumbling blocks which prevent the author from achieving the "ideal" literary effect.

Scholarship on Transcendentalism has been faced with such problems for a long time. The Transcendentalists have had a history of being caricatured by experts who have judged them by the standards of a particular specialty, beginning in 1836, when Francis Bowen "exploded" their philosophical pretensions.[14] Today they do not lack sympathetic scholarly attention, but the traditional problem of interpretation remains. Partly because the serious study of the movement has largely devolved upon students and professors of literature, analysis has tended to center on a few classic works—for example, Emerson's "Language" and "The Poet," Thoreau's *Walden,* and a half-dozen poems in *Leaves of Grass.* These are valued according to the degree to which they are seen as measuring up to modern standards of literary sophistication.[15] This narrowing of focus has led to some faulty interpretations. In Charles Anderson's view of *Walden,* for instance, exposition and narrative "are really only anti-structures"; the book's "true stylistic mode" is "the interplay of wit and metaphor."[16] Though there is much truth

[14] "Transcendentalism" and "Locke and the Transcendentalists," *Christian Examiner,* 21 (1837), 371–385; 23 (1837), 170–194.

[15] This trend may be said to have begun in earnest with F. O. Matthiessen's *American Renaissance* (New York: Oxford University Press, 1941). For an excellent short discussion that both criticizes and reflects subsequent developments in Emerson studies see Jonathan Bishop, *Emerson on the Soul* (Cambridge: Harvard University Press, 1964), pp. 1–8. For Thoreau, a roughly analogous discussion is Charles R. Anderson, *The Magic Circle of Walden* (New York: Holt, Rinehart & Winston, 1968), pp. 1–18.

[16] *Ibid.,* p. 38.

to this claim, in the long run it conveys a misleading impression of the man who once declared that "it is the style of thought entirely, and not the style of expression, which makes the difference in books" (*JT*, I, 344). The same can be said of Charles Feidelson's verdict that Emerson's theory of symbolism "has weight chiefly as a literary program," "his writings survive as literature," and "his literary theory and practice were limited by the philosophic issues that led him to symbolism." [17] Feidelson's essay brilliantly describes Emerson's affinities with modern symbolist aesthetics but understates the dependence of art upon belief in his writing. So does much recent Whitman criticism, despite that poet's repeated warning that "no one will get at my verses who insists upon viewing them as a literary performance, or attempt at such performance, or as aiming mainly toward art or aestheticism." [18]

Many scholars have of course continued to emphasize the spiritual bases of the Transcendentalist movement and its impact upon American thought and culture. Perry Miller, for example, has regarded Transcendentalism essentially as a religious phenomenon, in the context of the revivalism of the Second Awakening; William R. Hutchison has viewed it as a reform movement within Congregationalism; Stanley Elkins has (mistakenly, I believe) classified Transcendentalism as that species of northern bigotry which precipitated the Civil War.[19] But even as one takes account of the contributions of Transcenden-

[17] *Symbolism and American Literature* (Chicago: University of Chicago Press, 1953), pp. 121–123.

[18] "A Backward Glance O'er Travel'd Roads," *Leaves of Grass*, ed. Harold W. Blodgett and Sculley Bradley (New York: New York University Press, 1965), p. 574.

[19] Miller, *Life of the Mind;* Hutchison, *Transcendentalist Ministers;* Elkins, *Slavery: A Problem in American Institutional and Intellectual Life* (New York: Grosset & Dunlap, 1963), pp. 140–222. Elkins is corrected by Aileen Kraditor, *Means and Ends in American Abolitionism* (New York: Pantheon, 1967), pp. 11–38.

talism to our social and intellectual history, one is repeatedly struck by the movement's strongly aesthetic cast, which was unprecedented in the annals of American religious movements. Though Miller is right in saying that "Transcendentalism was not primarily a literary phenomenon" (*Tr*, p. 9), it remains that the Transcendentalists regarded "poetry [as] second only to religion," [20] and often inseparable from it. What John Holloway has said of the Victorians is true of them also: they are not committed to logical defense of particular propositions of beliefs so much as to stimulating their audiences to a new perception of things by appeals "to imagination as well as intelligence." [21]

A balanced study of Transcendentalist writing—and other nonfictional literature also—must therefore take into account its simultaneous commitment to beauty and truth, without scanting either. The techniques of explication developed by modern criticism must be adapted to such obviously sophisticated works as *Culture and Anarchy*, Emerson's essays, and Boswell's *Journals*, in a way that will illuminate their strengths as well as their shortcomings, that will not continually contrast them with what they might have been had their language been more metaphorical and their structure more closely knit, but that will demonstrate precisely how whatever message or vision they communicate enhances their imaginative subtlety and force. Or if the work seems to fail, the failure must be explained in terms of its own particular literary objectives. Conversely, the student of nonfictional literature must be prepared to show why the thought of an Emerson or an Arnold leads irresistibly to strongly poetic or rhetorical forms of expression rather than to a relatively unadorned argument or exposition.

Three principal approaches to these issues are employed in

[20] Cyrus Bartol, "Poetry and Imagination," *Christian Examiner*, 42 (1847), 251.
[21] *The Victorian Sage: Studies in Argument* (New York: Norton, 1965). pp. 9–10.

the present study. None is startlingly original, but if thought-fully applied they may yield some new insights.

(1) The first is to investigate ways in which the demands of vision and the demands of expression reinforce and qualify each other in Transcendentalist writing. The most challenging critical problem it poses consists not so much in its content per se (which is often half-baked) or in the style per se (which is often awkward and inchoate) as in such questions as What is the tone? To what extent is a given assertion serious or rhetorical? How much is left to implication and nuance? To what extent does the idea depend for its expression upon a circuitous, baroque, even obfuscatory style? As an example of the dimensions of the problem, consider the following passage from Emerson's Divinity School Address:

> If a man is at heart just, then in so far is he God; the safety of God, the immortality of God, the majesty of God do enter into that man with justice. If a man dissemble, he deceives himself, and goes out of acquaintance with his own being. [*W*, I, 122]

To the conservatives in Emerson's audience, this was one of the most obnoxious passages in the whole address—and with reason, since it seems to assert the identity of man with God. But does it really? Actually, it is quite unclear what, if anything, is being advanced. When one takes into account the qualifications with which Emerson surrounds his claims (the just man equals God is explained as meaning that "the safety of God" and so forth "do enter into that man with justice") the statement becomes quite tame: the just man partakes of the divine; the vicious man is alienated from his better nature. Yet this reading is not fair either, for it deprives the passage of all its boldness. Can it be that Emerson himself was unsure of what he meant? According to Theodore Parker, Emerson admitted precisely that to his former mentor, Henry Ware, Jr.; and Emerson's later writing would seem to bear Parker out. In "Self-Reliance," for example, changeableness in one's views of the nature of God is advanced as an argument in favor of inconsistency.[22] This assertion in turn makes one suspect that Emerson *didn't care* about being clear, that he was primarily writing for effect, to stir up his audience. The elegant balance of his sentences, with their paradoxes and antitheses, would seem to invite this suspicion. It is not at all unlikely that Emerson might have willingly departed from sober truth for the sake of coining two good aphorisms. Still, one cannot regard them simply as a rhetorical performance, any more than as a straightforward exposition of doctrine: Emerson's tone is far too urgent for that, and his journal for the period when he was formulating his thoughts for the address shows that they were the product of prolonged and conscientious meditation.[23]

The passage, then, dwells somewhere between metaphor and metaphysics, between the word as message and the word as art. If considered as either one alone it is unintelligible, coming across either as muddleheadedness or exhibitionism, neither of which characterizations is fair. It has to be seen from two angles at once. Emerson has a "truth" to communicate, but "truth" to him is a matter not of mathematical demonstration but of feeling. Accordingly, he prefers to make a striking general impression rather than to be exact. To the very casual or the very precise reader this approach may seem careless and sentimental.

[22] Parker to Elizabeth Peabody, 8 Jan. 1839, Massachusetts Historical Society, Boston. Cf. Mary W. Edrich, "The Rhetoric of Apostasy," *Texas Studies in Language and Literature*, 8 (1967), 547–560, which argues that the difference between Emerson's address and the Unitarian position was rhetorical rather than substantive. Ultimately the essay overstates its case, but not by much.

[23] For Emerson's state of mind at the time of the Address, see Emerson's Journal for 1838; Stephen Whicher, *Freedom and Fate: An Inner Life of Ralph Waldo Emerson* (New York: Barnes, 1961), pp. 72–76; and Conrad Wright, *The Liberal Christians: Essays on American Unitarian History* (Boston: Beacon, 1970), pp. 41–61. Neither scholarly account is, I think, strictly accurate: Whicher reads into Emerson's career too much of a thirst for greatness; Wright sees him as an irresponsible Unitarian. But both make clear Emerson's great emotional investment in the Address.

And indeed the passage does have a nonchalance which is typical
of Emerson. But in craftsmanship if not in tone the passage is
the reverse of casual; clearly much premeditation has gone into
its writing. It is the work of a keen mind and able craftsman;
it simply will not reveal its depths to those who ask no more of
it than "What does it say?" and "What are the rhetorical strategies?" One must further inquire, "What is the exact degree of
commitment? How much does the style work for and against it?
How much is the rhetoric an end in itself?"

In recent years such questions have been dealt with. To name
but three examples, Holloway's *The Victorian Sage,* J. Hillis
Miller's *The Disappearance of God,* and Jonathan Bishop's
Emerson on the Soul all contain admirable insights into these
matters. Unlike these works, however, I do not focus exclusively
on particular authors and their rhetorical methods but discuss
the Transcendentalists in the context of the principal genres or
formal traditions upon which they drew. This is the second
major way in which this book attempts to clarify the aesthetic
objectives of the Transcendentalists and of nonfictional literature in general. The distinctive qualities of such writing cannot,
I think, be fully appreciated without reference to whatever
stylistic conventions underlie them. Without such knowledge,
it is almost impossible to keep from thinking of nonfictional
literature as belonging to one large, nebulous category, to which
one then applies the conventions of the more familial genres
for purposes of evaluation. Thus *Walden* is praised because it
has elements of poetic structure, and *Sartor Resartus* attracts
attention because it is almost a novel. These analogies are often
illuminating, and I myself draw some below; but they hold only
to a point. On the whole, the Transcendentalists were exceedingly weak in the genres most in favor today (poetry, drama,
prose fiction); but they had strong affinities with other genres
and subgenres about which less is known but which, when once
defined, make Transcendentalist literature more comprehensi-
ble and interesting. The present study describes a number of

these generic traditions and how they apply to Transcendentalist writing: the conversation, the essay, the sermon, the literary travelogue or excursion, the catalogue, the diary, and the autobiography. In each case my method is to show the relevance of certain features of Transcendentalist thought to a given form of expression, the degree to which this form was traditionally practiced as an art as well as a vehicle for prophetic statement, and the ways in which Transcendentalist use of the form deviated from traditional practice.

A generic approach to any body of postromantic expressivist writing must of course be applied with caution. Works like *Walden* and *Nature* are to a large extent unique, and the problem of sorting out actual stylistic influences is insuperable. To call one an autobiography and the other a sermon is almost as simplistic as to call both poems. Such models are therefore used tentatively and in combination, to suggest a range of possibilities rather than to define within narrow limits; and each model is viewed as a cluster of motifs rather than as a fixed form.

Another risk of the generic approach is that it tends to make different authors seem too much alike. I have tried to compensate for this by indicating the range of dissent on major issues and by including one or more extended discussions of Emerson, Thoreau, Bronson Alcott, Margaret Fuller, Ellery Channing, Theodore Parker, Jones Very, and Walt Whitman. I could have put still greater emphasis on individual Transcendentalists and organized this study by author rather than by topic. Certainly there is a need for a survey of Transcendentalism that will do justice to the peculiarities of its lesser figures, just as there is an even greater need for a comprehensive history of the movement in all its aspects. But it seemed most useful for present purposes to organize in terms of unifying features, for such features surely exist. Despite their own vociferous protestations that no two of them thought alike, the Transcendentalists did have a great deal in common, such as their pride in their own individuality. As for their aesthetics, it is possible to distinguish not only shared critical principles but also a definite Transcendentalist rhetoric. Its leading characteristics are inchoate structure, prodigal imagery, wit, paradox, symbolism, aphoristic statement, paratactic syntax, and a manifesto-like tone. Examples include the passage quoted from the Divinity School Address, as well as most of Emerson's essays through 1844; Thoreau's *Antislavery and Reform Papers* and parts of his first two books; Alcott's *Doctrine and Discipline of Human Culture;* Brownson's *New Views of Christianity, Society and the Church;* and a number of Theodore Parker's sermons.

Literary Transcendentalism was not an isolated phenomenon; its hybrid mixture of religion and rhetoric had its origins in the cultural milieu from which the movement arose, namely Boston Unitarianism, cross-fertilized by English romantic thought and the antecedent tradition of platonic mysticism. A third way in which I attempt to clarify the relationship of style and vision in the Transcendentalist aesthetic is to examine it as an outgrowth of this intellectual heritage, or at least the most important part of it. Especially in Chapter 1, but throughout the book as well, I have much to say about the ways in which the Transcendentalists' situation as New Englanders seems to have preconditioned their relative allegiance to vision and expression in literary art. This subject has been less understood than one might expect. Commentators have generally pictured the heritage of Transcendentalism in panoramic terms as a legacy of the Puritans that suddenly resurfaced in reaction to Unitarianism, with the romantic movement as a catalyst. Although the study of any intellectual movement would seem properly to begin with an account of the immediate context in which it arose, not until the 1950s did scholarship attempt a thorough examination of Boston Unitarianism except as something the Transcendentalists repudiated. They themselves encouraged this omission, of course, with their caricatures of Unitarianism as "heartless" and "corpse-cold," and since then the myth has been kept alive by such influential statements as Perry

Miller's "From Edwards to Emerson." [24] But subsequent intellectual and church historians have shown that Unitarianism was considerably more complex and vital than had been supposed.[25] Building on their researches as well as my own, I take the position that Transcendentalism in all its aspects, including the aesthetic, is best seen not as a repudiation but an outgrowth of trends in Unitarian thought. This is not to deny the catalytic role of European influences. I also note these when it seems most appropriate, though for reasons of scope I do not go into much detail.

The major portion of this study is organized so as to emphasize what I take to be the three most significant intellectual and literary concerns of the Transcendentalist movement: spirit, nature, and man. Broadly speaking, Parts I and II describe in general terms how the Transcendentalists sought to express spiritual truth. Part III discusses their inquiries into the meaning of nature and, in particular, the ways in which the style and structure of some of their writings express conceptions of natural order. Part IV discusses the uses of personae in their writing and how these reflect their conceptions of the divinity of the self. Although this scheme is a matter of expediency as well as design and is not intended as a complete theoretical framework for the study of the Transcendentalists, it does have the value of highlighting the most complex and interesting areas of their intellectual and literary activity, and it also indicates the chief lines of relationship between their writing and American literature as a whole. To trace the literary "legacy" of Transcendentalism is not my major purpose here, but I try to

[24] *New England Quarterly,* 13 (1940), 589–617, rpt. in *Errand into the Wilderness* (New York: Harper, 1964), pp. 184–203.

[25] The scholars who have done the most significant work in this area are Howe, Hutchison, and Wright. In addition to their works cited above, see Wright, *The Beginnings of Unitarianism in America* (Boston: Starr King Press, 1955).

suggest the principal ways in which this can be done. Certainly the main tendencies in Transcendentalist writing discussed here —the impulses to prophesy, to create nature anew for oneself, and to speak in the first person singular—are three of the dominant motifs in American literary history.

PART I

BACKGROUND AND
GENERAL PRINCIPLES

The outstanding symbolic event in the history of Transcendentalism is Emerson's resignation from his Boston pastorate in 1832 in order to become a scholar-at-large. Most of the other Transcendentalists were also Unitarian ministers or in some sense lay preachers who came to distrust the institutional aspects of religion and were drawn to the literary life. A number of those who began as clergymen defected like Emerson; most of the rest pursued literary avocations on the side. The writings of laymen like Thoreau, Alcott, and Margaret Fuller also have a religio-aesthetic cast. The best-known Transcendentalist periodical was rightly subtitled "A Magazine for Literature, Philosophy, and Religion." Though individual Transcendentalists differed considerably on particular issues, they shared in common a lofty view of the relationship between religion and art: art (with a capital "A" always understood) is the product of the religious sentiment, and the religious sentiment, by its very nature, demands an imaginative expression. Though it was first of all a religious movement, Transcendentalism, as its first historian said, "was essentially poetical and put its thoughts naturally into song." [1] The purpose of Chapter 1 is to show why this was the case, by examining the relation between piety and aesthetics in early nineteenth-century New England, and the way in which the Transcendentalists redefined this relation in the course of their departure from Unitarianism.[2] Having thus seen their literary aspirations in this larger intellectual context, we outline, in Chapter 2, their views on the nature of literary craftsmanship per se, and show how these too are informed by spiritual considerations.

[1] O. B. Frothingham, *Transcendentalism in New England* (1876; rpt. New York: Harper, 1959), p. 134.

[2] Studies of the relationship between the religious views of Unitarians and Transcendentalists are copious, though until recently they tended to exaggerate both the conservatism of the one and the liberalism of the other and to see a sharper break between the two than was the case. Perry Miller's scholarship is, for the most part, a distinguished example of this position. An excellent short discussion of the factors within Unitarianism which made it first abet and then disown the Transcendentalist movement is Clarence H. Faust, "The Background of the Unitarian Opposition to Transcendentalism," *Modern Philology*, 35 (1938), 297–324. The best recent study of the theological and ecclesiastical relationship between Unitarianism and Transcendentalism is William R. Hutchison, *The Transcendentalist Ministers* (New Haven: Yale University Press, 1959). For two useful studies of the aesthetic side of Unitarianism, see Chapter 1, n. 4. Van Wyck Brooks's *The Flowering of New England* (New York: Dutton, 1936), in its impressionistic manner, also affords some valuable insights into the ways Unitarianism stimulated the literary side of Transcendentalism. Two works which discuss the relation between religious liberalism and aesthetic developments in America as a whole during this period are William Charvat, *The Origins of American Critical Thought, 1810–1835* (Philadelphia: University of Pennsylvania Press, 1936), and Neil Harris, *The Artist in American Society: The Formative Years, 1790–1860* (New York: Braziller, 1966), pp. 170–186, 300–316.

1 The Emergence of the Transcendentalist Aesthetic from American Unitarianism

Since the Puritan ministers were traditionally the cultural as well as the religious leaders of their people, it was natural that their successors should participate actively in the so-called flowering of New England letters during the early nineteenth century. The best of the literary and intellectual periodicals which mark the first stage of this process were thus run and written largely by clergymen: the *Monthly Anthology and Boston Review* (1803–1811), the *North American Review* (1815–1939), and the *Christian Examiner* (1824–1869). What is more noteworthy about these experiments is that their clerical supporters were almost exclusively Unitarian ministers. The Orthodox Congregationalists and other evangelical sects had their journals too—for this was the golden age of the religious magazine. But theirs were much more narrowly theological in scope.

Conversely, in the area of theology itself, the liberal clergy rarely approached the best of the evangelicals in depth, rigor, and thoroughness.[1] Just as Jonathan Edwards was a far more

[1] Jerry Wayne Brown's survey of theological developments during this period, *The Rise of Biblical Criticism in America, 1800–1870: The New England Scholars* (Middletown, Conn.: Wesleyan University Press, 1969), contains a lively and informative discussion of controversy between the Unitarians and the Orthodox during this period, but is too uniformly condescending toward the naivetés of both sides. The fact remains that the Unitarians tended to rely on common sense where the Orthodox had a passion for intellectual precision, essentially because they operated within

profound thinker than Charles Chauncy, his leading liberal opponent during the Great Awakening, so Chauncy's descendants were less sophisticated theologians than Samuel Hopkins, Nathaniel Taylor, Lyman Beecher, and Edwards A. Park. Among the Unitarians, only Andrews Norton had any claims to real distinction in this respect. Nor were they greatly concerned about this fact. Even among themselves, Unitarian divines were reputed more for other attainments. One Unitarian minister-historian, for example, after running fondly down the roster of the movement's early leaders, blithely declared that it was "difficult to say, out of hand, just what the Unitarian opinion is on any given matter, or what it is that Unitarians believe in." Indeed, he added, "I am a little impatient that they should ever be judged by their theology, which was so small a fraction of either their religion or their life!" [2] Among eminent early Unitarians, the two Henry Wares were respected primarily for their kindliness, piety, and devotion to duty; Orville Dewey for his eloquence; F. W. P. Greenwood for the beauty of his style; Buckminster and Channing for all of these. "An atmosphere of elegant taste pervades the denomination," as O. B. Frothingham says of this period. "Even where occasion calls for polemics the argument is usually conducted after the manner of one more interested in the style than in the dogmas under discussion, and who would gladly be let off from the duty of debate." [3] The imputation of lackadaisicalness here is unfair; but

---

a more dogmatic framework of belief. Most of the truly elegant monuments in the history of New England theology are therefore in the tradition of Edwards (as modified by his successors) rather than in that of Chauncy. See Frank Hugh Foster, *A Genetic History of the New England Theology* (Chicago: University of Chicago Press, 1907); and Sydney E. Ahlstrom, "Theology in America," in *The Shaping of American Religion,* ed. James Ward Smith and A. Leland Jameson (Princeton: Princeton University Press, 1961), I, 232–321.

[2] Joseph H. Allen, *Our Liberal Movement in Theology* (Boston: Roberts, 1883), p. 30.

[3] O. B. Frothingham, *Boston Unitarianism, 1820–1850: A Study of the*

the remark is correct in suggesting that what chiefly distinguished the liberal ministry from its evangelical counterparts
was its achievement in such avocations as essay-writing, literary
criticism, poetry, and a variety of other secular pursuits from
science to philosophy. Channing, for example, won international fame for his essays on Milton and Napoleon; the younger
Ware wrote an epic; his brother William invented a new literary genre, the Biblical novel; Jared Sparks and J. G. Palfrey
became two of the leading historians of their day.[4]

The difference in literary attitudes between liberal and Orthodox Congregationalism was great enough even to become a
point of dispute in the Unitarian controversy. The Unitarians
tended to look down upon Orthodox preachers as dogmatic and
narrow-minded ranters, while the Orthodox stigmatized Unitarian preaching and writing as hollow displays of elegance
which "please delicate tastes and itching ears, but awaken no
sleeping conscience." [5]

One must naturally beware of taking the language of controversy at face value. The Orthodox reviewer who condemned a

---

Life and Work of Nathaniel Langdon Frothingham (New York: Putnam,
1890), p. 261.

[4] The best general discussion of literary activity among Unitarian ministers is Daniel Howe's chapter on "Genteel Letters" in his impressive study,
The Unitarian Conscience: Harvard Moral Philosophy, 1805–1861 (Cambridge: Harvard University Press, 1970), pp. 174–204. For a more partisan
discussion, see George Willis Cooke, *Unitarianism in America: A History
of Its Origin and Development* (Boston: American Unitarian Association,
1902), pp. 412–435.

[5] "Review of Reviews," *Panoplist*, n.s., 3 (1810), 33. For some other comments by the Orthodox on Unitarian style see George B. Cheever,
"Thoughts on the Unitarian Controversy," *Quarterly Christian Spectator*,
5 (1833), 85–87, and review of *Lives of the Twelve Apostles*, in *Spirit of
the Pilgrims*, 1 (1828), 610. For Unitarians on Orthodox crudity, see
George Ticknor, "Dr. Parish's Eulogy," *Monthly Anthology and Boston
Review*, 10 (1811), 423–425; Joseph S. Buckminster, 'Dr. Griffin's Sermon,"
ibid., 8 (1810), 135; and 'Rhetorical Merits of Orthodox Preaching," *Christian Register*, 4 (1825), 102.

volume of liberal sermons as "a poisonous infusion in a deli-
cious bowl" showed considerable sensitivity to their beauties;
the Reverend Leonard Withington, who dismissed Channing
as a "nightingale of the moral grove," was himself an essayist
and poetaster.[6] Nevertheless the controversy did have a deeper
basis. Part of the explanation lay in the fact that a higher percentage of Unitarians than of any other American sect except
the High Church Episcopalians were people of sophistication
and refinement. But beyond this, their theological liberalism
led them to draw a closer analogy between religious and aesthetic experience than Orthodoxy would allow. The main impetus behind the Unitarian departure from Orthodoxy—the
shift from a Calvinist view of human nature as depraved to an
Arminian view of man as improvable—also helped to produce
a climate of opinion more favorable to the arts.[7] Believing that
the essence of religion is to stimulate the growth of moral character, the Unitarians tended to differentiate less sharply between "sacred" and "secular" pursuits and to view the arts as a
means of evangelism rather than as a threat to religion. Beauty
and truth came to seem inextricably intertwined. "There is no
such thing as naked truth, at least as far as moral subjects are
concerned," Channing declared. Such truth must come to us
"warm and living with the impressions and affections which it
has produced in the soul from which it issues." [8] Even the much
more conservative W. B. O. Peabody considered "poetry as not
distantly related to religion," as "alike" in its "tendency, which

[6] "Review of Buckminster's Sermons," *Christian Spectator*, 5 (1823), 152;
"Review of Channing's Works," *Literary and Theological Review*, 1 (1834),
304.

[7] As a William R. Hutchison explains, though the "nominal center" of
the Unitarian movement was the rejection of the doctrine of the trinity,
the "practical source" was the objection to the Calvinist view of human
nature (*The Transcendentalist Ministers* [New Haven: Yale University
Press, 1959], p. 4 and chap. i, passim.)

[8] *The Works of William Ellery Channing*, 4th ed. (Boston: Munroe,
1845), III, 142.

is to raise the thoughts and feelings above the level of ordinary life." [9]

Orthodox writers, though not entirely opposed to the arts, tended to be cautionary and restrictive. From this point of view, the *Panoplist* in 1808 endorsed a Presbyterian minister's estimate that five hundred out of every thousand novels were "so contemptibly frivolous, as to render the perusal of them a most criminal waste of time" and that four hundred ninety-nine of the remaining five hundred might "be considered as positively seductive and corrupting in their tendency." [10] The prejudice against prose fiction was such that even religious novels were suspect. The *Christian Spectator,* one of the most enlightened of early evangelical sect periodicals, did not have a good word to say for the genre until the 1830s. And Lyman Beecher, even in his old age, continued to fulminate against "effeminate, religious-novel-reading Christians." [11]

Liberal divines also fretted about "unsanctified literature," and the frivolity of novels in particular; some of Theodore Parker's sarcasms rival Beecher's.[12] But Unitarians tended to be much more permissive and positive in their criticism. "When we speak of a distinct moral aim as indispensable to the novelist," F. D. Huntington explained, "we do not mean that he should be constantly thrusting his moral into the reader's face, —one of the weakest pieces of folly an author can commit." [13]

[9] "Mrs. Barbauld's Works," *Christian Examiner,* 3 (1826), 305.

[10] "On Novel-Reading," *Panoplist,* n.s., 1 (1808), 205.

[11] *Autobiogrphy, Correspondence, . . . of Lyman Beecher, D.D.,* ed. Charles Beecher (London, 1863), I, 390.

[12] For a cross-section of early-nineteenth-century attacks on fiction, see G. Harrison Orians, "Censure of Fiction in American Romances and Magazines, 1789–1810," *PMLA* 52 (1937), 195–214. For Parker's criticisms of fiction, see *Sermons of Religion,* ed. Samuel A. Eliot (Boston: American Unitarian Association, 1908), p. 268, and "Theodore Parker's Experience as a Minister," *Autobiography, Poems and Prayers,* ed. Rufus Leighton (Boston: American Unitarian Association, 1911), p. 360.

[13] "Novels and Novel-writing," *Christian Examiner,* 42 (1847), 117.

Some liberal ministers even conceded that "the mind may be elevated and put in harmony with truth, even where no definite truth is conveyed." Specific moral or religious content is not necessary, as long as the work has an ennobling tendency, for *"whatever* inculcates pure sentiment, whatever touches the heart with the beauty of virtue and the blessedness of piety, is in accordance with religion." [14]

Such statements hardly sound revolutionary to our ears, but for their day they were avant-garde. As William Charvat observes in his study of early American periodical criticism, one of the most important developments that took place between 1810 and 1835 was the displacement of "the negative principle of religious restraint" by "the positive principle of moral idealism." The reviewer's question changed from "Does this book make vice attractive?" to "Does it make virtue beautiful?" [15] Although popular taste undoubtedly began to shift in advance of the reviewers, the Unitarian critics were the first group of intellectuals in New England to endorse the shift in significant numbers. They were quick to claim credit for their contribution too. One Unitarian scholar even claimed that nearly every eminent literary figure in nineteenth-century New England "was either a Unitarian or closely associated with Unitarian influences." [16]

"Unitarian influences" did not always improve one's critical discernment, though. However much the Unitarian critics praised art—especially poetry—in the abstract, when it came to passing judgment they followed Orville Dewey's stricture that "the moral character, or the effect upon the mind, must be the test." On this ground and this ground alone, Dewey denies the

[14] William Ware, "Tracy's Translation of Undine," *Christian Examiner,* 27 (1840), 399; Orville Dewey, *The Works of Orville Dewey, D.D.,* new ed. (Boston: American Unitarian Association, 1883), p. 125.

[15] *The Origins of American Critical Thought, 1810–1835* (Philadelphia: University of Pennsylvania Press, 1936), p. 15.

[16] Barrett Wendell, *A Literary History of America* (New York: Scribner, 1901), p. 289.

name of genius to Cooper, while F. W. P. Greenwood hails Joanna Baillie as the best dramatist since Shakespeare. Similarly, the highest compliment William Parsons Lunt can pay Bryant is, "His poetry is of that sort which is of *use*." [17] Altogether, Unitarian criticism was an uneasy mixture of the new and the old. On the one hand, liberal religion was able to provide a rationale, for the first time in New England history, for the intrinsic value of belles-lettres; to defend them, that is, not as decorations or even just as minor instruments of morality, but as inherently valuable by virtue of their beauty and emotional power. No Orthodox divine would have claimed, as Orville Dewey now could, that "the vocation of the really great singer . . . is as holy as the vocation of the great preacher." [18] But even while the Unitarians excited themselves by such daring remarks, they were holding hard to the very puritan, and Yankee, notion of art as justified by practical utility. For Dewey it is the singer's capacity for promoting holiness that makes his art worth praising.

It could hardly have been otherwise. So long as the Unitarians held revealed religion, at least in theory, higher than natural religion, they could not consistently depart from the position that human creation was at best a means of Christian influence. There was only one way of rescuing art from this position of subservience, short of denying its obligation to be moral or spiritual, which no self-respecting Unitarian would have done in public. The one alternative was to disclaim the specialness of revelation itself, or, in other words, to affirm that the utterance of art is (potentially) just as spiritual as that of the Bible. This is precisely what the more radical Transcendentalists did. To be sure, whatever they said in disparagement of the authority of revelation, they generally conceded that the Bible in

[17] Dewey, review of *The Bravo: A Tale,* in *Christian Examiner,* 12 (1832), 84; Greenwood, "Miss Baillie's *Dramas," ibid.,* 22 (1837), 1; Lunt, Bryant's *Poems," ibid.,* p. 68.

[18] *Works,* p. 126.

general and Jesus in particular were the most perfect expressions of the divine spirit which mankind has yet seen. But they also insisted, with varying degrees of intransigence, that other men are also capable of inspiration, that the difference between them and Jesus is at most one of degree. This being the case, Emerson said, "what shall forbid us to universalize the operations of God & to believe the operation of the Holy Spirit is the same in kind in the prophet Isaiah as in the poet Milton?" (*JMN*, III, 240). Indeed, if inspiration, or access to godhead, was available to all, then it seemed to follow that literary creation was not simply an amusement, or even a useful instrument, but a sacred act. "To create," Emerson says, "is the proof of a Divine presence. Whoever creates is God, and whatever talents are, if the man create not, the pure efflux of Deity is not his" (*JMN*, V, 341). Applied to art, this becoms a version of romanticist expressivism, just as its theological side might be called a romantic religion. The poet is an inspired demigod who, by creating, assumes God's role and re-enacts the creation. Conversely, Emerson holds, Jesus and the prophets are not figures of special authority but poets, whose sayings are to be taken as inspired utterances to stir us on to similar heights of vision rather than as a body of truths for us to formulate and follow.

The Divinity School Address is Emerson's most forceful statement of this position. Throughout Emerson uses the analogy of poetry to make his points about religion and the ministry. The prophets, including Jesus, are "holy bards," whose sayings "are sacred and permanent in proportion to their purity" (*W*, I, 126) but not binding upon us. Jesus' assertion that he was God and that we shall see God through him is an example of this sort. It was spoken in a "jubilee of sublime emotion." Unfortunately, his words, like all "doctrine of the Reason," have been corrupted into a doctrine of the understanding. "The understanding caught this high chant from the poet's lips" and made the dogma that Jesus was God. "The idioms of his language and the figures of his rhetoric have usurped the place of his truth; and churches are not built on his principles, but on his tropes. Christianity became a Mythus, as the poetic teaching of Greece and of Egypt, before" (*W*, I, 129). Jesus, Emerson affirms, had no disrespect for the earlier prophets; he was simply a true man: he was Self-reliant (*W*, I, 129–130), and by the same token we should not worship his person but respect ourselves (*W*, I, 130–132).

"Yourself a newborn bard of the Holy Ghost," Emerson exhorts his audience of fledgling ministers, "cast behind you all conformity, and acquaint men at first hand with Deity" (*W*, I, 146). "I look for the hour," he concludes, "when that supreme Beauty which ravished the souls of those Eastern men, and chiefly of those Hebrews, and through their lips spoke oracles to all time, shall speak in the West also." He even anticipates an improvement upon the scriptures:

The Hebrew and Greek Scriptures contain immortal sentences, that have been bread of life to millions. But they have no epical integrity; are fragmentary; are not shown in their order to the intellect. I look for the new Teacher ["some moral Bard," the journal version reads (*JMN*, V, 466)] that shall follow so far those shining laws that he shall see them come full circle; shall see their rounding complete grace. [*W*, I, 115]

Looking at the address as a whole, we see that Emerson at first uses the analogy of poetry pejoratively, to diminish the authority of historical Christianity. The prophets' utterances are only poetry; they are meant to inspire us, not to have authority over us. On the other hand, Emerson is also sounding the call for a priesthood of prophet-poets in his own day. He wants scripture read as literature, solely to inspire, while at the same time he wants new and better Bibles written by inspired contemporaries.

The turmoil caused by Emerson's address is well known. The Dean of the Divinity School thought it "odious"; Emerson's former mentor, Henry Ware, Jr., "refuted" it; the *Christian*

Examiner repudiated it. The atheist Abner Kneeland, according to Theodore Parker, delightedly read the discourse "to his
followers one Sunday, as better infidelity than he could write
himself." [19] Andrews Norton agreed, and prepared to demolish
Emerson in the next year's address. Less dogmatic Unitarians,
like Channing and the youthful Edward Everett Hale, criticized
Emerson for poor taste in casting aspersions on the clergy and its
doctrines within their own sanctuary.[20] And yet, as this last reaction should alert us, the conservative reaction was not uniformly
harsh. Channing, for one, claimed not to see any difference between Emerson's views and his own (though he could have, had
he looked closely enough). Even more interesting is Henry
Wadsworth Longfellow's impression, ten days after the event:
"The Reverend Dean Palfrey said that 'what in it was not folly
was impiety!' Oh! After all, it was only a stout *humanitarian*
discourse; in which Christ and Göthe were mentioned as great
Philosophers." [21] One would hardly expect a person like Longfellow to shed much light on the Transcendentalist controversy,
but this passage does. It is written with a layman's impatience
at dogmatic nitpicking. Longfellow obviously considers Emerson's idea as self-evident, and Palfrey as rather boorish and
unfair to dispute it, though technically Palfrey may have a
point. This perspective is especially interesting inasmuch as
Longfellow was a more or less conventional Unitarian. He respected the clergy; he regularly went to church, though he

[19] To George E. Ellis, 15 Oct. 1838; typescript, Massachusetts Historical
Society, Boston. Henry Ware's response was his sermon on *The Personality
of the Deity*. For Palfrey's reaction, see Frank Otto Gatell, *John Gorham
Palfrey and the New England Conscience* (Cambridge: Harvard University
Press, 1963), p. 75.

[20] Edward Everett Hale, Jr., *The Life and Letters of Edward Everett
Hale* (Boston: Little, Brown, 1917), I, 122–123; Elizabeth Peabody, *Reminiscences of Rev. Wm. Ellery Channing* (Boston: Roberts, 1880), pp. 377–
380.

[21] *The Letters of Henry Wadsworth Longfellow*, ed. Andrew Hilen
(Cambridge: Harvard University, 1966), II, 87.

didn't much like sermons; his muse was properly moralistic. If his reaction to the Address was at all typical of the kind of person whose father was an official of the American Unitarian Association and whose brother was later to become a Harvard Divinity School graduate (and a minor Transcendentalist), then the Unitarian community was much readier for Emersonian notions of art and religion than the acerbity of the miracles controversy would lead us to expect.[22]

It would be foolish, of course, to insist that Emerson and Andrews Norton really saw eye to eye. The Unitarians were quite right in claiming that the Address subverted their position on the special authority of the Christian revelation and, equally important, the way in which belief is validated. This, Emerson insisted, was entirely intuitive (which makes one's belief a philosophical certainty), whereas Norton claimed it was inductive, a process of reasoning from evidence (which makes belief at best a strong philosophical probability). But the process of subversion had been going on a long time, from within the ranks, and Norton himself was one of the culprits. As the leading Unitarian exponent of the "higher criticism" of the Bible—that is, the interpretation of scripture as a historical document, the creation of a particular milieu rather than the infallibly inspired word of God—Norton was making use of the German influences he deplored and, in a sense, leading his followers toward the "latest form of infidelity" of which he accused Emerson. As the Transcendentalists were quick to observe, Norton's magnum opus, *The Evidences of the Genuineness of the Gospels,* far from strengthening Christianity, in effect weakened it by casting doubts upon the authenticity of many parts of scripture and by seeming to deny to any but the expert the competence to interpret the Bible.[23]

---

[22] Cf. Mary W. Edrich, "The Rhetoric of Apostasy," *Texas Studies in Language and Literature,* 8 (1967), 547–560; and Introduction, n. 22, above.

[23] Orestes Brownson, 'Norton's Evidence," in *Tr,* pp. 205–213.

It was not just religious radicals who made such criticisms. When the Unitarian historian William Hickling Prescott, for example, tried to use Norton as a guide to his own Bible study, he gave up in despair. "It is vain to look for moral certainty in an affair of historic testimony, removed from us by so many ages," Prescott concludes. Norton's ascriptions of interpolation lead to "a conviction of credulity and superstition in the narrator" or of "corruption in the original text"; his interpretations of many passages as metaphorical open up "such an allegorical latitude of expression, as will shake the solidity of every doctrine and declaration in the Scriptures." Prescott's only refuge was to retreat into religious sentimentalism. Yes, the Bible may be riddled with cruxes and errors, he admitted, but, in the long run, "who, whatever difficulties he may meet with in particular incidents and opinions recorded in the Gospels, can hesitate to receive the great religious and moral truths inculcated by the Savior, as the *words of inspiration?*" [24] Despite Unitarianism's claims to being a "rational religion," this was really the basis of belief for most of its worshipers: a vague but ardent core of poetic feeling.[25]

Unitarians of an aesthetic bent were unlikely to follow Norton's analyses even as closely as Prescott. To the extent that his approach influenced their faith, it tended to reinforce a loosely poetic view of the Bible. The eighteenth-century researches of Lowth and Herder had called attention to the Bible's literary qualities; the higher criticism now seemed to show that much of what was not actually poetry was to be interpreted metaphorically also. A good example of the state of mind thus induced can be seen in a report by the future Transcendentalist

[24] *The Literary Memoranda of William Hickling Prescott,* ed. C. Harvey Gardiner (Norman: University of Oklahoma Press, 1961), I, 209–212.

[25] Daniel Howe and Conrad Wright have effectively disposed of the myth that Unitarianism was "corpse-cold." Howe gives a good account of the pietistic strain within Unitarianism in his chapter on "The Religion of the Heart," in *The Unitarian Conscience,* pp. 151–173.

poet-minister Charles T. Brooks of the teaching of Henry Ware, Sr., who was *the* professor of divinity to Harvard undergraduates between 1805 and 1843.

Dr. Ware began with stating the importance of the books both because of the momentous nature of their contents and the fact of their authors being inspired. Then he gave the different views of this inspiration that had been held. Some thought it plenary; others only a general superintendence of the Divine Spirit, leaving all minor matters to each author's taste. But at any rate, we didn't doubt that they were extraordinarily gifted writers, etc.[26]

As this example shows, biblical criticism without rigor leads to a dreamy mishmash. Whatever degree of mental discipline Ware's pupils achieved in later life was not due to him. All the eulogies agree that his chief attributes as a teacher were kindliness, tolerance of dissent, and reluctance to come down hard on any side of an issue. "He trusted truth enough to give error every fair chance" was one such epitaph.[27]

But it was not the likes of Norton or Ware who excited the younger generation of the 1820s and early 1830s so much as the superb oratory of Edward Everett and especially William Ellery Channing.[28] Everett was the example par excellence of the

[26] *Poems, Original and Translated, by Charles T. Brooks, with a Memoir by Charles W. Wendte,* ed. W. P. Andrews (Boston: Roberts, 1885), p. 15.

[27] J. G. Palfrey, 'Henry Ware," in *American Unitarian Biography,* ed. William Ware (Boston: Munroe, 1880–1881), I, 245. See also Edward Brooks Hall, "Memoir of Henry Ware," *Christian Examiner,* 40 (1846), 279.

[28] See *W,* X, 329–340, and *JMN,* VIII, 268–271; Cyrus Bartol, "William Ellery Channing, D.D.," *Monthly Miscellany of Religion and Letters,* 7 (1842), 275–288; Elizabeth Peabody, *Reminiscences of Rev. Wm. Ellery Channing, D.D.;* Theodore Parker, "Channing," in *The American Scholar,* ed. George Willis Cooke (Boston: American Unitarian Association, 1907), pp. 126–171; W. H. Channing, *The Life of William Ellery Channing, D.D.* (Boston: Crosby, Nichols, 1848), II, 285–295. The best scholarly discussion of Channing's impact on the Transcendentalists is David P. Edgell, *William Ellery Channing: An Intellectual Portrait* (Boston: Beacon, 1955),

minister in the process of transforming himself into a man of the world; Channing was the minister as sublime saint. He above all other Unitarians prepared the way for the Emersonian synthesis of religion and art. He did this, primarily, by the example of his preaching. His method was to inspire rather than to instruct, to celebrate rather than to argue closely—an approach always congenial to youth. In addition, Channing extended the analogy between art and religion to the farthest limits Unitarianism could bear, by taking seriously, so to speak, the idea of poetic inspiration, with which his colleagues only flirted.

To attribute the creative impulse to the hand of God is an ancient way of accounting for the mystery of creation. In English criticism it is as old as the anecdote of Caedmon by the Venerable Bede. Even in the Age of Reason one finds variants of the idea.[29] But in general the eighteenth century and the Unitarians of Channing's generation, who were mainly children of the Enlightenment in their philosophy, used the notion of art as inspired not for the sake of argument so much as for embellishment, taking the idea metaphorically, or in a classical rather than a Christian sense. They considered the creative impulse as a "humbler inspiration" or "something bordering upon inspiration," rather than the real thing. Channing was bolder. In his essay "Milton" especially, he explicitly endorses Milton's

---

pp. 113–149. Conrad Wright, however, argues that Edgell and others have somewhat overstated the affinities between Channing and Transcendentalism: v. "The Rediscovery of Channing," *The Liberal Christians: Essays on American Unitarian History* (Boston: Beacon, 1970), pp. 22–40. Everett's influence on Transcendentalism itself was indirect and therefore has been less frequently discussed; most scholarship relies on the Emerson essay cited above.

[29] See Murray Roston, *Prophet and Poet: The Bible and the Growth of Romanticism* (London: Faber and Faber, 1965). Ernest Tuveson calls attention to the affinities between Lockean psychology and an aesthetics of inspiration, in *The Imagination as a Means of Grace* (Berkeley: University of California Press, 1960).

opinion that "of all God's gifts of intellect . . . poetical genius [is] the most transcendent," a genuinely divine infusion.

Channing's defense of this claim is remarkable for the way its assumptions about religion lead to a conclusion about poetry that is clearly Emersonian. "No doctrine is more common among Christians than that of man's immortality," he begins, "but it is not so generally understood, that the germs or principles of his whole future are now wrapped up in his soul," as the plant is contained in its seed. Consequently, the soul "is perpetually stretching beyond what is present and visible . . . and seeking relief and joy in imaginings of unseen and ideal being. This view of our nature . . . carries us to the very foundation and sources of poetry." "In an intellectual nature, framed for progress and for higher modes of being, there must be creative energies . . . and poetry is the form in which these energies are chiefly manifested." Therefore, although poetry may be in a literal sense false, "it observes higher laws than it transgresses" and "far from injuring society, is one of the great instruments of its refinement and exaltation." [30]

Channing's article, particularly this section of it, was widely read and quoted. Emerson came to regard the essay as a landmark in American criticism (*W*, X, 339); Bryant quoted a long passage (on the importance of poetry to society) to conclude his lecture on "The Value and Uses of Poetry"; Alexander Everett, in an 1835 essay on Channing, gave the highest praise to "Milton" and singled out the passage on the nature of poetry— "doubtless familiar to many of our readers"—as the "most powerful" part of the essay.[31]

This last remark shows that the Unitarians were prepared to accept a certain dose of inspiration. But Everett goes on to criticize Channing for ascribing to poetry what properly belongs to

[30] *Works,* I, 7–9.
[31] *Prose Writings of William Cullen Bryant,* ed. Parke Godwin (New York: 1884), I, 22–24; Everett, "Channing," *North American Review,* 41 (1835), 375.

religion alone. Other Unitarians questioned Channing's pronouncements about religion itself—his claims for what he called
man's "Likeness to God," the essential divinity of human nature.[32] On the other hand, Channing would never have gone so
far in his literary theory as to say with Emerson that the poet
"is the true and only doctor" (*W*, III, 8), nor would he have endorsed the idea of the divine madness of the poet, or any other
theory of inspiration that emphasized its irrational aspects.
Channing habitually criticized reverie and dreaming—staples
of the romantic poet—as a waste of time. He also shared the
Unitarians' reflexive distrust of all forms of religious emotionalism, although he himself had had a conversion experience in
his youth the validity of which he seems not to have questioned.
Probably he would have agreed with the sentiments of John
Brazer's widely respected "Essay on the Doctrine of Divine Influence," which argued that there is such a thing as inspiration
but that its workings are indistinguishable "from the ordinary
operations of the human mind." [33] The realization of this conservatism underlying Channing's tributes to human nature ultimately alienated the more extreme Transcendentalists, although most of them later mellowed and freely acknowledged
their debt to him.

Altogether, the Transcendentalist movement was more an
evolution than a revolt from Unitarianism, although there were
also basic philosophical differences that should not be glossed
over. Transcendentalism was in almost every way a logical end
result of the momentum of the Unitarian movement, just as
liberalism has led to radicalism in the moral thought of the
last two decades. The Unitarians arrayed themselves against
the Orthodox as the party of free inquiry; and up until the late
1830s, they elevated this principle, in many a peroration, to

[32] Everett, *ibid.,* p. 378; Andrews Norton, "Channing's Dedication Sermon," *Christian Examiner,* 4 (1827), 61–66.

[33] *Christian Examiner,* 18 (1835), 238. For the conservative side of
Channing's thought, see Wright, *The Liberal Christians,* pp. 36–38.

giddy and intoxicating heights—not just Channing, but even some ministers who later accused the Transcendentalists of atheism. In the 1836 Dudleian Lecture at Harvard, for example, John Brazer told the undergraduates:

Let nothing come in competition with the established claims, the rightful supremacy, of your religious capacities and powers. Let nothing mar, debase, or impair them. Let the idea of God sit enthroned, as God, within you. Let the authentic and imperative voice of conscience be ever, and under all circumstances, implicitly obeyed. Honor it. Reverence it. Fall down before it. Give it the entire homage of your entire soul.[34]

This was not *quite* Transcendentalism, but under the circumstances it was an invitation to disaster. After hearing this sort of rhetoric from their seniors, Emerson and Parker were understandably surprised by the reaction they provoked. They were not so naive as to be unconscious of playing the role of *enfants terribles,* but they were genuinely taken aback by the depth of Unitarian resentment toward them. Partly this was because they themselves retained a strong tinge of intellectual conservatism, as we shall soon see.

The foregoing discussion has pointed up two aesthetic trends. First, increasingly greater claims are made for the importance of the arts as Orthodoxy gives way to Unitarianism and Unitarianism to the Transcendentalism of Emerson's Divinity School Address. Second, despite this tendency, art continues to be justified on religious grounds, rather than for its own sake alone. Though Emerson elevated the poet to a position superior to that of the minister, he still prized poetry for spiritual reasons, for "the feeling of Immortality it awakens" (*JMN,* VII, 314). "The highest originality," he says, "must be moral": the Bible and other sacred scriptures are the only really original

[34] "Review of the Argument in Support of Natural Religion," *Sermons* (Boston: Crosby and Nichols, 1849), p. 367.

books, compared to which even Shakespeare is derivative (*W*, IV, 357). "When we speak of Poet in the great sense, we seem to be driven to such examples as Ezekiel & St. John & Menu with their moral Burdens; and all those we commonly call poets become rhymsters & poetasters by their side" (*JMN*, VIII, 229).

Emerson's literary objective, then, was twofold: to unite "seer" and "sayer," spiritual insight and beautiful expression. This ambivalence is reflected by the image of the poet-priest in the Address and pervades all his literary criticism. Like the ideal preacher, Emerson's "Poet" must be the "reconciler" (*W*, III, 37), perfect in both inspiration and utterance (*W*, III, 37). In *Representative Men*, Shakespeare and Swedenborg personify the two poles. "For executive faculty, for creation, Shakespeare is unique"; his power of expression is incomparable (*W*, IV, 212); but he had no conscious purpose beyond beauty and amusement, Emerson thinks (*W*, IV, 217 f). Swedenborg, on the other hand, was a seer with the vision of a great poet, but his mind was warped by its "theologic determination," and so his work is often dull and ugly (*W*, IV, 134). What is needed, Emerson concludes, is a "poet-priest, a reconciler, who shall not trifle, with Shakespeare the player, nor shall grope in graves with Swedenborg the mourner; but who shall see, speak, and act, with equal inspiration" (*W*, IV, 219). Not surprisingly, he looked in vain for the poet he described (*W*, III, 37).

Nor was Emerson's aesthetic position wholeheartedly endorsed by all Transcendentalists, even though most did look up to Emerson as "the best of us all." [35] A broad range of variance existed within the movement.

To begin with, a number of the Transcendentalist ministers who still saw possibilities in organized religion and maintained a stronger reverence for historical Christianity distrusted the antinomian tendency in Emerson's thought (as he himself did at times) and regarded his poetic style and theories as beautiful but somewhat frivolous. Frederic Henry Hedge, James Freeman

[35] W. H. Channing to Fredrika Bremer, reported in her *The Homes of the New World* (New York: Harper, 1853), I, 73.

Clarke, William Henry Channing, Parker, and Cyrus Bartol all voiced criticisms of this sort. Their impatience with Emerson's rhapsodies tended to vary in proportion to their social conscience. Bartol, for instance, was himself an aesthete who affected an oracular style; his objection was little more than a slight, decorous quibble over Emerson's heterodoxy.[36] W. H. Channing, however, took Emerson severely to task for ivory towerism, beginning with a review of "The American Scholar." "Not as a scholar, not with a view to literary labor, not as an artist, must he go out among men—but as a brother man," Channing declares.[37] For pastors and reformers intent on communicating the new views to ordinary people, the literary model Emerson presented was a positive encumbrance. The raptures of prophecy, after all, had to be made intelligible to the understanding. Most of the Transcendentalist ministers maintained, like more conservative Unitarians, that "Literature should be the handmaid of Religion," considering it "simply another aspect of man's attempt to better himself."[38] Significantly, when Emerson tried to channel the missionary impulses of two of his friends—Bronson Alcott and Jones Very—in a more literary direction, he met with stiff resistance. One of Alcott's severest strictures on Emerson is that he was too narrowly literary in his interests.[39]

[36] "Poetry and Imagination," *Christian Examiner*, 42 (1847), 259–260; *Ralph Waldo Emerson: A Discourse in West Church* (Boston: Williams, 1882).

[37] "Emerson's *Phi Beta Kappa Oration*," *Boston Quarterly Review*, 1 (1838), 116. See also Orestes Brownson, "Mr. Emerson's *Address*," *ibid.*, pp. 500–516, which is much less sympathetic to the Divinity School Address than the excerpt in *Tr*, pp. 198–200, would lead one to believe.

[38] Quotations from Samuel Osgood, "The Old World and the New," *Western Messenger*, 2 (1836), 202; and Russel B. Nye, "The Literary Theory of Theodore Parker," *Papers of the Michigan Academy of Science, Arts, and Letters*, 32 (1946), 457. See also Virgil Michel, *The Critical Principles of Orestes A. Brownson* (Washington, D.C.: Catholic University of America Press, 1918), pp. 7–47.

[39] *JA*, pp. 90–91 and passim. The Emerson-Alcott relationship is discussed at great length in Odell Shepard, *Pedlar's Progress: The Life of*

For another group of Transcendentalists, on the other hand, the Emersonian aesthetic did not go far enough. One of these was Margaret Fuller, who felt that Boston culture was insensitive to "the poetical side of existence" for its own sake, not "poetry in its import or ethical significance, but in its essential being, as a recreative spirit that sings to sing." Her cosmopolitanism was part of what eventually drew her away from the orbit of Boston to New York and Europe.[40] John Sullivan Dwight, Christopher Cranch, Ellery Channing, and, to some extent, Henry Thoreau, were also closer to the purely artistic temperament than Emerson. "How could there be a religion without music?" Dwight asks, and he answered the question for himself by quitting the ministry after one year and devoting the best part of his active career to the criticism of music.[41] Cranch, also a ministerial dropout,[42] and Channing, who never got through

---

Bronson Alcott (Boston: Little, Brown, 1937), and Hubert H. Hoeltje, *Sheltering Tree: A Story of the Friendship of Ralph Waldo Emerson and Amos Bronson Alcott* (Durham, N.C.: Duke University Press, 1943). For the Emerson-Very relationship, see Edwin Gittleman, *Jones Very: The Effective Years, 1833–1840* (New York: Columbia University Press, 1967), pp. 162–167 and 232–352 passim.

[40] "Entertainments of the Past Winter," *Dial*, 3 (1842), 46. The most forceful scholarly statement of this contrast between Fuller and Emerson is Frederick A. Braun, *Margaret Fuller and Goethe* (New York: Holt, 1910), pp. 71–147, which overstates its case, however, in its attempt to disassociate Fuller from Transcendentalist moralism and present her as a child of Goethe. A more balanced view of Fuller's aesthetic opinions is Helen Neill McMaster, "Margaret Fuller as a Literary Critic," *University of Buffalo Studies,* 7 (Dec. 1927), 31–100.

[41] "Music," in *Aesthetic Papers*, ed. Elizabeth P. Peabody (New York: Putnam, 1849), p. 32. Dwight's criticism is to be found chiefly in the *Christian Examiner, The Harbinger,* and *Dwight's Journal of Music.* His aesthetic opinions are discussed in George Willis Cooke, *John Sullivan Dwight: Brook-Farmer, Editor and Critic of Music* (Boston: Small, Maynard, 1898).

[42] Cranch wrote little criticism, but was a prolific creative writer and would-be artist. His literary activities are discussed in Leonora Cranch

his first year as a Harvard undergraduate, were both essentially dilettantes who pursued long and rather troubled careers as painter-poet and poet-conversationalist, respectively. Both concluded rather pathetically after the fact that they were temperamentally unsuited for the prophetic role. Channing, for instance, was quite clearly cut out to be a writer of witty joux and mellow descriptive sketches rather than a bard of the profound; perhaps his most successful work, still unpublished, is a series of thirty New England situation comedies called "Fashionable Dialogues." [43] Thoreau had more of the prophetic spirit, but was wary of the oppressive moralizing in which the Transcendentalist ministers and (to a lesser extent) Emerson were prone to indulge. Though his own social and ethical writing is also in this vein, Thoreau liked at the same time to maintain an aesthetic distance from his own jeremiads: "What offends me most in my compositions is the moral element in them," he once declared (*JT*, I, 316).[44]

But neither Thoreau nor Fuller nor the *Dial* aesthetes deviated appreciably from the *ideal* of the poet-priest. Channing repeatedly celebrates it in his poetry ("So sacred is his Calling, that no thing / Of disrepute can follow in his path," etc.), and

---

Scott, *The Life and Letters of Christopher Pearse Cranch* (Boston: Houghton Mifflin, 1917), and F. DeWolfe Miller, *Christopher Pearse Cranch and His Caricatures of New England Transcendentalism* (Cambridge: Harvard University Press, 1951).

[43] bMS Am 800.6, Houghton Library, Harvard University. See Chapter 9, below, for a detailed discussion of Channing's writing.

[44] The question of whether Thoreau should be approached mainly as a moralist or an aesthete is broached in the Introduction and reappears below in different contexts, in Chapters 7, 8, and 11. The most ambitious attempt to dissociate Thoreau's aesthetics from Transcendentalist moralism is Joel Porte, *Emerson and Thoreau: Transcendentalists in Conflict* (Middletown, Conn.: Wesleyan University Press, 1965), which overstates its case in the same way as Braun does for Margaret Fuller (see note 40, above) but is useful in calling attention to the real differences between Thoreau and Emerson.

for a time, with Emerson's encouragement, even dared to think that *he* might be destined to become the bard of New England. Fuller, in reviewing Emerson, returns with a vengeance to the Emersonian party line: "A man who has within his mind some spark of genius or a capacity for the exercises of talent should consider himself as endowed with a sacred commission. He is the natural priest, the shepherd of the people." The poetry and criticism of the *Dial* breathe this same spirit almost in unison.[45] Even the Transcendentalist ministers and reformers partook of it, albeit more sparingly. Samuel Osgood conceded that "the Beautiful is the rightful priest of the True"; Theodore Parker, who censured the sort of piety which thrives on art but never translates itself into moral action, nevertheless praised Emerson both as a greater artist than Milton and as the foremost religious writer alive.[46]

The list of instances could be extended indefinitely. Altogether there is little doubt that Emerson's romanticist image of the poet-priest was generally accepted by other Transcendentalists as the model for the role of the artist, though they differed considerably in their dedication to it, their disposition for it, and their opinions of its importance. For some it became a life-style—for better or for worse; for others it was primarily a splendid ideal to dream about in one's idle moments. The literary among them naturally made more of it than the minister-reformer contingent. But even the latter adopted it at least to the extent of attaching great importance to inspiration and imagination in preaching.

This was quite understandable. It followed from Transcen-

[45] Margaret Fuller, "Emerson's Essays," *Life Without and Life Within*, ed. Arthur B. Fuller (Boston: Brown, Taggard and Chase, 1860), p. 192. For an informative, though unsympathetic, account of *The Dial*'s critical orientation, see Helen Hennessy, "*The Dial*: Its Poetry and Poetic Criticism," *New England Quarterly*, 31 (March 1958), 66–87.

[46] Quotation from *Tr*, p. 166. For Parker's opinions, see *Autobiography, Poems and Prayers*, p. 360; *Sermons of Religion*, p. 268; *American Scholar*, p. 74.

dentalism's central principle, the affirmation of man's ability to
experience God firsthand. This is a doctrine which has to be
communicated more by re-creation than analysis. The experience can of course be talked *about* in the language of analysis;
its probability can be established by induction, and so forth.
Hence the great importance of the erudition of Ripley, Hedge,
and Parker to the Transcendentalist movement. But because
spiritual experience is inherently a nonrational thing, indeed a
denial in itself of reason and logic, it will not bear to be talked
about for very long in the language of the understanding, as
Emerson noted. To make it convincing demands all the resources of which language is capable. Sensing this, Emerson
wisely accompanied his call for an original relation to the universe (in *Nature*) with a call for original use of language.

The basis for the idea of the poet-priest was of course also
partly temperamental. It is impossible to say just where principles began and personality left off. Had Emerson not been a
dreamy, poetic youth, he would not have become a literary man.
Perhaps his formidable Aunt Mary Emerson made the profoundest comment on her nephew when she declared that no
Emerson "is capable of deep investigation or of long-continued
thought." [47] He himself once said of the attraction of the poet's
role that "the provocation is not that the Law is there, but the
means are alluring" (*JE*, VI, 144). Had not a number of Transcendentalists felt the same way, the movement might have expressed itself much less in the area of literature and more in,
say, abolitionism. Philosophically most of the Transcendentalists were against slavery at least as much as they were for poetry,
but being cultivated intellectuals, for the most part they chose
to express this protest in a literary way.

Similarly, the central message of Transcendentalism itself,
the idea of divine immanence, was not just a stage in the orderly
unfolding of religious thought in New England, but the natural

[47] Quoted in George Tolman, *Mary Moody Emerson,* ed. Edward Waldo
Forbes (n.p., 1929), p. 17.

expression of certain particular temperaments to be found in any age. Parker and Brownson, for example, report that as young children they experienced a deep and intimate sense of God's presence and felt called to the ministry.[48] They were headed for Transcendentalism before the Unitarian controversy had well begun. Something of the same can be said of Walt Whitman, whose affinities with the Transcendentalists are probably best explained by the fact that he was like a number of them to begin with: dreamy, rather adolescent, unambitious in a conventional way, optimistic yet confused about his identity. All this was chiefly what made Whitman simmer to the point where Emerson could bring him to a boil.

The Transcendentalist ferment might not have amounted to anything, however, had it not been for the particular position of the ministry and the institutional church at this point in history. The ministry had traditionally been the recognized vocational option in New England for young men of altruistic and literary impulses; but the satisfactions of the clerical life were not now what they once were. No longer was the frugal, sometimes penurious, existence of the average preacher offset by the compensation of being revered as a local patriarch, the shepherd of his people. Though according to one estimate the ratio of church members to total population in America nearly doubled between 1800 and 1835,[49] the connection between pastor and people was actually weakened. Advances in the educational system and in the mass media eroded the minister's traditional status as the most learned man in the community, even on religious matters. Sectarian disputes divided his congregations and sapped his energy. He had to fight (or join) as never before a

---

[48] Brownson, *The Works of Orestes A. Brownson,* ed. Henry F. Brownson (Detroit: Nourse, 1882–1907), V, 5–6; Parker, *Autobiography, Poems and Prayers,* p. 290.

[49] Winthrop S. Hudson, *Religion in America* (New York: Scribner, 1965), p. 129. The ratio of church *attendance* to total population Hudson estimates at 40 and 75 per cent respectively.

range of secular outlets for the religious impulse: temperance, antislavery and other reform societies, the lyceum, the religious press, and the like, all of which undermined the uniqueness of the church. By the same token, these organizations, plus opportunities in the west and the sudden proliferation of church-related colleges across the country, created a more enticing variety of alternative vocations for a minister than ever before. As a result, pastoral removals and changes of occupation become so common by 1835 that one observer wondered "whether any will hereafter close their life in the sacred office, unless they are taken away in the very flower of youth." [50]

Needless to say, his fear was premature; but among those who did remain in the ministry one often finds paeans to the dignity of the profession alternating with confessions of clerical self-distrust. Orville Dewey, for example, frequently complains about the disparity between the "superstitious reverence and false respect" accorded a minister and the feebleness of his actual influence. "We grapple with the world's strife and trial, but it is in armor. . . . We are a sort of moral eunuchs," Dewey exclaims in one such mood.[51]

For the Congregational clergy the loss of social influence was particularly acute, since theirs had been the established church in New England up until the Revolution (and much later in some states). And among Congregationalists, the Unitarians felt the most aggrieved. Though the early years of the movement were a time of exhilaration, during which the Unitarians imagined that they were spearheading a mass reformation in American religion, by the 1830s it had become clear that Unitarianism

[50] "Sermons by the Late Rev. Ezra Shaw Goodwin," *New England Magazine,* 7 (1834), 248. For a thorough scholarly dicsussion of the status of the clergy at this time, see Daniel Calhoun, *Professional Lives in America: Structure and Aspiration, 1750–1850* (Cambridge: Harvard University Press, 1965), pp. 88–177.

[51] Orville Dewey, *Autobiography and Letters,* ed. Mary E. Dewey (Boston: Roberts, 1883), pp. 231, 88. See also Dewey, "Dignity of the Clerical Office," *Christian Examiner,* 12 (1832), 349–375.

was destined to be only a small wave in the tide of religious awakening which was sweeping across the country. In a period of phenomenal growth in the evangelical sects, the Unitarians made little headway; though their ranks included many of the leading men in New England, their denominational strength was confined mainly to Massachusetts. The Orthodox soon counteracted much of their influence within Congregationalism itself by reforms of their own, and as a result by 1855 they outnumbered the Unitarians by almost twenty to one.[52] In retrospect it is clear that from the start the Unitarians were in an untenable position. On the one hand, they would not compete in their proselytizing with evangelical protestantism because their distrust of emotionalism made them unwilling to use revivalistic tactics. On the other hand, their appeal to the large body of deists and ethical humanists was limited because they insisted in preserving the vestiges of revelation.

Some Unitarians blamed their lack of success on the Transcendentalists, for discrediting organized religion and for disrupting the life of the church. But Transcendentalism was, as we have seen, a symptom rather than a cause. Seldom have the recognized leaders of a denomination been so critical of it, almost from the start, as were the Unitarians'. Henry Ware, Jr., was sometimes so critical of Unitarians that "it was often said . . . that he was no Unitarian." [53] Channing always spoke disparagingly of sects, liked to think of himself as not belonging to one, and predicted "that our present religious organizations will silently melt away." [54] John G. Palfrey, Dean of the Harvard Divinity School during the 1830s, publicly averred that for the half-century preceding his generation, the Congregational clergy were "with highly honorable exceptions . . . con-

[52] Timothy L. Smith, *Revivalism and Social Reform in Mid-Nineteenth-Century America* (New York: Abingdon, 1957), p. 14.

[53] Edward Brooks Hall, "Memoir of Henry Ware," *Christian Examiner*, 40 (1846), 279. Hall rejects the allegation, however.

[54] Letter to *Western Messenger*, 2 (1836), 167.

sidering their obligations and advantages, an exceedingly' imbecile class of men." Palfrey professed to think better of his contemporaries, yet he also described the student body of the Divinity School "as being made up of mystics, skeptics, and dyspeptics." [55] Such criticisms, motivated by a variety of factors—liberal inclination, personal pique, economic problems—naturally conspired to undermine morale. The Transcendentalist controversy brought the problem to the surface and intensified it. After 1840, the younger Ware observed, it became the fashion among ministers of the liberal stamp to "claim nothing on account of our office; nothing but for our character and services." Ware deplored this policy as "suicidal," which was quite correct,[56] but there was little that could be done about it at that late date except for conservatives to retrench against the liberal faction, as they did.

Meanwhile, fewer young men were going into the ministry. The percentage of Harvard graduates who became clergymen had dropped fairly steadily since the seventeenth century, from more than 50 per cent in Harvard's early years to 15 per cent between 1800 and 1830 to 10 per cent between 1830 and 1850, until the class of 1855 produced no ministers at all.[57] Of those students who did graduate work in divinity at Harvard through 1850, only 70 per cent were ordained (as compared to 80 per cent at the rival Orthodox seminary at Andover) and 25 per cent of those ordained later left the ministry.[58] "A man enters the D. School but knows not what shall befall him there, or where he shall come out of its tortuous track," wrote Emerson

[55] *A Sermon Preached at the Installation of Rev. Samuel Kirkland Lothrop* (Boston: Hale, 1934), p. 10; T. W. Higginson, *Cheerful Yesterdays* (Boston: Houghton Mifflin, 1898), p. 101.

[56] "The Pastoral Office," *Christian Examiner,* 32 (1842), 61.

[57] *Catalogus Senatus Academici . . . in Universitate Harvardiana* (Cambridge: Metcalf, 1857).

[58] *General Catalogue of the Divinity School of Harvard University* (Cambridge: Harvard, 1915); *General Catalogue of the Theological Seminary, Andover, Massachusetts: 1808–1908* (Boston: Todd, 1909).

in 1841. "Some reappear in trade, some in the navy, some in Swedenborg chapels, some in landscape painting" (*JMN*, VIII, 119). The situation was not critical, but it was highly disturbing, especially when the defectors from the ministry had the prestige of an Emerson or a Ripley. The period of indecision which young men normally went through before becoming clergymen was now protracted; even the most devout hesitated to commit themselves. All Theodore Parker's friends, for example, "advised [him] against the ministry—it was 'a narrow place, affording no opportunity to do much' ";[59] and though Parker eventually rejected this advice (not without misgivings for some years) he always retained a prejudice against ministers in general, maintaining his self-respect only by believing that he was an exception to the rule.

In short, by the 1830s the state of liberal religion in New England was such as to disaffect a significant number of young men and women of altruistic and/or aesthetic bent who just a generation or so before would have been able to find enough satisfaction in conventional piety, for whom art and personal rapport with nature were more uplifting than sermons and church worship and for whom writing, lecturing, and social action were more rewarding and effectual when done outside the church than within. This was the state of mind underlying Transcendentalism and the vision of the self-reliant poet-priest.

Small wonder, then, if that image was such a nebulous one. There was no institutionalized outlet for the ambitions of the Transcendentalists, no socially recognized name for what they wanted to do. They were going through the most severe crisis of identity ("vocation" was their word for it) that New England had seen; they were the first really modern American generation in that respect, as in several others. Henry Nash Smith and other scholars have rightly noted that it was a favorite Tran-

[59] *Autobiography, Poems and Prayers,* p. 294. Cf. Tilden Edelstein, *Strange Enthusiasm: A Life of Thomas Wentworth Higginson* (New Haven: Yale University Press, 1968), pp. 18–67.

scendentalist pastime to brood about one's vocation.[60] The answers they hit upon were always metaphorical and grandiose. "I would fain be a fisherman, hunter, farmer, preacher, etc., but fish, hunt, farm, preach other things than usual," says Thoreau (*JT,* VI, 45); and again, "My profession is to be always on the alert to find God in nature" (*JT,* VI, 472). Impractical? No matter, for as Emerson said, "a little integrity is better than any career" (*W,* VI, 189). When John Sullivan Dwight lost his job as a minister in Northampton, Elizabeth Peabody encouraged him to be of good cheer for "the Ravens shall feed thee," and to remain on the spot "and minister in a truly transcendental way to a true church of friends . . . without money & without price—celebrating the communion of the Lord." [61] Such exuberance had its tragic side, in the long run. "All Emerson's young men," Sherman Paul points out, "had trouble in choosing careers; indeed, in looking back over that generation one finds in the wake of Transcendentalism a series of personal failures." [62]

Almost all the Transcendentalists with literary aspirations fell into this category. Emerson encouraged Alcott, Channing, Very, Thoreau, and Fuller in their writing, but if anything his influence kept them from literary success, at least as the world measures it. This was partly because he encouraged them to be uncompromisingly high-minded, partly because his view of the literary vocation was as vague as it was extravagant. Emerson

[60] Smith, "Emerson's Problem of Vocation—A Note on 'The American Scholar,'" *New England Quarterly,* 12 (1939), 52–67, rpt. in *Emerson: A Collection of Critical Essays,* ed. Milton R. Konvitz and Stephen E. Whicher (Englewood Cliffs, N.J.: Prentice-Hall, 1962), p. 60–71; Whicher, *Freedom and Fate: An Inner Life of Ralph Waldo Emerson* (New York: Barnes, 1961), pp. 126–130 and passim; Sherman Paul, *The Shores of America: Thoreau's Inward Exploration* (Urbana: University of Illinois Press, 1958), pp. 1–48.

[61] Elizabeth Peabody to John S. Dwight, 24 June 1841, Boston Public Library.

[62] Paul, p. 16.

considered himself a poet, "in the sense of a perceiver and dear lover of the harmonies that are in the soul and in matter, and specially of the correspondences between these and those." [63] This was an eloquent summation of the relationship between his poetic and pietistic impulses, but it did not readily translate into a practical program for making a living. Thoreau, following in Emerson's footsteps, complained about having experienced "a fullness of life, which does not find any channels to flow into. I feel myself uncommonly prepared for *some* literary work, but I can select no work" (*JT*, II, 467). Emerson's lecture on "The Transcendentalist" paints an unconsciously pathetic picture of the younger generation waiting in disaffected aloofness for the call which, as yet, has failed to come.

When the Transcendentalists did achieve literary success on their own terms, they almost inevitably fell short of popular acclaim. "Essays on 'The True, the Beautiful, and the Good,' " as James F. Clarke remarked to a friend, "are in no demand out of the vicinity of Boston." [64] In most cases, therefore, the Transcendentalists made their way in the world only to the extent that they abandoned the ideal of the poet-priest in favor of such institutionalized roles as minister, journalist, surveyor, and housewife. Lecturing in the lyceum was as close as they came to converting a truly transcendental mode of utterance into a popular success. This indeed seemed to be a forum in which unfrocked ministers could display their talents to best advantage. Lecturing involved many of the same oratorical techniques as preaching; it was a rapidly expanding field; and above all, it was open-ended. Anything was possible in the lecture room. "You may laugh, weep, reason, sing, sneer, or pray, according to your genius," Emerson told Carlyle.[65] But as it turned out,

[63] *The Letters of Ralph Waldo Emerson,* ed. Ralph L. Rusk (New York: Columbia University Press, 1939), I, 435.

[64] Clarke, *Autobiography, Diary and Correspondence,* ed. Edward Everett Hale (Boston: Houghton Mifflin, 1891), p. 262.

[65] *The Correspondence of Emerson and Carlyle,* ed. Joseph Slater (New York: Columbia University Press, 1964), p. 171. In the early years of the

only Emerson and Parker among the Transcendentalists had much success in the lyceum. The other Transcendentalists found that the demand there, just as in preaching, was mainly for the entertaining, the easily intelligible, and the morally inoffensive. Without the notoriety of a Parker or the mystique of an Emerson, the Transcendentalist could not expect much more than an occasional honorarium.

In retrospect, it would appear that the Transcendentalist literati were in a doubly anomalous position, in relation to their times. On the one hand, they were in advance of their public in claiming more for the role of the poet than most of New England was prepared to admit. But on the other hand, they were also in a sense seeking to preserve the Puritan conception of the literary life in an era when that conception was fast becoming extinct. In picturing the role of the Poet in essentially religious terms, the Transcendentalists sought, in effect, to subsume their aesthetic impulses within the traditional theocentric framework of New England culture. As a result, in many respects they have more in common with Timothy Dwight and Edward Taylor than with the newly emerging class of literary professionals, such as Irving, Cooper, Poe, and even Hawthorne and Melville.

As we proceed to examine the Transcendentalist aesthetic in more detail, we should keep in mind these anomalies in their position. Not for sympathy's sake, since most of them have won their posthumous laurels, but as a reminder that the sort of literary vocation they had in mind cannot be easily pigeonholed. They themselves were vague about what they wanted, and what

---

lyceum, ministers appear to have been much better represented than any other occupational group. Of those persons listed as having lectured at the Concord Lyceum during its first fifty years (1829–1878), for example, about 30 per cent were ministers (*Proceedings on the Fiftieth Anniversary of the Organization of the Concord Lyceum* [Concord: Tolman and White, 1879]). For a short history of the lyceum movement, especially in New England, see Carl Bode, *The American Lyceum: Town Meeting of the Mind* (New York: Oxford University Press, 1956).

they wanted was not simply aesthetic or spiritual but a combination of the two. To a modern reader it may well seem that
their criticism and their art were vitiated by the intermixture,
but the reverse is actually more true. The view of the artist's
vocation as profoundly religious, for which the Unitarian movement had prepared the way, was a liberating conception for
them. If it helps account for their shortcomings, it is also a key
to their power.

2 Transcendentalist Literary Method: Inspiration versus Craftsmanship

We have witnessed the Transcendentalists' admiration for the vocation of the poet-priest. But what exactly does such an individual do? What sort of utterance is demanded of him, and what sort of discipline must he master if he is to achieve it?

At first sight, the Transcendentalists' ideas about literary method seems rather desultory, even abortive. The couplet inscribed on Emerson's gravestone would have made a good epitaph for the group as a whole: "The passive Master lent his hand / To the vast soul that o'er him planned." All Transcendentalist attempts to describe how art is to be created, and the impact which it should make upon its audience, begin and end with the idea of inspiration.[1] "Genius" is lauded, "talent" dis-

[1] For previous discussions of the idea of inspiration and its importance relative to craftsmanship in Emerson's thought, see Norman Foerster, "Emerson on the Organic Principle in Art," *PMLA*, 41 (1926), 193–208, rpt. in *Emerson: A Collection of Critical Essays*, ed. Milton Konvitz and Stephen E. Whicher (Englewood Cliffs, N.J.: Prentice-Hall, 1962), pp. 108–120; F. O. Matthiessen, *American Renaissance* (London: Oxford University Press, 1941), pp. 24–29; Vivian Hopkins, *Spires of Form* (Cambridge: Harvard University Press, 1961), pp. 17–62. For Thoreau, see Paul O. Williams, "The Concept of Inspiration in Thoreau's Poetry," *PMLA*, 79 (1964), 466–472. For Very, see Edwin Gittleman, *Jones Very: The Effective Years, 1833–1840* (New York: Columbia University Press, 1967), pp. 77–79, 87–92, 304–305. For Brownson, see Virgil Michel, *The Critical Principles of Orestes A. Brownson* (Washington, D.C.: Catholic University of America Press, 1918), pp. 20–21, 37–40.

paraged. "There can be no will in composition," Alcott insists.
"The spirit within is the only writer" (*JA*, p. 206). The poet
"does not seek his song," says Brownson, "it comes to him. It is
given him." [2] Jones Very even professed to value his poems "not
because they were his but because they were not." [3] Emerson
agreed. "A work of art," he says, "is something which the Reason created in spite of the hands" (*JMN*, V, 206), lasting "in
proportion as it was not polluted by the wilfulness of the writer,
but flowed from his mind after the divine order of cause and
effect" (*W*, XII, 466). At such times as these, Emerson sounds
like those early protestants who claimed that good works are
actually an impediment to salvation.

But even as Emerson seems to be recommending a sort of
automatic writing, he is apt to come out with a shrewd remark
which suggests the opposite, as in his objections to Very and
Ellery Channing: "Is the poetic inspiration amber to embalm
& enhance flies & spiders? . . . Cannot the spirit parse &
spell?" [4] Although Emerson was a fanciful theorist, he could be
a demanding editor and good practical critic. Another example
is his mixed opinion of Wordsworth and Tennyson. Wordsworth, most Transcendentalists agreed, had genius; [5] Tennyson
had talent; each seemed deficient in the other category. In
principle, Emerson was prepared to venerate Wordsworth and
disparage Tennyson as "a beautiful half of a poet" (*JMN*, VII,
83). But he did not rest in this view. Picking up a new volume
of Wordsworth in 1835, for instance, Emerson reminds himself
(as if about to take medicine) that "I may find dulness & flatness,
but I shall not find meanness & error." But on the next day he
exclaims: "What platitudes I find in Wordsworth. 'I poet be-
stow my verse on this & this & this.' Scarce has he dropped the

[2] "Wordsworth's Poems," *Boston Quarterly Review*, 2 (1839), 143.

[3] Quoted in *JMN*, VIII, 52.

[4] *The Letters of Ralph Waldo Emerson*, ed. Ralph L. Rusk (New York:
Columbia University Press, 1939), II, 331.

[5] Brownson's review (see note 2 above) was the only dissent.

smallest piece of an egg, when he fills the barnyard with his cackle" (*JMN*, V, 99, 100). After such fatuities, Tennyson comes as "a godsend." [6] In the one essay in which they are compared, "Europe and European Books," Emerson moves with an obvious sense of relief from the former to the latter.

Again, Emerson was often carried away by what he took to be a new genius, in whom he placed "a faith approaching to superstition," as Alcott said; [7] but he was quick to have second thoughts. Alcott, Carlyle, Charles King Newcomb, Walt Whitman, and Emma Lazarus were all warmly praised at first, then coolly reappraised in much the same manner as Very and Channing. The famous letter to Whitman, so often taken as a key link in the great causal chain to which one reduces American literature for mythological purposes, is only one instance of the recurring syndrome, in Emerson's criticism, of high praise giving way to critical reservations followed by qualified respect. Nor was Emerson totally spontaneous when it came to his own writing. No method of composition could have been less spontaneous, indeed, than his practice of piecing together mosaics from journal to lecture to essay.

The same common sense, underneath a rhetoric of inspiration, can be found in all the other Transcendentalists with any claim to literary importance except for Channing and Very, and even Channing revised his manuscripts. Contrasting Byron and Goethe, Margaret Fuller concluded that untutored genius was great but cultivated genius was greater.[8] Thoreau, similarly, accepted the theory of inspiration, but with the proviso that "we blunder into no discovery but it will appear that we have prayed and disciplined ourselves for it" (*JT*, IX, 53). This statement represents pretty well the actual, as opposed to the apparent, consensus among the major Transcendentalists on the subject of inspiration. They were all enamored of the *idea* of inspiration, and hastened to ascribe as much as possible to it, even the

[6] *Letters*, III, 74.   [7] *Concord Days* (Boston: Roberts, 1872), p. 38.
[8] *Literature and Art* (New York: Fowlers and Wells, 1852), I, 50.

literary grubwork. (Witness Emerson's declaration that the process of revising over a period of time does not negate his theory, because each part of the composition comes to the writer in a flash of insight (*JMN,* VII, 216–217). But as refined and sensitive people, they demanded satisfaction from the finished product. Discipline, then, was a hidden but genuine part of the Transcendentalist aesthetic. Even Jones Very served an apprenticeship in sonneteering before he wrote his "inspired" pieces, though he may not have regarded it as such.

In some ways the Transcendentalist view of the creative process resembles the attitude taken toward the workings of grace in the covenant theology of the Puritans.[9] In each case, the individual is theoretically powerless and the spirit does the work. All believe and delight in the absolute sovereignty of God or the Muse as the case may be. But the doctrine of sovereignty is hedged about with qualifications as to the importance of individual preparation. These qualifications were muted enough to expose both Puritans and Transcendentalists to the charge of antinomianism, but distinct enough to allow both to repudiate it.

The analogy must not be pushed too hard, or it will make Emerson, with his fondness for the Plotinian theory of the poet's divine madness, seem altogether too respectable; but the resemblances that do exist are more than coincidental, as the Transcendentalists' use of biblical language to talk about the creative process should have suggested. However much it relies for its expression on such literary jargon as genius/talent, imagination/fancy, and classic/romantic, their theory of creativity begins, like the concept of the poet-priest itself, with their intui-

[9] My knowledge of this subject derives chiefly from Perry Miller's discussions in chapter x of *The New England Mind: The Seventeenth Century* (New York: Macmillan, 1939), and in his essay "The Marrrow of Puritan Divinity," in *Errand into the Wilderness* (Cambridge: Harvard University Press, 1956).

tions about religious experience. Inspiration did not mean for them a great idea for a poem or story, so much as the experience of that Truth or Reality of which the finished work was to be the expression. We must bear in mind this equation of creativity with spiritual or intellectual fulfilment if we are to understand not only the theoretical importance they attached to inspiration but also their practical attention to craftsmanship. Though these attitudes might seem incompatible, both are consistent with the Transcendentalists' peculiar beliefs as renegade Unitarians. Their chief weapon against Unitarian "rationalism," as we have seen, was to insist that all men have direct access to the deity. And yet none of them, except Jones Very and perhaps Theodore Parker, seem to have been steady partakers in the divine experience they celebrate. No Transcendentalists wrote diaries like those of many pious evangelicals, with their almost daily attributions of particular events to providence. To be sure, this is explicable partly on technical grounds. The Transcendentalists, like the Unitarians, tended to discount such claims as superstitious, at best quaint, at worst delusive. They viewed spiritual fulfilment in terms of human, natural excellence rather than in terms of supernatural intervention. "Which is greater & more affecting?" Emerson asks, "to see some wonderful bird descending out of the sky, or, to see the rays of a heavenly majesty of the mind & heart emitted from the countenance & port of a man?" (*JMN*, VII, 236). The true mystical experience, that is, is a transfiguration from within and not a message or thunderbolt from without. But even this sort of experience is rarely recorded by the Transcendentalists. If one excepts their obviously fictitious recreations of ecstasy, like "Bacchus" and "Merlin," as merely vicarious and wish-fulfilling, there are not more than a score of mystical experiences reported by the whole lot of them to rival in emotional intensity the habitual fervor of some of the great American revivalists. Alcott and Fuller each had several; Orestes Brownson had vi-

sions in his childhood; Charles King Newcomb and Ellery
Channing record none.[10] Emerson gives us something like the
real article in "Each and All" and the two anecdotes in the first
chapter of *Nature*—crossing the common and becoming a transparent eyeball; but all three of these are literary elaborations of
observations which are reported in a comparatively matter-of-
fact way in his journal. The closest thing to a detailed account
of an ecstatic experience to be found in all his writing is the
description of his illumination in Mt. Auburn Cemetery in
1834 (*JMN*, IV, 272–273). Thoreau's writings are almost as un-
mystical. Judging from his frequent complaints in later life of
a loss of spontaneous perception, it may well be, as Ethel Seybold says, that he was "a youthful mystic" who later "lost the
ability to enter the ecstatic state." [11] In any case, he left little
record of such experiences, with the exception of a few journal
passages (e.g., *JT*, VIII, 43–45) and three more literary descriptions, all written during the 1840s: two in *A Week* (on "Monday" night and "Tuesday" morning) and one in "Ktaadn." [12]
For the most part Thoreau's writing conveys the sense of a
highly self-conscious and rational intelligence.

This hasty census suggests that despite what the Transcendentalists said about inspiration, they were nearly as Unitarian in

[10] Odell Shepard, *Pedlar's Progress: The Life of Bronson Alcott* (Boston:
Little, Brown, 1937), pp. 437–439; *Ossoli*, I, 140–142, 288–289, 308–309;
Brownson, *The Works of Orestes A. Brownson*, ed. Henry F. Brownson
(Detroit: Nourse, 1882–1907); V: *The Convert*, pp. 5–6; Charles King
Newcomb, *The Journals of Charles King Newcomb*, ed. Judith Kennedy
Johnson, Brown University Studies, 10, Americana Series, No. 1 (Provi-
dence, 1946), p. 85; Ellery Channing manuscript journals, bMs Am 800.6,
Houghton Library, Harvard University.

[11] Ethel Seybold, *Thoreau: The Quest and the Classics* (New Haven:
Yale University Press, 1951), p. 73.

[12] One cannot dogmatize about Thoreau, however. Some readers might
also wish, for example, to include Thoreau's excitement near the end of
"Spring" and his moment of cosmic reassurance in "Baker Farm," although
I myself find the first too naturalistic and the second too self-consciously
mythical as well as a bit tongue-in-cheek.

their emotional restraint as they were in their distrust of particular providences. Emerson, for example, disliked the "restlessness and fever" of Fuller's religious enthusiasm (*Ossoli*, I,
309). "He who trusts to sudden flashes of good feeling and excitement, follows no safe guide," says the persona in one of
Cranch's parables.[13] Altogether, Transcendentalism was not so
much an antirational reaction to Unitarianism as it was, in
Clarence Gohdes' admirable phrase, "Unitarianism in the process of 'getting religion.' "[14] Theirs was a highly intellectual,
almost a hypothetical mysticism, more talked about than felt.
It was not so much that they lacked the emotional capacity for
such experience, but that they were too sophisticated to be uninhibited about it, and also too conscientious or unselfish to
want to wall themselves up forever with God, without trying
to communicate with others. "One must not seek to dwell always in contemplation of the Spirit," Emerson cautioned, lest
he become indolent and helpless (*JMN*, VIII, 188). "The spiritual life," another Transcendentalist minister agreed, "demands, rather contains in itself, the germ which produces . . .
utterance of word, utterance of deed."[15] It may be significant
that the most passionate men among the Transcendentalists,
Brownson and Parker, were also the most committed to logic,
as if they felt compelled to rationalize their emotion, and that
both found fulfilment in religio-social causes: Catholicism in
Brownson's case, theological and social reform in Parker's.
Parker's temperament was especially paradoxical. Time and
again he insists that belief is a matter of intuition not subject
to proof, and from such sermons as "The Delights of Piety" it
would seem that he experienced this feeling as much as any
man. But at the same time he feels driven to bolster his intui-
tionalism by copius demonstration and encyclopedic reference.

[13] "The Lightning and the Lantern," *Western Messenger*, 5 (1838), 374.
[14] *The Periodicals of American Transcendentalism* (Durham, N.C.: Duke
University Press, 1931), p. 10.
[15] Thomas T. Stone, *Sermons* (Boston: Crosby, Nichols, 1854), p. 101.

He seems to have had a farm-boy's simple trust in the power of knowledge, as well as a farm-boy's simple faith. Parker pushes the intuitions still further into the background by insisting upon the moral life as the test of piety. "Parkerism," as a result, is as much rationalism and social gospel as it is Transcendentalism, though the latter is its starting point.

Nowhere are the Transcendentalists' lurking reservations about the validity of inspiration more evident than in their reaction to Jones Very. None of the Transcendentalists were much impressed with Very's messianic claims, not even Alcott, who was most sympathetic. They realized that he spoke reason in madness, but it was still madness. James Freeman Clarke, for instance, draws the following conclusion from Very's insistence to Dr. Channing that he did everything "in obedience to the spirit," even so small an act as walking across the room and leaning on the mantel: "And, indeed, if it has become a habit of the soul to be led in all things, great and small, why not in this too? Only, I suppose, that most of us would not think it worth while to consult the Spirit in such a purely automatic action as this." [16] This is the voice of urbanity curbing the misguided enthusiast, the same voice which speaks in Emerson's comments about Brook Farm, or the Chardon Street Convention, or Edward Palmer, the man who wanted to abolish money. In a way, Yvor Winters was quite right when he said that Very "had the experience which Emerson merely recommends." [17] Emerson admitted as much himself: " 'Tis remarkable that our faith in ecstasy consists with total inexperience of it" (*W*, VI, 213). Indeed, as his writings show, the faith thrived on the inexperience: after the late 1830s, Emerson's praise of inspiration actually gets more effusive the more he complains about his own lack of it. As he felt his powers of perception wane, inspiration seemed progressively more wonderful.

[16] Jones Very, *Poems and Essays,* ed. James F. Clarke (Boston: Houghton Mifflin, 1886), p. xxv.

[17] *Maule's Curse* (Norfolk, Conn.: New Directions, 1938), p. 127.

Still, Emerson sold himself short, with characteristic modesty. Nor should we judge the other Transcendentalists by their reactions to Very. Though they fell short of hierophancy, and were skeptical of Harvard tutors who suddenly claimed to be prophets, there is no question that they experienced inspiration of a sort, perhaps many times. At least they thought so. Emerson, Hedge, Parker, Thomas Stone, and Thoreau all undertook to give a general description of what it felt like.[18] The best-known accounts are Emerson's descriptions of afflatus in "The Poet" and "The Over-Soul." But one gets a better idea of the experiential basis for these idealized pictures if we turn to a passage with a more personal ring.

We say I will walk abroad, and the truth will take form and clearness to me. We go forth, but cannot find it. It seems as if we needed only the stillness and composed attitude of the library to seize the thought. But we come in, and are as far from it as at first. Then, in a moment, and unannounced, the truth appears. A certain wandering light appears, and is the distinction, the principle, we wanted. But the oracle comes because we had previously laid siege to the shrine. It seems as if the law of the intellect resembled that law of nature by which we now inspire, now expire the breath . . . , the law of undulation. [*W*, II, 331–332]

The "inspiration" reported here is modest, but genuine. Everyone has encountered it in some form. It is not the road to Damascus or the Pentacostal fire, but a very natural thing, as natural as breathing, but also mysterious and involuntary, although Emerson is careful to note that we can prepare for it to some extent. It was this sort of phenomenon which formed the primary existential basis for the Transcendentalist theory of literary inspiration. When they talk, that is, of the poet as hav-

[18] In addition to previous citations, see Parker, *A Discourse of Matters Pertaining to Religion,* ed. Thomas Wentworth Higginson (Boston: American Unitarian Association, 1907), pp. 203–205; Hedge, "The Transfiguration: A Sermon," *Western Messenger,* 5 (1838), 82–88; Stone, *Sermons,* pp. 87–108.

ing direct access to godhead, their confidence derives mainly from having known such flashes of insight. When they talk of the possibility of a "perpetual revelation," they probably have in mind such insight extended and intensified to the nth power —not so much delirious transport as perfect powers of perception and sensitivity to one's surroundings. It was the failure to gain this anticipated level of awareness, rather than a deep allegiance to the idea of the divine madness in itself, which led Emerson during his middle years to overdramatize the process of inspiration as an almost supernatural event.[19]

Applying the same line of thought to religious experience as well as the intellectual illumination just quoted, one might contend that there was no real difference between the kind of inspiration felt by Transcendentalists and by other Unitarians, and by many modern believers, for that matter. This is suggested, for example, by Parker's description of comfort after prayer as a true inspiration. Some conservatives might have quibbled with his definition even as they shared precisely the same experience. Actually, as we have seen, the Unitarians did not categorically deny that there was such a thing as inspiration, and that it might be at work in such a case as Parker cited; they simply claimed less, claimed that it did not imply an identity of the soul with God, that its workings were indistinguishable from other mental acts. Conversely, while the Transcendentalists considered inspiration as a special experience, the most exciting fact of life, they did not think that it should take violent or perverse forms of expression. "It is no turbulent emotion," cautions F. H. Hedge, "no fever of the blood—no unnatural heat. It has nothing of the whirlwind or the tempest, but that repose which belongs alike to nature and to mind in their most healthy moods—the calmness of the sunshine—the

---

[19] For a sensitive account of the contradictions and changes in Emerson's statements about the nature of spiritual experience, see J. A. Ward, "Emerson and 'The Educated Will': Notes on the Process of Conversion," *ELH*, 34 (1967), 495–517.

tranquillity of intense contemplation." [20] Similarly, for most
other Transcendentalists, as Howard Mumford Jones has said,
"religion was an experience above, not beneath, the rational
faculty." [21] Father Edward Taylor, with his uninhibited sallies
of earthy rhetoric, qualified as inspired; Jones Very, when he
started to prophesy in garbled Old Testamentese, became suspect.

The fact remains, however, that once the Transcendentalists
began to dwell upon the glories of inspiration, they found it
hard to apply the brakes. The sense of exuberance one feels in
his best moments; the effort of striving to recapture it; the delight of believing that man is truly divine; the awareness that
inspiration comes by surprise—all these considerations led them
to condone and even to cultivate an extravagance of statement,
if not behavior, which goes well beyond what they said in their
more sober moments. So it was quite natural that Emerson, in
his criticism, should regard genius as implicitly including
craftsmanship and yet at the same time choose to view the whole
creative process as a divine mystery. Although he knew very well
the importance of discipline to writing and to inspiration itself,
he believed so strongly that the decisive factor in composition
was unpredictable and he attached such a cosmic significance
to it that he couldn't bring himself to praise discipline very
highly. Though F. O. Matthiessen oversimplifies in saying that
the Transcendentalist notion of art as inspiration is necessarily
"in sharp opposition" to the idea of art as craftsmanship, such
did prove to be the case in some instances, not so much for
Emerson and Thoreau as for some of the less gifted Transcendentalists.[22] The reluctance of Very and Channing to comply
with Emerson's editorial requests has been alluded to. Alcott
and Fuller might also have taken more pains with their writing

[20] Hedge, "The Transfiguration," p. 84.

[21] *Belief and Disbelief in American Literature* (Chicago: University of
Chicago Press, 1967), p. 54.

[22] *American Renaissance,* p. 25.

had they not been discouraged so quickly by the task of getting their insights down on paper. John S. Dwight came to grief as a preacher when, for a time, he took literally the principle of spontaneity and did not prepare. W. H. Channing could deliver beautiful extemporaneous orations but he wrote turgid prose; his biographer rightly says that he dissipated his talents. So did Cranch, who upbraided himself in old age for having "wooed too many mistresses." [23]

Despite this list of casualties, however, distrust of discipline per se was probably less of a problem for the Transcendentalists in the long run than confusion as to the nature of discipline. They recognized no distinction between art and life. They imbibed too eagerly the critical commonplace of their day, that to be a great artist one must be a good man. If an "immoral" person (like Goethe) seemed to have written a great book, then either the man really did have a great soul underneath or the book itself was somehow flawed.[24] This assumption is philosophically defensible; the real difficulty came when the Transcendentalists tried to reverse the idea and claim that the good man will be a good writer. That is exactly the position Emerson takes in "The Poet," in prescribing an ascetic regime for his bard: "Never can any advantage be taken of nature by a trick. . . . The sublime vision comes to the pure and simple soul in a clean and chaste body" (*W*, III, 28). Thoreau's version of this idea is easier to misread but also adamant: "Nothing goes by luck in composition. It allows of no tricks. The best you can write will be the best you are. Every sentence is the result of a long probation. The author's character is read from title-page

---

[23] Cranch, "Note Book," p. 193, Massachusetts Historical Society, Boston; O. B. Frothingham, *Memoir of William H. Channing* (Boston: Houghton Mifflin, 1886), pp. 7–8, 466–469; George W. Cooke, *John Sullivan Dwight* (Boston: Small, Maynard, 1898), pp. 35–36.

[24] Cf. Margaret Fuller, *Life Without and Life Within*, ed. Arthur B. Fuller (Boston: Brown, Taggard and Chase, 1860), pp. 13–60; and Brownson, "Bulwer's Novels," *Boston Quarterly Review*, 2 (1839), 265–297.

to end" (*JT*, I, 225–226). Here too the speaker dedicates himself to a discipline, and at first it seems to be the craft of writing. But it is not. Sincerity and moral seriousness are really what he is after. "The problem of the artist for Thoreau," Sherman Paul sums up, "was a question of depth," not of expertise,[25] and the same is true in even greater measure of the other Transcendentalists.

Given the times in which the Transcendentalists lived, their viewpoint is not at all surprising. The idea of art as an expression of character was a standard romantic assumption; it was also a classical assumption, and a Christian assumption too. It was drummed into Harvard students by every Boylston Professor of Rhetoric, beginning with John Quincy Adams. What is provocatively unique about the Transcendentalists is the seriousness with which they took it. It was no mere cultural shibboleth with them. Here, as at several other points, what differentiates them from the great English romantics as well as such compatriots as Hawthorne and Poe is not so much their critical principles as the strictness with which they applied them. Thus Coleridge's response to the gap between Wordsworth's theory of language and its practice was to criticize the theory, whereas Brownson's was to criticize the practice, to take Wordsworth to task for writing in a too artificial manner.[26] Likewise, the Transcendentalists took the messianic implications of the poet-priest more seriously than all English romantics except Blake and Shelley.

In their more worldly moments, the shrewdest Transcendentalists conceded that morality and art didn't always go hand in hand, as when Margaret Fuller went out of her way to insist that Byron's dissipation did nothing to impair his power as a writer.[27] Most of them, indeed, were sensitive to the power of

[25] Sherman Paul, *The Shores of America: Thoreau's Inward Exploration* (Urbana: University of Illinois Press, 1958), pp. 211–212.

[26] "Wordsworth's Poems," *Boston Quarterly Review*, 2 (1839), 155–156.

[27] *Literature and Art*, I, 76.

language as an independent instrument; they simply considered
it trivial if not employed in the service of truth. Such high-
mindedness prevented them from grappling with the technical
problems of craftsmanship as effectively as they might have
otherwise. They preferred to jump from fact to essence, from
the nuts and bolts of technique to affirmations like "The true
poem is not that which the public read"; "Life is the Poem;
Man is the Poet," and so forth. Because of this attitude, they
quickly became dissatisfied with art as a whole, for it was obvious that even the greatest works do not fully realize the inspiration that gave rise to them. Not even the writers of the Bible,
Andrews Norton had shown, had been able to do that. Like
Shelley, the Transcendentalists regarded art as at best a fading
coal, a feeble replica of the original experience. They tended to
be hardest on the best books, as being the most pretentious.[28]
Tennyson was declared lovely but facile, Wordsworth noble
but dull, Coleridge and Carlyle provocative but bigoted,
Goethe splendid but dilettantish, Shakespeare great but morally
unsound. By keeping their eye so scrupulously on the absolute,
the Transcendentalists thus short-circuited themselves both as
critics and artists. When confronted with a work of art which
came close to meeting their standards, which did seem worthy
of discussion, they were unable to account for it, let alone rival
it. And this, in turn, reinforced their sense of creativity as
miraculous.

   An interesting case of this sort is Cyrus Bartol's response to a
Madonna of Raphael which he saw in Dresden. This picture
captivated him, especially the eyes of the child, in which

there is, in what manner I know not, by what art or inspiration
painted I surely cannot tell, a supremacy of control which princi-
palities above or below might well fear to disobey, as though that
were the final authority of the universe.
   . . . Long did I inspect, and often did I go back to re-examine,

   [28] See especially *ibid.*, II, 2–4, where Fuller argues that serious literature
should be judged by higher standards than popular literature.

this mystery, which so foiled my criticism, and constrained my wonder, and convinced me, as nothing visible beside had ever done, that if no picture is to be worshipped, something is to be worshipped; that is to be worshipped which such a picture indicates or portrays. But the problem was too much for my solving.[29]

Clearly Bartol *wants* to remain mystified. He wants badly to draw a pious conclusion from this encounter, as he does from all the other "pictures of Europe" presented in his book. But it is clear too that he has approached the picture not just as a minister but as a critic; he has made a great effort to understand it, and failed. His praise of the artist's inspiration is a confession of personal inadequacy as well as an act of reverence.

This very Jamesian image of the preacher-aesthete overcome by the European masterpiece makes a good epitome of the Transcendentalist writer's predicament. His New England background had trained him to be a connoisseur of piety rather than of art, yet led him to the conclusion that great art was a high expression of piety. But how was he to be an artist, or even a critic, when his forte was the moral life? He might be aware that the Madonna was composed of brushstrokes and paint, but he could appreciate it only as the expression of spirit. This dilemma was almost as severe for Thoreau as it was for Bartol. Though Thoreau was a lot closer to being a professional writer and rated D.D.'s lower than chickadees, he could no more than Bartol be satisfied with a conception of art as craft.

Fortunately the problem implied its own solution, namely an expressivist-didactic form of art in which one's thought or experience or perception was uttered and regulated as deftly as possible but was still the dominant element. At best, if one was lucky or worked hard enough, the result would have the roundness of a masterpiece as well as the authenticity of truth. If not, it would at least be heartfelt, which was more than one could say for most art; it would be emancipated from the kind

[29] *Pictures of Europe, Framed in Ideas* (Boston: Crosby, Nichols, 1855), pp. 203–204.

of triviality which the Transcendentalists disparaged in "men of talent" like Longfellow. Indeed a little roughness might be a good thing: "The kingly bard/ Must smite the chords rudely and hard," says Emerson's Merlin (*W*, IX, 120). One representative literary model for the sort of utterance the Transcendentalists wanted was the ancient bard or prophet, a man of high seriousness, "rude and massive proportions" rather than "smooth and delicate finish,"[30] who would express himself with vehemence and enthusiasm in gnomic, picturesque speech.

> He may not stoop to pander to the herd,
>   Their fickle tastes and morbid appetites,
> He hath upon his lips a holy word,
>   And he must heed not if it cheers or blights,
> So it be Truth.[31]

Thus spake Cranch—a representative view of the poet's role. He himself was not too successful in his imitation of it, to say the least, nor was most Transcendentalist poetry. Thoreau tries in his doggerel:

> Conscience is instinct bred in the house,
> Feeling and Thinking propagate the sin
> By an unnatural breeding in and in.
> I say, Turn it out doors,
> Into the moors.   [*Wr*, I, 75]

But this sounds less like the bard than like the local crank. Very had a better sense of the prophetic tone:

> Thou art more deadly than the Jew of old,
> Thou hast his weapons hidden in thy speech;

---

[30] *Wr*, I, 378–379. See also Nelson F. Adkins, "Emerson and the Bardic Tradition," *PMLA*, 63 (1948), 662–677. The *direct* influence of bardic poetry on the Transcendentalists was slight; the bard was important rather as an image of the type of role they envisioned—a combination of artist and lawgiver. Among literary examples of the prophetic mode, the Bible was far more important to the Transcendentalists than any other.

[31] "The Poet," *Western Messenger*, 6 (1838), 90.

> And though thy hand from me thou dost withhold,
> They pierce where sword and spear could never reach.[32]

But his imagery is usually so derivative that his utterance seems like a pastiche or masquerade rather than the real thing. Perhaps Emerson came closest in his Channing Ode:

> Virtue palters; Right is hence;
> Freedom praised, but hid;
> Funeral eloquence
> Rattles the coffin-lid. [*W*, IX, 77]

On the whole, though, prose was a more congenial medium for the Transcendentalists, especially if the occasion happened to be a lecture or sermon:

Nothing changes more from age to age than the doctrines taught as Christian, and insisted on as essential to Christianity and personal salvation. What is falsehood in one province passes for truth in another. The heresy of one age is the orthodox belief and "only infallible rule" of the next. Now Arius, and now Athanasius, is lord of the ascendant. Both were excommunicated in their turn, each for affirming what the other denied. Men are burned for professing what men are burned for denying. [*Tr*, p. 266]

This passage, from Parker's "The Transient and Permanent in Christianity," comes closer than the poetry just quoted to what "Merlin" calls for: artful thunder. It has a truly prophetic sweep and intensity, combined with aphoristic bite. Emerson's Divinity School Address is in the same vein, though Parker is harder-hitting and much more explicit and orderly than Emerson (which explains why Parker aroused more opposition). The pervasiveness of this sort of rhetoric throughout Transcendentalist writing can be seen by glancing through any anthology. It appears in staccato in Brownson's *News Views:*

I do not misread the age. I have not looked upon the world only out from the window of my closet; I have mingled in its busy

[32] *Poems and Essays*, p. 88.

scenes; I have rejoiced and wept with it; I have hoped and feared, and believed and doubted with it, and I am but what it has made me. I cannot misread it. It craves union. [*Tr*, p. 123]

Where Brownson is merely strident, Thoreau likes to make his point more obliquely, by elaborating his exempla:

The best men that I know are not serene, a world in themselves. For the most part, they dwell in forms, and flatter and study effect only more finely than the rest. We select granite for the underpinning of our houses and barns; we build fences of stone; but we do not ourselves rest on an underpinning of granitic truth, the lowest primitive rock. Our sills are rotten. What stuff is the man made of who is not coexistent in our thought with the purest and subtilest truth? [*Wr*, IV, 470]

This is the Emersonian technique of showing man's shabbiness by comparison to nature, with the Thoreauvian twist of contrasting the poverty of our inner lives with the quality of our possessions.

The manifesto-note is not the only one the Transcendentalists favored, although it is the easiest to hear. Much of the time, they employed what we would regard as a normative or conventional style of writing. Nor, when they strove for special effects, did they always try to play Jeremiah or Taliessen, any more than Renaissance poets tried to write only epics. Another style, for instance, of which several of them were equally if not more fond, was the ruminative, especially in a pastoral setting. Thoreau's reflection on autumn flowers, in *A Week,* is an example:

There is a peculiar interest belonging to the still later flowers, which abide with us the approach of winter. There is something witch-like in the appearance of the witch-hazel, which blossoms late in October and in November, with its irregular and angular spray and petals like furies' hair, or small ribbon streamers. Its blossoming, too, at this irregular period, when other shrubs have lost their leaves, as well as blossoms, looks like witches' craft. Certainly it blooms in no garden of man's. There is a whole fairy-land on the hillside where it grows. [*Wr*, I, 318–319]

This passage gives us the prophet off-duty, so to speak, relaxing. Instead of lofty didacticism for public purposes, we see him playing with the significance of things. His vehemence has diffused into the dreamy atmosphere of fairyland. But it is still moral art: much as he loves nature for herself, Thoreau is not content to stay on the descriptive level alone, even in his later work where there is much less of reverie.

Some other Transcendentalist works which use this style, in whole or in part, are Emerson's "Musketaquid," "Saadi," "Woodnotes," "Stonehenge" (in *English Traits*), and the second essay on "Nature"; Judd's *Margaret;* Fuller's *Summer on the Lakes;* some of Very's nature poems; and much of Ellery Channing's verse. Next to Thoreau, Channing was fondest of pastoral meditation. His poetry in this vein (the best of which is better than it has been given credit for being, as I attempt to show in Chapter 9) ranges widely in content between description and didacticism, and between a leisurely and a compressed style. "Moonlight" is an example of his compression:

> He came and waved a little silver wand,
> He dropped the veil that hid a statue fair,
> He drew a circle with that pearly hand,
> His grace confined that beauty in the air;—
> Those limbs so gentle, now at rest from flight,
> Those quiet eyes now musing on the night.[33]

The stock imagery here is largely redeemed by the poem's compactness and elusive quality: who "he" is is not at first apparent; the last two lines suggest both Luna and someone ob-

[33] *The Collected Poems of William Ellery Channing the Younger,* ed. Walter Harding (Gainesville, Fla.: Scholars' Facsimiles and Reprints, 1967), p. 88.

serving her. As with the passage from Thoreau, the evocation of atmosphere is primary here, but it is an atmosphere in which one is induced to look for meanings.

Prophecy and meditation, manifesto and reverie, the bardic and the pastoral, Merlin and Saadi—much of Transcendentalist writing oscillates between these opposites. The charm of *Walden*, for instance, consists to a large extent in Thoreau's way of alternating between them. Such formulations are simplistic, of course; we shall need to look much more closely at the range of stylistic conventions underlying Transcendentalist literary expression. For now, the point to recognize is that the Transcendentalist idea of craftsmanship, however vaguely articulated, is not a contradiction in terms. Though their theory of inspiration kept them from coping with the practical problems of their craft as clear-sightedly as they might otherwise have done, most of the Transcendentalists interpreted the theory as explaining but not precluding literary labor. Although the kinds of expression which chiefly interested them emphasized message and tone at the expense of asthetic symmetry and logical precision, the Transcendentalists were by no means insensitive in their understanding and use of the intricacies of those points of style best suited to their ends.

PART II

THE LIVING WORD

When it came to putting their literary theories into practice, the Transcendentalists naturally relied to a large extent on the models most readily available to them. The next two chapters describe two such models, conversation and preaching, which may be regarded as those forms of self-expression most familiar to such provincial and aesthetically unsophisticated men and women as the Transcendentalists were upon entering adulthood. Generally speaking, they were far more sensitive connoisseurs of conversation and preaching than of the fine arts, and they tended to adapt the two forms for their own special purposes. Although the leading literary figures in the movement did not regard either conversation or preaching as an end in itself, elements of each recur continually in their writing and help to give it its special coloring. Tracing the Transcendentalists' awareness and use of these elements, furthermore, will give us a better idea of the complex relationship between the aesthetic and didactic impulses in their work. As we shall see, they tended to inhibit the art of conversation by making it into an instrument of education, but to liberalize the sermon by turning it into an art form.

3 From Conversation to Essay

> *Garrison made the Convention*
> *Greeley made the Newspaper,*
> *Emerson made the Lecture,*
> *and*
> *Alcott is making the Conversation.*
> —A. B. Alcott

If a writer believes that inspiration is more valuable than expression and that it cannot be fully expressed in any case, he is bound to ask himself at times, "Why bother to write at all?" The Transcendentalists often did. Partly for that reason, much of the spirit of the movement was never recorded in a lasting and memorable form. As an organized movement, Transcendentalism can almost be said to have begun and ended as a discussion group. Much of its internal ferment and a good deal of its external impact can be attributed to talkers like Alcott and Margaret Fuller; even its writing is largely oral literature, in the sense of having been composed originally for the pulpit or the lyceum.[1]

Alcott's choice of "Conversation" as his proper medium is understandable. He was, first of all, a teacher by vocation, a

[1] The most important contemporary published accounts of transcendental conversations are, for Alcott, *Conversations with Children on the Gospels*, 2 vols. (Boston: Munroe, 1836–1837); and conversations on "Woman," 'Plato," and "Personal Theism," reported in *The Radical*, 5 (1869), 89–102, 177–200, and 6 (1869), 22–33. In addition, see Alcott's scrapbook of newspaper clippings ("Autobiographical Collections") and his unpublished journals, Houghton Library, Harvard University; and the manuscript collection of reports on Alcott, "Notes of Conversations," Concord Free Library, Concord Massachusetts. For Fuller, see *Ossoli*, I,

teacher who believed in the value of dialogue with the student. The basis of his pedagogy was the idea of education in its root sense, a "drawing out" of the pupil by a combination of induction and response, a method which he did not fail to note was "the ancient mode of instruction," sanctioned by the greatest of teachers, Socrates and Jesus. In his use of it to teach young children, he seemed alarmingly radical for his times, especially when he began to imitate Jesus too closely and make the Oversoul a part of his curriculum.[2] But in his general fondness for informal and spoken discourse he was quite typical of his age. As Mason Wade observes, "it was far more a vocal than a literary era." [3] The contemporary Americans whom the Transcendentalists most respected as young people—Channing, Everett, and Daniel Webster—were pre-eminently public

---

345–347, as re-edited by Perry Miller in *The American Transcendentalists* (New York: Doubleday, 1957), pp. 102–103; and Caroline H. Dall, *Margaret and Her Friends* (Boston: Roberts, 1895).

The best source of information about the meetings of the Transcendental Club or Symposium is Alcott's unpublished journals. See also Odell Shepard, *Pedlar's Progress* (Boston: Little, Brown, 1937), pp. 246–261. "Alcott's 'Conversation' on the Transcendental Club and *The Dial*," a newspaper account re-edited by Clarence Gohdes, *American Literature*, 3 (1931), 14–27, has some interesting reminiscences. Two modern attempts to reconstruct the atmosphere of a public conversation are, for Alcott, *Pedlar's Progress*, pp. 231–246, and, for Fuller, Granville Hicks, "A Conversation in Boston," *Sewanee Review*, 39 (1931), 129–143. Madeline Stern's portrait of Fuller as a conversationalist in *The Life of Margaret Fuller* (New York: Dutton, 1942), pp. 181–198, is well researched though effusive.

[2] *Table-Talk* (Boston: Roberts, 1877), p. 91. For Alcott's references to Socrates and Jesus, see *JA*, pp. 63–64, 104; and "The Doctrine and Discipline of Human Culture," in *Conversations with Children on the Gospels*, I, xxxiv–xxvi. For studies of Alcott's teaching, see Shepard, pp. 180–218; Dorothy McCuskey, *Bronson Alcott, Teacher* (New York: Macmillan, 1940); and Charles Strickland, "A Transcendentalist Father: The Child-Rearing Practices of Bronson Alcott," *Perspectives in American History*, 3 (1969), 5–73, which gives a full and absorbing account of how Alcott applied his theories in his own home.

[3] *Margaret Fuller, Whetstone of Genius* (New York: Viking, 1940), p. 63.

speakers; three of their foremost European literary heroes—Goethe, Coleridge, and Madame de Staël—were also famous talkers.[4] In cultivated Boston society, the conversation club was also in fashion, commonly as a nexus for some literary enterprise. The affairs of the *Monthly Anthology* were transacted at the meetings of the Anthology Society. Andrews Norton, J. G. Palfrey, the Everetts, and other establishment literati formed a later group which met for dinner and talk. For the Transcendentalists, the best-known group, the Symposium or Transcendental Club of the later thirties was only one of several. It was preceded by a Cambridge group which gathered around Margaret Fuller, as well as a Boston group formed by Elizabeth Peabody, and followed by a club organized in the late 1840s by James Freeman Clarke and ultimately by the Radical Club. Those Transcendentalists who wanted to go respectable in their middle age could also join the Saturday Club or the short-lived Atlantic Club. And in addition to these organizations, of course, were innumerable ad hoc gatherings at Brook Farm, Fruitlands, Concord, and Boston.

Much of the interest of those Transcendentalists who participated in such groups can doubtless be explained in terms of the fashion of the day, the lack of other entertainment, and the perennial desire of intellectuals to talk together. But for the truly devoted, such as Alcott, Fuller, and Emerson, conversation was not just a pastime but also a fine art and fit subject for philosophy. Conversation had a special mystique for the Transcendentalists because of its spontaneous nature. As the

[4] See *Coleridge the Talker: A Series of Contemporary Descriptions and Comments,* ed. Richard W. Armour and Raymond F. Howes (Ithaca: Cornell University Press, 1940); *Goethe: Conversations and Encounters,* ed. and trans. David Luke and Robert Pick (Chicago: Regnery, 1966); and Emile Deschanel, *Histoire de la Conversation* (Brussels: Office de Publicité, 1857), pp. 161–166. The Transcendentalists would have been especially stimulated by Mme de Staël's remarks on conversation in *Germany;* Coleridge's *Table Talk;* and Margaret Fuller's translation of Johann Eckermann's *Conversations with Goethe* (Boston: Hilliard, Gray, 1839).

least studied form of expression, it approached most closely the ideal of a continuous inspiration. Good talk was perpetual discovery and improvisation. The inspired talker could also take more satisfaction in his performance than the writer because the formal requirements were less strict. In conversation one needed simply to express each thought as it came. This unfettered quality also appealed to the Transcendentalists for the range and versatility it permitted. "The magic of liberty" in such moments, as Emerson put it, makes "the world like a ball in our hands" (*W*, III, 32). "All we have, all we can, all we know, is brought into play, and as the reproduction, in finer form, of all our havings" (*W*, XI, 408–409).

Then, too, conversation was an available art. It was not the property of an elite, like the creation or connoisseurship of painting, but a universal ability. Of course it did require special gifts; Alcott periodically asserts that there is "nothing rarer than great conversation," that indeed he has never found any "surpassing talkers." [5] At the same time, conversational success was in reach of any thoughtful person, without extensive training. Thus conversation appealed to the Transcendentalists both as equalitarians of the spirit and as aesthetic amateurs, people of sensitive tastes with a largely untechnical interest in art.

Finally, conversation came closer than all other arts to realizing the Transcendentalists' idea of the proper relation between art and life. They believed in the romanticist notion of sincerity as a test of literary merit, that the reader should be able to sense a man behind the work. Whitman was proud to be able to say "Who touches this touches a man." Although most Transcendentalists looked down upon Byronic egoism and Rousseauistic confessional as perverse, they were equally romantic in insisting that literature seem to be an utterance from the depths of one's being, a human communication. Thus Emerson liked Montaigne because "the sincerity and marrow

[5] *Concord Days* (Boston: Roberts, 1872), p. 74; *JA*, p. 223.

of the man reaches to his sentences. . . . It is the language of conversation transferred to a book. Cut these words, and they would bleed; they are vascular and alive" (*W*, IV, 168). From this point of view, as Emerson's analogy suggests, conversation could be thought of as superior to writing. If the end of writing is communication, if literature is essentially a conversation between writer and audience, then how much more noble is conversation itself. "By it I come nearer the hearts of those whom I shall address than by any other means," Alcott wrote (*JA*, p. 104). "The lecture is too formal. It is, beside, presuming. Man doth not meet his fellow on equal terms. . . . And similar deficiencies are felt in regard to the book. Only the living, spoken, answered, word, is final." [6] At the best it leads to a truly communal inspiration, "a pentecost of tongues, touching the chords of melody in all minds." [7]

Not all Transcendentalists were as enthusiastic conversationalists as Alcott. Emerson, for instance, sometimes wearied of Alcott's marathon capacity for talk, though he enjoyed his company as much as any man's.[8] "Good as is discourse, silence is better, and shames it" (*W*, II, 311), Emerson concludes, in such a mood. Thoreau professed to think even less of talk. Devotees of conversation struck him as trying to "eject themselves like bits of packthread from the tip of the tongue." [9] When he himself was pressed to participate against his will, Thoreau liked to give his interlocutor the silent treatment. This usually proved discomfiting, which Thoreau took as a sign that he had exposed a false facade in the other person. Alcott and Margaret Fuller, on the other hand, were people whose best inspirations

[6] "Diary for 1838," p. 23, *MS* 59M–308 (11), Houghton Library, Harvard University.

[7] *Tablets* (Boston: Roberts, 1868), p. 76.

[8] For works on the Emerson-Alcott relation, see Chapter 1, note 39, above.

[9] "Conversation," *The First and Last Journeys of Thoreau,* ed. Franklin B. Sanborn (Boston: Bibliophile Society, 1905), I, 114.

came in company. "Conversation is my natural element," Fuller
put it. "I need to be called out, and never think alone, without
imagining some companion" (*Ossoli*, I, 296). With George
Ripley it was evidently somewhat the same way. "If he could
preach as he talks," Theodore Parker told a friend, "he would
surpass all." [10] Even Emerson, Alcott once declared, was better
at conversation than lecturing (*JA*, p. 425). And as for Thoreau,
despite his crusty pose, he admitted that "I love society as much
as most" (*Wa*, p. 140); and Franklin Sanborn agreed that
Thoreau, like Emerson, "was ever ready in conversaton." [11]

This combination of individual talent and romanticist
ideology had the effect of making talk a Transcendentalist in-
stitution. The informal club became a rallying point; Fuller
and Alcott became professional conversationalists. The three instances of Transcendentalist conversation which had the most
public impact were the original Transcendentalist Club (1836–
1840), Fuller's series of conversations in Boston (1839–1844),
and Bronson Alcott's long career, first as an elementary school
teacher and then as a conductor of adult discussion groups from
New England to Iowa. Taking the extant records of these ses-
sions as our principal texts, so to speak, let us try to see what
the art of conversation meant for the Transcendentalists in
practice. Though what is on record was more or less organized
for special occasions, it may for that reason be all the more
revealing.

Unfortunately, our texts are all quite corrupt, except for the
Conversations with Children on the Gospels, which is the least
typical because the conversations were geared specifically for
"infant instruction." "I am at the mercy of reporters," Alcott
complained in old age. "My subjects, and extemporizing these,

[10] To George E. Ellis, 27 May 1838; typescript, Massachusetts Historical
Society, Boston. Emerson also praised Ripley as a conversationalist (*Ossoli*, I, 320).

[11] *The Life of Henry David Thoreau* (Boston: Houghton Mifflin, 1917),
p. xii.

leave me open to misconception and frequent mortification" (*JA*, p. 535). Almost all accounts of such meetings are written either with unconscious pomposity or deliberate intent to caricature. Take for example the closest approach to a detailed account now in print: Margaret Fuller's session with the women of Boston on the subject "What Is Life?"

March 22, 1841. The question of the day was, "What Is Life?"

"Let us define, each in turn, our idea of living." Margaret did not believe that we had, any of us, a distinct idea of life.

A[nna] S[haw] thought so great a question ought to be given for a written definition. "No," said Margaret, "that is of no use. When we go away to think of anything, we never do think. We all talk of life. We all have some thought now. Let us tell it. C[aroline Sturgis], what is life?"

Caroline replied, "It is to laugh, or cry, according to our organization."

"Good," said Margaret, "but not grave enough. Come, what is life? I know what I think; I want you to find out what you think."

Miss P[eabody] replied, "Life is division from one's principle of life in order to a conscious reorganization. We are cut up by time and circumstance, in order to feel our reproduction of the eternal law."

Mrs. E[merson]: "We live by the will of God, and the object of life is to submit," and went on into Calvinism.

Then came up all the antagonisms of Fate and Freedom.

Mrs. H[ooper] said, "God created us in order to have a perfect sympathy from us as free beings."

Mrs. A[lmira] B[arlow] said she thought the object of life was to attain absolute freedom. At this Margaret immediately and visibly kindled.

C[aroline] S[turgis] said, "God creates from the fulness of life, and cannot but create; he created us to overflow, without being exhausted, because what he created, necessitated new creation. It is not to make us happy, but creation is his happiness and ours."

Margaret was then pressed to say what she considered life to be.

Her answer was so full, clear, and concise, at once, that it cannot but be marred by being drawn through the scattering medium of my memory. But here are some fragments of her satisfying statement.

She began with God as Spirit, Life, so full as to create and love eternally, yet capable of pause. Love and creativeness are dynamic forces, out of which we, individually, as creatures, go forth bearing his image; that is, having within our being the same dynamic forces by which we also add constantly to the total sum of existence, and shaking off ignorance, and its effects, and by becoming more ourselves, i.e., more divine—destroying sin in its principle, we attain to absolute freedom, we return to God, conscious like himself, and, as his friends, giving, as well as receiving, felicity forevermore. In short, we become gods, and able to give the life which we now feel ourselves able only to receive.

On Saturday morning, Mrs. L[idian] E[merson] and Mrs. E[llen] H[ooper] were present, and begged Margaret to repeat the statement concerning life, with which she closed the last conversation. Margaret said she had forgotten every word she said. She must have been inspired by a good genius, to have so satisfied everybody—but the good genius had left her. She would try, however, to say what she thought, and trusted it would resemble what she had said already. She then went into the matter, and, true enough, she did not use a single word she used before.[12]

In this case, the scribe is the unconsciously pompous one, with the editor, perhaps, as the caricaturist. Introduced by a preface in the breezy, ironic style with which Miller usually handles the Transcendentalists, the selection effectively deflates their pretensions to high seriousness. Cliché and incongruity abound. Instead of the salon, we have the schoolroom or quiz program setting ("The question of the day was . . . "). Who would think of calling Caroline's reply "good," let alone "not grave enough"? One has the general impression of novices trying to talk above their heads: Mrs. E "went on into Calvinism"; "Then came up all the antagonisms of Fate and Freedom." For a while,

[12] *Ossoli*, I, 345–347; re-edited in *The American Transcendentalists: Their Prose and Poetry*, ed. Perry Miller (New York: Doubleday, 1957), pp. 102–103).

one remains hopeful of Margaret, who at first only puts questions. But then comes the rosy, effusive digest of her "satisfying statement," "drawn through the scattering medium of my memory" by the adoring scribe. It is the usual neoplatonic stuff, only worse. We proceed to rank Margaret with the other ladies, equal in kind if somewhat more glib. The ending clinches this impression. When pressed to recapitulate, "true enough, she did not use a single word she used before." No doubt this is meant in admiration but it can be taken as additional proof of flightiness.

This report, then, hardly explains Fuller's reputation as a conversationalist and the admiration obviously felt for her by the scribe, except on grounds of mutual fatuity. The same is true of extant reports of other conversations. They seem either elliptical or rhetorical. However they may have been received at the time, on the printed page they are dull. The fact is that Transcendentalism lacked a Boswell, so we can never be certain whether it deserved one, though the mutual admiration of the group suggests that it did.

Even a totally accurate text of a Transcendentalist conversation might not explain very much about its success or failure. The effect of speech is inevitably distorted by transcription; nonverbal factors may have been as important to the effect as any words spoken. The general atmosphere of the gathering, the decorations in the room, the historical occasion, Alcott's pale blue eyes and air of serenity, Fuller's flushed animation and elegance of manner and dress—all these were noticed by their contemporaries but are lost to us.

Still, some facts about Transcendental conservation are evident. First, it was serious, especially in any public session, where it was being used essentially as an "organ of instruction." "What avails any conversation but the sincere?" Emerson asked (*JMN*, VIII, 17). Geniality alone would not suffice. You had to be grave enough. "The fault of literary conversation in general," says William Hazlitt, "is its too great tenaciousness. It fas-

tens upon a subject and will not let it go. It resembles a battle
rather than a skirmish, and makes a toil of pleasure." Hazlitt
would not have enjoyed the Transcendental Club. He thought
the long-winded Coleridge a conversational failure; presumably
Alcott would have struck him the same way.[13] For Hazlitt, conversation was essentially a recreation and a social grace; but the
Transcendentalists gathered not for witty banter but to trade
ideas on such knotty topics as "Does the Species Advance beyond the Individual?" and "Mysticism in Christianity." Usually
the meetings inspired Alcott to write pages of abstruse meditation on the issue at hand. His own conversations, likewise, he
took very seriously as an instrument for converting the world
to the spiritual philosophy. His topics were equally grandiose:
The Corporeal Relations of the Soul, The Doctrine of the Godhead, Instinct, Behavior, Private Life, and—inevitably—Conversation itself, since part of his mission was to vindicate his
method. It might indeed be argued that discussions on such
mind-bending and preset topics as these should not be called
conversations so much as informal seminars.

Margaret Fuller's announced goal, in opening her conversations for the women of Boston, was somewhat more secular
than Alcott's but just as ambitious in its own way. "It is to pass
in review the departments of thought and knowledge, and endeavor to place them in due relation to one another in our
[i.e., female] minds. . . . To ascertain what pursuits are best
suited to us, in our time and state of society, and how we may
make best use of our means for building up the life of thought
upon the life of action" (*Ossoli*, I, 325). In short, she intended
not only to supply the ladies with a comprehensive liberal education but to come up with some sort of practical program for
improving the lot of women in society.

Of course few are going to approach an ordinary, friendly

[13] "On the Conversation of Authors," *Selected Essays of William Hazlitt*, ed. Geoffrey Keynes (London: Nonesuch Press, 1930), pp. 456–457.
See pp. 461–465 for comments on Coleridge.

conversation with such zeal, even if they are Transcendentalists. Their tone in speaking of their public conversations derives partly from the sense that they are bringing light to the gentiles, partly from the awareness that they must use some sort of come-on to attract a public. In private Fuller at least was more quotidian. Indeed she struck Emerson, upon first acquaintance, as frivolous, "for I was, at that time, an eager scholar of ethics, and had tasted the sweets of solitude and stoicism, and I found something profane in the hours of amusing gossip into which she drew me" (*Ossoli,* I, 202). The thing to note here is that Emerson found her manner *both* tempting *and* unsatisfactory. Clearly the young Transcendentalist enjoyed those "profane" pleasures, but unlike the middle-aged Brahmin who is writing the memoir, he resolutely suppressed them as inferior to the higher conversation with the soul.

This element of sublimation in Transcendentalist relationships is characteristic. The trivial must be symbolic to be worth anything; the initial love is always giving way to the demonic and the celestial. Every Transcendentalist had his familiar side, but not in his capacity as Transcendentalist. Thoreau, for example, liked children and town characters and got along with his family, but when it came to associating with his fellow mystics he stiffened. Thus Emerson told Sanborn that he never had "the least social pleasure" with Thoreau, "though often the best conversation." [14] Even toward those Transcendentalist friends most devoted to him, Channing and Blake, Thoreau condescended. Unrequited friendship was indeed a universal byproduct of the Transcendentalist seriousness. The Fuller-Emerson relation is another instance, and the Alcott-Emerson relation perhaps the most interesting of all. Although Alcott was in a way the epitome of Transcendental abstruseness, his conversation as abstract as his diary, he was temperamentally a sociable person who longed in particular for Emerson's affection. When Emerson did not fully reciprocate, Alcott chalked

[14] Sanborn, p. 297.

it up to his friend's reserve, classifying him as a "pent personality from which his rare accomplishments have not yet liberated his gifts, nor given him unreservedly to the Muse and mankind." [15] But Emerson on his side seems to have concluded much the same thing. Put off by the abstruseness of Alcott's conversation, he described him as "a man quite too cold and contemplative for the alliances of friendship" (*W*, X, 341). One might say that the two men were trapped in a convention of serious conversation. At any rate, it was a convention. Thus when Jones Very came to Emerson's house and insulted all the guests, they did not cry breach of decorum or bad fellowship because what Very said was profound (*JMN*, VII, 124).

Also because it was "charming." The Transcendentalists did not value in conversation any more than they did in writing the kind of profundity or seriousness which was merely "sound" or "weighty." The highest compliment to pay a participant was "So-and-so said *fine* things," not "*weighty* things." Emerson's habitual way of recording conversations in his journals, in fact, was to note down the best aphorisms. Sallies of wit, even puns, were preferable to elaborate reasoning and logic-chopping. Parker and especially Brownson, who called for continuity and definition of terms, were often an annoyance. When Margaret Fuller asked her friends to say something grave, what she had in mind was a few good apothegms, not an elaborate speech.

This, then, was a second characteristic of Transcendentalist conversation which somewhat qualified the first. It was serious, but its method was desultory, sometimes to the point of caprice. The Club met not in order to reason, argue, or even come to a consensus, but to be mutually stimulated and speak as the spirit moved. Alcott and Fuller, in their public conversations, also liked to proceed by having each participant speak to the topic or leading question with a minimum of guidance from the coordinator and without criticism of what others had said.

[15] *Ralph Waldo Emerson: An Estimate of His Character and Genius* (Boston: Williams, 1882), p. 51.

Both also liked to give introductions, and sometimes conclusions too, and if they were warm and their audience cold this could make the session very one-sided. Both were periodically accused of monopolizing discussion in this way, just as Coleridge was; and given the fact that they both thought of conversation as a means of instruction and themselves as instructors, they must often have been tempted to hold forth. But each really wanted to draw the company out in the manner just described and felt that they had failed if they didn't.

The method had its risks, as in any nondirective discussion: vagueness, disjointedness, the tendency to play around the edges of topics rather than to confront them in depth. But it did not follow from this that the speakers were careless in what they said. On the contrary, the desire to be both grave and clever must have led to a great amount of premeditation, at least as much as in a good undergraduate seminar. To come up with anything like "life is division from one's principle of life in order to [effect] a conscious reorganization" (assuming Elizabeth Peabody actually said this—and it isn't at all out of character) is pretty difficult to do on the spur of the moment. Their frequent cross-allegations of personal coldness, their praise of the "eloquence" and "brilliance" of each other's conversation suggest that the Transcendentalists rarely let themselves go in each other's company.

"What is life?" bears out this impression of Transcendentalist conversation as carefully calculated. Each lady chirps out her gem in the proper order. Anna Shaw begins first, and lowliest, by trying to be let off the hook. Then we get the commonsense definition (Caroline), the pedantic definition (Miss P.), the Calvinist definition (Mrs. E.), the Unitarian definition (Mrs. H.), and finally the Transcendentalist definition Margaret likes (Mrs. A. B.), which Caroline tries to outdo, until at last we are ready for the rhapsody of Margaret. The whole process is a model of inductive method, of drawing out your pupils by getting them to make progressively better generalizations. Perhaps Miller included it in his anthology for this reason too, in addition to its humorous aspects. In its formal tightness, it proves that Transcendentalist conversation could take on the symmetry of a work of art, even though that symmetry is a denial of the principle of spontaneity upon which conversation is supposedly based.

A professional conversation is naturally apt to be more patterned than those in which there is no coordinator. Both Fuller and Alcott, being ex-teachers and missionaries of a sort, inevitably sought to steer their audiences around to certain pet ideas, with varying degrees of tact. Alcott sometimes made preliminary outlines of the topics he wanted to cover and, as he grew older, even used note cards. In the reports of his and Fuller's public conversations, therefore, one usually finds at least an inchoate structuring of some sort, although in no case is it as pronounced as in "What is Life?" Presumably they were not so schoolmasterish with their friends. But, as I have pointed out, even the informal intercourse of the Transcendentalists seems to have had a sculptured quality to it. Hawthorne made the definitive comment when he said of one casual gathering that everybody seemed to be straining to say the profoundest thing that had ever been said. This self-consciousness, common in some degree to all cultivated people, was intensified in the Transcendentalists by their devotion to what they called "self-culture," meaning, roughly, the total growth of one's intellectual-moral-spiritual faculties, the ultimate in liberal education. Their literary source for this idea was Goethe; but essentially it was another of Unitarianism's legacies to the movement, formulated most memorably by Dr. Channing, for whom the idea was the quintessence of the Unitarian principle that religion consists chiefly in the improvement of the character.[16]

[16] "Self-cultivation was the essence of Massachusetts Arminianism," notes Daniel Howe (*The Unitarian Conscience* [Cambridge: Harvard University Press, 1970], p. 110). Howe has much to say on this subject throughout his book.

Almost by definition, self-culture encourages a view of life as an art, the converse of the notion that art is subordinate to life. All the Transcendentalists flirted with this idea; in some, notably Margaret Fuller, it threatened to become a ruling passion. According to Emerson, Fuller "looked upon life as an art, and every person not merely as an artist, but as a work of art. She looked upon herself as a living statue, which should always stand on a polished pedestal, with right accessories, and under the most fitting lights. She would have been glad to have everybody so live and act" (*Ossoli,* I, 238). Throughout her *Memoirs* her biographers tend to describe her through the analogy to art: "She wore this circle of friends . . . as a necklace of diamonds about her neck"; "Like a moral Paganini, she played always on a single string, drawing from each its peculiar music,—bringing wild beauty from the slender wire" (*Ossoli,* I, 213, 97–98). From our perspective it is clear that such behavior was as much a matter of compulsion as wiles, that her biographers perhaps half saw and disguised that fact. Her overtures to Emerson, for instance, were more spontaneous than he was willing to admit. Still, consciously or not, Fuller was a collector and manipulator of personalities, a virtuoso of friendship. One gets much the same impression from what Alcott, Emerson, and Thoreau have to say about friendship. The sense of personal longing and unfulfilment is continually being stiffened into high-minded rationalizations for ever more noble, more distant relationships.

Seeing this pitfall in the Transcendentalist ethos, the danger of becoming too enmeshed in the self-conscious pursuits of the art of life, one is tempted to reverse the emphasis of the previous chapter and suggest that far from having an excessive regard for spontaneity the Transcendentalists had too little. Craftsmanship in art they undervalued, but they more than made up for this by harping on the craft of life, which must have been a continuous frustration to them. "Emerson," reports Ellery Channing, "was never in the least contented. . . . The

Future,—that was the terrible Gorgon face that turned the
Present into 'a thousand bellyaches.' 'When shall I be perfect?
When shall I be moral? when shall I be this and that? when
will the really good rhyme get written?' Here is the Emerson
colic. Thoreau had a like disease." [17] He who would make self-
culture his ideal, warns Hedge in "the Art of Life the Scholar's
Calling," "must become a living sacrifice." "Let him who
would build this tower consider well the cost" (*Tr*, pp. 473,
472). Hedge goes on to praise the ideal, but his metaphors suggest only too well the emotional casualties of Transcendentalism.

Nevertheless the Transcendentalists continued to value conversation as a high art, whatever their frustrations, both in private and in public; and Alcott and Fuller even won a share of
public acclaim. Both were erratic, but Fuller had charisma and
Alcott at least had atmosphere and sometimes even mystique.
Though to the modern reader their seances seem amateurish,
stilted, and slightly bizarre, they were historically significant
as harbingers (along with the lyceum) of the adult education
movement and anticipations of modern nondirective pedagogy.
And as an art form, the conversation came as close to a truly
transcendental utterance as the movement ever attained.

Neither Alcott and Fuller nor any other Transcendentalist
was content to rest in conversation alone. Characteristically, the
Transcendental Club talked from the first about launching a
new journal. Alcott and Fuller became professional conversationalists only after despairing of success as writers, and even so
they never resigned their literary ambitions, but later returned
to writing. Alcott confessed to having "a profound superstition
about books" (*JA*, p. 526). The first sentence of his *Table-Talk*,
ironically, reads: "One cannot celebrate books sufficiently." [18]

[17] *Thoreau the Poet-Naturalist* ed. F. B. Sanborn, new ed. (Boston:
Goodspeed, 1902), p. 132n.
[18] *Table-Talk*, p. 5.

After the modest success of *Tablets* and *Concord Days* his hope revived that he might "add a syllable or two to the living literature of my time" (*JA*, p. 462), though he always remained very modest about his chances. Nor could Fuller help but feel that being better at talk than writing "bespeaks a second-rate mind" (*Ossoli*, I, 107). The other Transcendentalists were usually quite unequivocal about the superiority of writing. In the long run, "conversation is an evanescent relation—no more," Emerson cautions (*W*, II, 208). On the other hand, he regarded conversation also as a sort of model for the best literary works, like Montaigne's. Altogether, the Transcendentalists as a group valued conversation less as an autonomous art form than as a quality in literature. To a degree, their prose reflects this quality.

To begin with, the Transcendentalists composed a fair number of literary dialogues, in the manner of Landor's *Imaginary Conversations,* which Emerson, Fuller, and Alcott all admired.[19] These included, for example, Ellery Channing's *Conversations in Rome,* "Fashionable Dialogues," and "Walks and Talks" (in *Thoreau the Poet-Naturalist*); Margaret Fuller's dialogues in the *Dial;* Brownson's in the *Boston Quarterly Review;* and, on the fringes of the movement, the young Lowell's *Conversations with a Critic.* In somewhat the same vein are two poetic dramas Channing wrote in old age: *Eliot* and *John Brown, and the Heroes of Harper's Ferry.* These performances vary in content and tone from theology to farce. But none is of much literary consequence, partly because the language is too stilted to sound conversational, partly because the writers are less interested in drama than monologue. The conversation is usually just a device for presenting ideas in a loose form, as Lowell frankly admits in his preface. As an approximation of actual speech, only Channing's manuscript dialogues come close.

[19] Helen Neill McMaster, "Margaret Fuller as a Literary Critic," *University of Buffalo Studies*, 7 (1928), 79; *JA*, p. 184; *W*, XII, 337–349.

The same percentage holds true for the rest of Transcendentalist writing, contrary, it would seem, to their expressed purposes. In their criticism, they all incorporated in some form or
other the Wordsworthian dictum that the writers should use
the language of common speech. Brownson even went so far as
to praise the style of newspaper-writing and to make popularity
a test of literary merit.[20] But he himself did not use a colloquial
style. Emerson even grew away from it—the plain prose of
his early sermons is much closer to ordinary speech than the
baroque style of the essays. Walt Whitman had a point when he
declared of Emerson's writing that "no performance was ever
more based on artificial scholarships and decorums at third or
fourth removes" and compared Emerson's work to porcelain
statuettes.[21] Far from attempting the kind of familiar style
praised by Hazlitt and Lamb, Transcendentalist conversation
and prose seems continuously to be striving to rise above the
colloquial to a more literary level.

The picture changes, though, when one considers the prose
tradition that the Transcendentalists inherited. The principal
forms in which a serious-minded young Bostonian of literary
inclinations could respectably express himself were oratory, the
sermon, the highbrow review, and the periodical essay. For the
latter, which was the only "informal" one of the four, *The
Spectator* was still the primary model (Addison rather than
Steele, of course, and often alloyed with Samuel Johnson);
Irving was still looked upon in some quarters as bohemian.[22]

[20] "American Literature," *Boston Quarterly Review,* 2 (1839), 17–22.
See also *W,* I, 110–112; and XII, 284–290.

[21] "Emerson's Books (The Shadows of Them)," *Prose Works, 1892,* ed.
Floyd Stovall (New York: New York University Press, 1964), II, 515.

[22] E.g., W. H. Prescott, "Essay Writing," *North American Review,* 14
(1822), 319–350. For the way in which the young Emerson was influenced
by the prejudices of his elders, see *JMN,* I, 172. For information on the
background of the essay tradition in America, I am indebted to Martin
Christadler, *Der Amerikanische Essay, 1720–1820* (Heidelberg: Winter,
1968), particularly chapters xiii–xvii.

Even Addison was really revered, at least in public, more for his moral soundness than for the familiar aspects of his style. And in their own writing, Bostonians tended to compartmentalize these two elements: either they played it straight, writing on a rather ceremonious level with a minimum of wit and rambling, or else (like Hawthorne in his sketches) they made it plain that they were not really trying for high seriousness.[23] Their notion of the style in which matters so significant as the subjects of Emerson's major essays should be discussed was in short very conservative, to the point that when Emerson first discovered in himself a taste for the more desultory forms of journal-writing and seventeenth-century prose as a way of expressing his deepest thoughts he was somewhat apologetic about it (*JMN*, I, 25, 268). Indeed he never outgrew the suspicion that his writings were inferior because they were not more elaborate and systematic.

The style of his essays, nonetheless, is actually a reaction against the finished evenness of American Unitarian Association prose in the direction of a less formal, more fanciful and discontinuous, more "individualistic" style which would better express nuance of meaning and tone but which would remain morally serious and intellectually tough. In varying degrees, other Transcendentalists followed Emerson's example. For inspiration the Transcendentalists drew both upon elements within their native culture which will be discussed later on and upon such European models as Carlyle and other romanticist visionaries; the analects of Coleridge, Luther, and others (including Socrates); the metaphysical rhetoric of Sir Thomas Browne; and the Senecan tradition of epigrammatic, asymmetrical rambling prose from Plutarch through Montaigne. The Transcendentalists' indebtedness to these writers can be

[23] The *Monthly Anthology and Boston Review* is an excellent example of this dichotomy. For excerpts and a scholarly analysis of the periodical, see Lewis Simpson, *The Federalist Literary Mind* (Baton Rouge: Louisiana State University Press, 1962).

and has been studied at great length.[24] For our purposes it can
be epitomized, however, in terms of the idea of conversation. In
general, what the Transcendentalists learned from the models
just named was how to inject a conversational note into moral
discussion, how to give the impression of obiter dicta rather
than treatise.

Perhaps the most striking example of this quality in Transcendentalist writing is its fondness for aphorism, which of
course is both a hallmark of good conversation and a condition
to which analects and moral essays aspire. W. H. Channing was
attracted to Margaret Fuller because "she knew how to concentrate into racy phrases the essential truth gathered from wide
research, and distilled with patient toil" (*Ossoli*, II, 20). Emerson, similarly, declared "compression," or "the science of
omitting," a cardinal virtue of rhetoric and advised him who
would attain to it to read his compositions aloud (*W*, XII,
290–291). Part of the reason Alcott composed his "Orphic
Sayings," very likely, was to capture an aspect of his conversation. At first glance they of course seem to fail miserably.
"Thou art, my heart, a soul-flower, facing ever and following
the motions of thy sun, opening thyself to her vivifying ray,"
and so on—what could be more un-conversational? [25] Certainly
it must be a pale imitation of his public manner. But it probably *is* an imitation, either of himself or of Socrates, insofar as
good intellectual conversation tends to become a series of
aphorisms. "Orphic Sayings" could be read as a literary dialogue with the interlocutor left out.

Another resemblance between conversation and Transcendentalist prose is its desultory, improvisational quality. "Its
beauty," as Alcott said of Emerson, "consists in its suggestive-

[24] See especially Edmund G. Berry, *Emerson's Plutarch* (Cambridge:
Harvard University Press, 1961), pp. 242–248; Charles L. Young, *Emerson's
Montaigne* (New York: Macmillan, 1941), pp. 52–79; and Vivian Hopkins,
"Emerson and Bacon," *American Literature*, 29 (1958), 410–413.

[25] *Tr*, p. 303. Alcott was somewhat more successful in the aphoristic
mode in his lesser known *Table-Talk* (1877).

ness, unexpectedness, saliency; it vaults the passes, flashes the whole of things upon the imagination at a glance, sets life and things anew for the moment." [26] It was this quality which led Alcott to nickname Emerson "The Rhapsodist." The following passage illustrates it well:

How many volumes of well-bred metre we must jingle through, before we can be filled, taught, renewed! We want the miraculous; the beauty which we can manufacture at no mill,—can give no account of; the beauty of which Chaucer and Chapman had the secret. The poetry of course is low and prosaic; only now and then, as in Wordsworth, conscientious; or in Byron, passional; or in Tennyson, factitious. But if I should count the poets who have contributed to the Bible of existing England sentences of guidance and consolation which are still glowing and effective,—how few! Shall I find my heavenly bread in the reigning poets? Where is great design in modern English poetry? [*W*, V, 256]

This is a quite literary style of writing on the whole, but it also has the scattershot, staccato quality of lively talk, as in the sudden tonal shifts from amused impatience to high-minded yearning to hardheaded criticism to exasperated outburst. As always in Emerson, the thoughts have gaps between them, as if the author were thinking them up and throwing them out off the top of his head. Twice his syntax breaks in mid-sentence. Finally, there is a kind of nonchalance mixed in with the precision and subtlety of detail: "jingle through," "heavenly bread" (to go with Bible), the dismissal of all of modern English poetry—"of course" it is "low and prosaic," one sketchy epithet sufficing for each poet.

This casualness is typical of Emerson, and even more of Thoreau, since he is more unpredictable and also more aware of being casual.

Our life is frittered away by detail. An honest man has hardly need to count more than his ten fingers, or in extreme cases he may add his ten toes, and lump the rest. Simplicity, simplicity, simplicity!

[26] *Table-Talk*, p. 84.

I say, let your affairs be as two or three, and not a hundred or a thousand; instead of a million count half a dozen, and keep your accounts on your thumb nail. [*Wa,* p. 91]

Again, the utterance is formal; it stays within the convention of the jeremiad; but the prophet is so earthy and droll ("frittered away," "lump the rest," "keep your accounts on your thumbnail") it seems almost as if Thoreau is deliberately burlesquing himself—as some commentators have in fact alleged.[27]

Still another unconventional prose stylist was Theodore Parker. Parker was as contemptuous of the stuffiness of his colleagues' pulpit manner as he was of their theology, and in his own writing he tried to inject colloquialisms and common references. It was typical of him to enter the miracles controversy in the rustic disguise of "Levi Blodgett." As that pamphlet shows, Parker was not always successful in conversationalizing his theology, but he made some interesting attempts. His homiletic specialty, as far as experimentation in colloquial style is concerned, was to drive home his point with a mixture of hard-hitting exhortation and curt, sometimes even vulgar sarcasm:

It is a good thing to get up pious feeling; there is no danger we shall have too much of that. But the feeling should lead to a thought, the thought to a deed, else it is of small value; at any rate, it does not do all of its work for the individual, and nothing for any one beside. This religious sentimentality is called Mysticism or Pietism, in the bad sense of those two words.[28]

As in much of Parker's writing, the passage maintains a certain level of decorum, which even assumes a scholarly air at the end. But the emotional thrust is supplied by the salty colloquialisms in the first sentence and the last clause of the second, and in the contrast between the level of these and the literariness of the rest.

[27] Charles Anderson, *The Magic Circle of Walden* (New York: Holt, Rinehart & Winston, 1968), pp. 19–29.

[28] *Sermons of Religion,* ed. Samuel A. Eliot (Boston: American Unitarian Association, 1908), p. 263.

The analogy between the style of conversation and that of Transcendentalist prose has definite limits, even in Thoreau, as these passages suggest. Emerson's citation of Socrates as a model of the "low style" (*W*, XII, 287) which writers ought to cultivate shows that the low he had in mind was still pretty high. Compare Parker's sermons with Henry Ward Beecher's, or any Transcendentalist essay with the journalism of Poe and it becomes clear that Emerson and his circle came nowhere near a truly popular style of expression. The very way in which they put this ambition refutes them: "Plain speech is always a desideratum," says Thoreau (*JT*, I, 342); "I embrace the common, I explore and sit at the feet of the familiar, the low," Emerson effuses (*W*, I, 111). Indeed it was almost impossible to be earthy after being processed at Harvard by Professor Edward Tyrell Channing, whose reputation for producing great writers is utterly undeserved. Channing discouraged the bombastic and the illogical but he brought out the didactic, the moralistic, the abstract, and the conventional in his young charges—most of which it took Thoreau and Emerson ten years to begin to outgrow.[29]

A more important reason, however, why the Transcendentalists did not pursue the idea of writing as conversation as far as Hawthorne or Poe, not to mention Lamb and Hazlitt, was of course their own intellectual seriousness. To picture them as essentially conversationalists, in any recognizable sense of the word, is to misrepresent them as dilettantish, nonchalant patricians; to picture them as committed to a colloquial standard in writing is to mistake their understandable endorsement of a romanticist cliché with democratic overtones for an indispensable doctrine. In the long run, the very thing which most attracted them to conversation limited its appeal. They became fascinated with the mystique of conversation less for its own sake than as the primary example from ordinary life of the transmission of the living word from soul to soul. This vision, of an eloquence which, as Emerson put it, could "alter in a

[29] For a good account of E. T. Channing's limitations, see Henry S. Canby, *Thoreau* (Boston: Houghton Mifflin, 1939), pp. 51–54.

pair of hours, perhaps in a half hour's discourse, the convictions and habits of years" (*W*, VII, 64), was the deepest basis of the Transcendentalists' admiration for great literature and oratory, as well as for conversation, and it was most responsible for the analogies they drew between the three.

The ultimate value of studying Transcendentalist conversation, therefore, is in calling attention to the importance of personal communication in Transcendentalist aesthetics: the idea of the superior man speaking through his art to fulfil himself and inspire other men. To have begun with the artistic successes of the movement, like *Walden,* and worked from explication of them into their expressivist and didactic implications would have largely reversed the order of priorities, for Transcendentalist literary works are less aesthetic products than aesthetic processes—forms of communication, transitional links between author and reader. Emerson and Thoreau are quite explicit about this in the contrasts they draw between the imperfectness of the vehicle of expression and the nobility of the thing expressed; and their pronouncements should not be disregarded because they are hyperbolic. For one thing, they tell a part of the truth about literature which modern literary criticism tends to leave out: art does not simply mean, or even be; it is also a communciation between artist and reader. Secondly, to accept this fact is to alter in certain important ways one's assumptions about literary excellence. When art is seen as a process of communication rather than as a product, static elements like structural patterning seem less important than kinetic elements like the flow of images or ideas; and clarity (or ambiguity) and refinements of diction in general seem less important, in themselves, than sheer impact or suggestiveness, though the one may of course result from the other. The present study assumes the validity of these alternative criteria, in view of the Emersonian dicta that "there is higher work for Art than the arts" (*W*, II, 363); "the poetic gift we want, as the health and supremacy of man,—not rhymes and sonneteering"

(*W*, VIII, 63–64). This old-fashioned view of art as the vehicle of inspiration will not satisfy the demands of modern formalist criticism, but neither will the latter suffice to explain Transcendentalist aesthetics. In judging a conversation held by Alcott or Fuller, for instance, one would want to demand continuity rather than unity, provocativeness rather than precision, edification rather than elegance, and (in some cases) tone or atmosphere or ambience rather than the exchange of words itself. The same is also true to a marked degree of the literary forms of expression favored by the Transcendentalists.

Of these forms, the traditional moral essay is of course the most evident, since it furnished the concept of topical meditation used in the organization of the most central oeuvre of the movement, Emerson's essays. To establish a kinship with Montaigne and Bacon takes one but a limited distance, however, into the intricacies of Transcendentalist literature, for the category "moral essay" defies close specification, and the special contexts in which the Transcendentalists altered the tradition of the essay are much more important for our purposes than affinities with the tradition as a whole. The moral essay cannot be defined much more narrowly than as a short, unsystematic meditation on a given abstract issue, often marked by curtness, lack of transition, and aphoristic statement. All of these qualities are indeed prevalent in Transcendentalist prose. Its more particular themes and techniques, however, are better understood in terms of the conventions of form discussed in the remainder of this book. The manner in which the Transcendentalists approached moral issues, for example, becomes fully clear only when one sees it as an outgrowth of their special religious concerns and the conventions of religious discourse which they inherited and adapted, especially the sermon. These will be the subject of the next chapter.

4 From Sermon to Scripture

One of Hawthorne's minor tales, "Passages from a Relinquished Work," presents the confessions of an itinerant storyteller who finds that he has an alter ego, a wandering preacher. The storyteller is a runaway from home, a novice at his trade, painfully self-conscious of his inadequacies, aware that he is a charlatan. Even as he is telling his most famous story (which just happens to be called "Mr. Higgenbottam's Catastrophe"), he has to admit to himself that he has no idea how it will end. Altogether he feels shamefaced and guilty about his calling, which he has taken up against the wishes of his guardian. The preacher, though also a figure of ridicule, haunts him as the symbol of the moral orientation that he has forsaken.

To some extent the storyteller who cannot shake off the preacher within himself is of course Nathaniel Hawthorne, or nearly any New England artist of the day. Art was a vocation to be embarked upon with misgivings, ethical as well as economic, which were compensated for by continual reaffirmations of the moral responsibility of the artist. As long as he kept his eye on the church, like the voyeuristic speaker in Hawthorne's "Sunday at Home," he might be excused from attending the service. This vigil was not just a sop to the times, but a matter of instinct. Even as the speaker describes his alienation from the conventional forms of religion, he feels a spiritual influence tugging at him like a magnet.[1]

[1] It must have appealed to Hawthorne's sense of irony that he was singled out as a target for evangelism by Jones Very, who reminded him

The same ambivalence is to be found in all the major American renaissance authors. Religious conventionalism was their favorite target for satire, but largely because they saw themselves in competition with it. Their own genius was deeply religious; among their most important literary models are the Bible, hymnody, John Bunyan, and the sermon; the deepest purpose in their writing often seems to be an inquiry into the meaning of the universe. Emily Dickinson's poems on spiritual themes; Poe's *Eureka;* Melville's *Moby-Dick, Clarel,* and *The Confidence-Man* are all at least nominally fictive, but they are metaphysical writings before they are anything else.

It is often said that such works represent a transitional stage in the history of American thought, when theology had lost its hold as dogma but still dominated the imagination, whose energy was released in the form of creative writing now that the old channels of belief had broken down.[2] This is too simple an explanation, but it is true in its main lines, as can be seen by examining the affinities between the sermon tradition and Transcendentalist prose. Many of the Transcendentalist writings which are read today are either sermons (like Emerson's Divinity School Address and Parker's *Discourse of the Transient and Permanent in Christianity*) or at one remove from sermons, like Emerson's *Nature* and Brownson's *New Views.* *Walden* and Emerson's essays were, in large part, originally delivered as lectures in the lyceum, the conventions of which were in turn strongly indebted to the pulpit. The same is true of the critical writing in most of the Transcendentalist periodicals: the *Western Messenger* and *Boston Quarterly Review, The Present* and *The Harbinger* are all in different

---

strongly of the preacher in his "Relinquished Work." For information about their relationship, see Edwin Gittleman, *Jones Very: The Effective Years* (New York: Columbia University Press, 1967), pp. 283–285.

[2] The most eloquent statement of this idea which I have seen is Allen Tate, "Emily Dickinson," in *Reactionary Essays on Poetry and Ideas* (New York: Scribner, 1936), pp. 3–25.

ways openly evangelistic, and the philosophic and religious
essays in *The Dial* are scarcely less so. To appreciate the literary
aims of the Transcendentalists, therefore, one needs to understand the conventions of contemporary religious discourse, particularly those of the sermon, which was still the main literary
form of religious expression and the first one that the majority
of the Transcendentalist writers had to master in their professional careers.

The subject has not been well researched, undoubtedly because of scanty background information about the sermon
form. The structure of the Puritan sermon has been analyzed
quite thoroughly,[3] but little has been written about the literary
qualities of the genre after the Great Awakening.[4] Part of the
reason, perhaps, is that after 1750 New England became frag-
mented into sects whose styles of worship were so diverse that
one cannot speak of *a* prevailing tradition in preaching. As the
nineteenth century progressed, furthermore, the sermon be-

[3] See for example chapters x and xi of Perry Miller, *The New England
Mind: The Seventeenth Century* (New York: Macmillan, 1939); chapter
iv of William Haller, *The Rise of Puritanism* (New York: Columbia
University Press, 1938); and Babette May Levy, *Preaching in the First
Half Century of New England History* (New York: Russell, 1945).

[4] The closest approximation is still Lewis Brastow, "The Preaching of
the United States," *The Modern Pulpit: A Study of Homiletic Sources
and Characteristics* (New York: Macmillan, 1906), pp. 318–435, a sketchy
overview including all major Protestant denominations. A more recent
survey, *Preaching in American History*, ed. Dewitte Holland, Jess Yoder,
and Hubert Vance Taylor (Nashville: Abingdon, 1969), is highly selective
in scope, and organized more in terms of subject matter than homiletical
method. For a detailed study of the immediate backgrounds of the developments traced in this chapter, see my "The Unitarian Movement and
the Art of Preaching in 19th Century America," *American Quarterly,* 24
(1972), 166–190; and Daniel Howe, *The Unitarian Conscience* (Cambridge: Harvard University Press, 1970), pp. 151–173. The only significant
previous discussion of the sermon form vis à vis Transcendentalist style
is A. M. Baumgartner, " 'The Lyceum Is My Pulpit': Homiletics in
Emerson's Early Lectures," *American Literature,* 34 (1963), 477–486.

came a less important form of literary expression: secular literature was much more sophisticated than before the Revolution,
and immensely more prolific. Ironically, the preaching of this
later period is also of greater literary interest than ever, especially to the student of Transcendentalism. Up until 1850, the
best American sermons were still on the whole the best literature that America was producing. Critics of the day were painfully self-conscious about the mediocrity of native belles-lettres,
but they did not hesitate to claim that American sermons were
as good or better, as literary performances, than any in the
world.[5] The same softening of the dogmatic structure of American protestantism which made possible the emergence of the
Transcendentalist aesthetic as described in Chapter One had a
similar liberalizing effect upon religious writing itself. During
the nineteenth century the idea of the sermon as a means of
expounding and enforcing doctrine tended to give way to the
idea of the sermon as an inspirational oration. Much more was
made of imagination and creativity in preaching than had been
the case before.

To examine Transcendentalist literature, for the moment, as
an outgrowth of this larger trend, as an attempt to develop
lyric possibilities to the fullest within the confines of an
essentially homiletic mode of expression, may help us to appreciate some of the peculiarities of Transcendentalist writing. I
think especially of the intermixture of high seriousness and
apparent dilettantism which makes it so hard to compare the
Transcendentalists either with their Puritan ancestors or with
their more literary descendants. The fact is that the nature of
their commitment to truth and beauty is simply different, because of their distrust of doctrine on the one hand and of fiction

[5] James D. Knowles, "American Literature," *Christian Review*, 1 (1836),
583; John G. Palfrey, "Pulpit Eloquence," *North American Review*, 10
(1820), 204; Timothy Dwight, *Travels in New England and New York*,
ed. Barbara Solomon (Cambridge: Harvard University Press, 1969), IV,
313.

on the other. Their literary allegiance is to the expression of
noble and virtuous impulses on the philosophical rather than
the dramatic or narrative level, but in such a way as to satisfy
the aesthetic sense as well as the intellect, because they conceived of religious concepts as for the most part metaphorically,
not literally, true. Altogether, what the Transcendentalists were
after was a sort of solemn but joyful spiritual ballet, a continuous improvisation around those few abiding central themes
which constituted their core of belief. And in this respect, they
were quite representative of their times; the sermons and other
devotional writings of their great liberal contemporaries exhibit the same qualities just described. "What is the office of a
Christian minister?" asked the young Emerson. "'Tis his to
show the beauty of the moral laws of the Universe . . . , to see
the creation with a new eye, to behold what he thought un-
organized, crystallize into form, to see the stupendous temple
uplift its awful form, towers on towers into infinite space,
echoing all with rapturous hymns" (*JMN*, III, 152). If this
seems like the fantasy of a future poet, nevertheless it has a
basis in the preaching of those who later rejected Emersonianism as heretical.

In the trend toward greater imagination and literary refinement in sermon writing during the nineteenth century, the
Unitarians were in the vanguard, being the least dogmatic and
the most highly cultured of the American Protestant sects.
"The Unitarians," James Walker modestly explained, "have
had more eminent preachers, in proportion to their numbers,
than any other sect, . . ."

owing partly to the greater attention paid by them, as a body, to
intellectual culture, and partly to the greater freedom and scope
allowed them in the choice and treatment of their subjects. The
consequence has been, that among them native force and originality, where these existed, have commonly been regulated by good

taste, without being restrained or shackled by the artificial conventionalities of the pulpit.[6]

One might dispute Walker's value judgment, but not his general diagnosis. Theological liberalism undoubtedly did encourage ministers to pay less attention to particular points of theology and more to eloquent appeals to their flocks to lead a moral life. "We all *know* enough," as Walker said on another occasion. "The great principles of religion . . . are few and simple. To be understood they need but to be stated." The problem was rather how "to urge these common truths upon the consciences of men." What was needed was "not so much moral *instruction* as moral *impression*." [7]

Well before the Unitarian movement was identified as such liberal Congregationalist ministers had moved away from traditional sermon conventions. To begin with, they largely discarded the old-fashioned sermon structure of text-doctrine-application, which prevailed through the eighteenth century. Traditionally, the minister would begin by reading the text, follow with a brief explication or preface, leading to the "proposition," or concise statement of his subject. In the main part of the sermon, he would first expound the doctrine, in a series of clearly marked steps, and then draw practical admonitions or inferences from his exegesis, with the same explicitness. He would then end with a short peroration. This scheme was suited to sermons which based their practical morality solidly upon dogma, but for a preacher to whom religion was mostly a matter of moral guidelines, the method was inappropriate. All the nineteenth-century Harvard professors of rhetoric, therefore, taught that "in point of form [the sermon] is precisely the

[6] James Walker, "Martineau's Discourses," *Christian Examiner,* 36 (1844), 182.

[7] *A Sermon, Preached in Brooklyn, Connecticut, at the Installation of Rev. Samuel Joseph May* (Boston: Russell, 1824), p. 7.

same, as the demonstrative oration," [8] and the ministers they trained almost universally complied.

The movement away from formalism in both theology and homiletical structure made it easier to introduce secular subjects and references, which had traditionally been considered outside the pulpit's regular scope. F. W. P. Greenwood preached on "The Religion of the Sea"; the young Emerson preached on "Astronomy"; Thomas Starr King on "Religious Lessons from Metallurgy"; Orville Dewey on business ethics; W. B. O. Peabody "On Reading Works of Fiction." Peabody's preliminary explanation of the appropriateness of his topic to the pulpit expressed the view of most of his colleagues: "I cannot think it improper to discuss any subject here in which our improvement is concerned." [9] Any subject that could provide food for moral reflection was theoretically legitimate, and as the title of one of Dewey's sermons had it, "Everything in Life Is Moral."

Related to this broadening of the scope of preaching was an increasingly freer and more creative handling of scriptural themes. Under the impact of the higher criticism, which was introduced into America by Joseph Stevens Buckminister shortly after 1800 and quickly absorbed by all liberal thinkers,[10] Unitarian ministers had rejected the idea of the literal inspira-

[8] John Quincy Adams, *Lectures on Rhetoric and Oratory* (Cambridge: Hilliard and Metcalf, 1810), I, 340.

[9] *Sermons by the Late William B. O. Peabody, D.D., with a Memoir*, ed. O. W. B. Peabody, 2d ed. (Boston: Greene, 1849), p. 367. For the other sermons referred to see *The Miscellaneous Writings of F. W. P. Greenwood, D.D.* (Boston: Little, Brown, 1846), pp. 278–289; *Young Emerson Speaks*, ed. Arthur C. McGiffert, Jr. (Boston: Houghton Mifflin, 1938), pp. 170–179; King, *Christianity and Humanity: A Series of Sermons*, ed. Edwin P. Whipple (Boston: Osgood, 1878), pp. 348–362; Bartol, *Discourses on the Christian Spirit and Life* (Boston: Crosby and Nichols, 1850), pp. 55–70; and *The Works of Orville Dewey, D.D.*, new ed. (Boston: American Unitarian Association, 1883), pp. 234–279.

[10] Jerry Wayne Brown, *The Rise of Biblical Criticism in America, 1810–1870: The New England Scholars* (Middletown, Conn.: Wesleyan University Press, 1969), pp. 10–26.

tion of the Bible; one result was that the role of the scriptures
in preaching tended to shrink from the status of authoritative
source for proofs to a storehouse of analogies and illustrations.
Nathaniel Frothingham, for example, became famous within the
denomination for his creative use of offbeat texts: for instance,
"Jesus answered, are there not twelve hours in the day?"; and
"Aha, I am warm, I have seen the fire." [11] At his best Frothingham weaves his text throughout his discourse like a leitmotif,
resulting in a much more polished, though also more glib,
performance than was achieved by the traditional method of
making the separate phrases of the text the division headings in
the sermon. Another group of ministers liked to paint portraits
of biblical scenes or retell Bible stories. "Imagine the scene for
a moment," says F. W. P. Greenwood of Luke XVIII:16
(Jesus receiving the children: "Suffer little children to come
unto me . . ."): "The disciples are standing aside, abashed and
subdued; the gratified feelings of mothers and fathers are
flowing forth in tears; and the multitude looks on, in respectful
sympathy, while he who commanded the wind and sea, and they
obeyed him, receives with outstretched arms the children who
are brought to him." [12] Here we have the beginning of biblical
fiction—a genre invented by another Unitarian minister, William Ware.

As the Greenwood passage shows, there is a strong tendency
in Unitarian preaching when dealing with biblical and doctrinal subjects not to confront the issues directly but to substitute one's own poetic imagery. For example, in attempting to
discredit the Orthodox idea of hell, William Ellery Channing
hurriedly passes over the substantive argument that all occurrences of the word in the Bible are metaphors or mistransla-
tions in order to lament the "unspeakable injury to Christianity" which has resulted from the Orthodox view.

[11] *Sermons, in the Order of a Twelvemonth* (Boston: Crosby, Nichols,
1852), sermons 3 and 31.

[12] Greenwood, *Sermons* (Boston: Little, Brown, 1844), I, 100.

It has possessed and diseased men's imaginations with outward tortures, shrieks, and flames; . . . turned their thoughts to Jesus, as an outward deliverer; and thus blinded them to his true glory, which consists in his setting free and exalting the soul. Men are flying from an outward hell, when in truth they carry within them the hell which they should chiefly dread. The salvation which man chiefly needs, and that which brings with it all other deliverance, is salvation from the evil of his own mind.[13]

Channing's method is consistent with his beliefs: he indicts Calvinism for a too literal interpretation of the idea of hell through the eloquence of his appeal to the better nature of his audience, rather than by arguing doctrine or citing chapter and verse. Elsewhere Channing may be more deliberate, but to conquer by force of rhetoric is his most effective strategy.

Other Unitarian preachers were less rhetorical; indeed the denomination as a whole prided itself on its "rational" approach to religion, as we have seen. But more concerned with morality than theology, they tended to proceed rather in the manner of Adam Smith or Samuel Johnson than in the manner of Edwards or Lyman Beecher, as in Joseph Stevens Buckminster's distinction between "the desire of approbation and the desire of admiration":

The former we rarely condemn; the latter always. The former is often connected with a tender conscience; the latter, always with a vain imagination. The one relates to our motives and to the heart; the other, to our manners and to the exterior. Approbation is the reward of good intentions; admiration, of good appearances. The desire of being approved is a passion which may include God himself among the objects of its concern. . . . But the desire of being admired can have no reference to God, for God cannot admire. Admiration is an emotion unknown to the mind of omnipotence. He, in whose sight all worldly glory is but a glimmering exhalation, low in its origin, transitory in its continuance, delusive in its

[13] *The Works of William E. Channing,* 4th ed. (Boston: Munroe, 1845), III, 221.

effects, cannot be dazzled by splendor, or deceived by appearances. He who wishes to be admired, must not look above the earth.[14]

This is moral preaching at its most inventive and ingenious. Buckminster spins out his distinction in an exquisitely discriminating way, piling his nice antitheses one atop the other until he reaches his rhetorical culmination in the penultimate sentence, which he caps with a terse aphorism to sum up his whole critique. The passage is a literary construct as much as it is a homiletical appeal.

The standard set by Buckminster and Channing was hard for less creative preachers to imitate; Unitarian preaching below the first rank tends toward pedantry or effusiveness. The Unitarians were further inhibited by their distrust of emotional display (Buckminister's passage, for instance, has a coldness to it, and even Greenwood is precious rather than fervent) and by a lingering conservatism that kept them from innovating beyond a certain point. Frothingham's textual improvisations, for example, show a reluctance to let go of old forms. "As a matter of taste," his son tells us, he would not "have spoken of a sonata of Beethoven in a sermon, [though] there was nothing in his philosophy to render secular allusions improper." [15] Henry Ware, Jr., in his Divinity School courses on homiletics, recommended that his students make use of narrative, anecdote, and analogy; but he felt constrained to warn against references to the arts and common life as, for the most part, too profane.

Altogether, the Unitarians developed a mildly innovative sort of religious discourse. In their specifications for content and style, they were relatively unrestrictive: the sermon had only to be religiously uplifting, intelligible, and consistent with Unitarianism's somewhat ill-defined principles. It was expected that the minister would preach most of his sermons on themes

[14] Buckminster, *Sermons,* 3d ed. (Boston: Wells and Lilly, 1821), pp. 70–71.
[15] O. B. Frothingham, *Recollections and Impressions, 1822–1890* (New York: Putnam, 1891), pp. 7–8.

suggested by the New Testament, particularly the Gospels, but he was welcome to sermonize on secular topics if he pleased. A sermon might run anywhere from, say, eight to thirty pages in length. The Unitarian sermon was a supple enough model to allow liberal ministers of a literary bent to gratify their creative impulses within its framework, even as their less inventive colleagues continued to preserve old homiletical motifs and formulas; and at the same time it provided those radicals like Parker who were discontented with even the vestiges of religious traditionalism with a useful point of departure in the evolution of their own style. Conservatives may not have recognized the discourses of Emerson and Parker as sermons, but they themselves regarded them as such, and justly so. We shall now see why.

The issue is complicated by the fact that the division between Unitarian and Transcendentalist views of literary style is no more clear cut than it is in respect to world-view. On the one hand, the sermons and essays composed by the Transcendentalist ministers who remained in the clergy generally conformed to middle-of-the-road Unitarian practice in respect to style. Cyrus Bartol's sermons in *The Christian Spirit and Life,* for example, were considered so unexceptionable by the *Christian Examiner* reviewer that he could make no criticism of them.[16] George Ripley's *Discourses on the Philosophy of Religion* was criticized by one Transcendentalist for being too Unitarian in tone.[17] Nor can the rhetoric of W. H. Furness, James F. Clarke, Convers Francis, or the young Emerson be distinguished, except by the practiced eye, from that of Greenwood or Frothingham or Henry Ware, Jr. Whatever their theological orientation, in point of style their prose is not what we think of as "Transcendental." Between the latter (epitomized by the essays of

[16] A. P. Peabody, "Bartol's Sermons," *Christian Examiner,* 48 (1850), 120.

[17] Samuel Osgood, "Review of Discourses," *Western Messenger,* 3 (1837), 580–583.

Thoreau and the mature Emerson) and Unitarian discourse there seems to be a sharp break.

This contrast can be well illustrated by juxtaposing the passage from Emerson's Divinity School Address quoted in the Introduction, above, with a parallel excerpt from Channing's most Transcendental sermon, "Likeness to God."

1. If a man is at heart just, then in so far is he God; the safety of God, the immortality of God, the majesty of God do enter into that man with justice. If a man dissemble, he deceives himself, and goes out of acquaintance with his own being. [*W*, I, 122]

2. [Man's likeness to God] has its foundation in the original and essential capacities of the mind. In proportion as these are unfolded by right and vigorous exertion, it is extended and brightened. In proportion as they are perverted and overpowered by the appetites and passions, it is blotted out.[18]

The two men differ more here in language than in substance. Channing makes his point as deliberately as possible; Emerson uses paradox and antithesis (the just man is God; he goes out of acquaintance with his own being) to drive home his point— whatever it is. In their works as a whole, the contrast is the same. Channing is at great pains not to lose his reader; Emerson often does not even seem to care about being orderly or straightforward: he prefers to speak metaphorically. When one considers that Channing himself was suspected of being carried away by his eloquence, it is clear that an Emerson discourse, not only in its content but in its style, would not have served as a Unitarian sermon. The liberties Emerson took with language were unintelligible to conservatives. They eventually came to terms with him only by pigeonholing him as a "poet," a talented eccentric. They regarded him as one with Carlyle, rather than with themselves, and the distrust was reciprocated.[19]

[18] *Works*, III, 228.

[19] Cf. Channing's statement in "Unitarian Christianity": "It is not the mark of wisdom, to use an unintelligible phraseology, to communicate what is above our capacities, to confuse and unsettle the intellect by

The prose styles of Alcott, Ellery Channing, Thoreau, Dwight, Cranch, and the early Brownson all partake of Emerson's oracular quality to some degree. Faced with the obvious difference between their prose and Unitarian prose, one initially fails to perceive the affinities between them and is tempted to explain Transcendentalism as a foreign importation, as both sides in the controversy in fact alleged. Nevertheless, important lines of relationship do exist. One is the figurative approach to truth. The free and creative use the Unitarians made of scripture and doctrine was a significant legacy to Transcendentalist style as well as thought. Their approach to the Bible was a near anticipation of the Emersonian habit of interpreting its supernatural elements metaphorically. Channing's passage on hell is a prime example. There and elsewhere, one of Unitarianism's chief weapons against Orthodoxy was a strategy of redefinition by appealing to essence. Its high point, perhaps, came when Orville Dewey—who as a former Calvinist was a master of the technique—defined the Unitarian belief in terms of the Calvinist doctrines of atonement, depravity, regeneration, and election, interpreting each one, however, beyond anything a Calvinist would have accepted.[20] "Atonement" now meant the "reconciliation" of man to God (instead of vice versa), the realization of God's love for man in sending Christ.[21]

---

appearances of contradiction" (*Works*, III, 69). This sort of admonition, here directed against Calvinism, was easily applied to Transcendentalism also.

[20] *Works*, pp. 345–351. For a Calvinist reaction to this sort of approach, see Anon., "On the Figurative Character of the Sacred Writings," *Spirit of the Pilgrims*, 4 (1831), 15–21.

[21] This definition of atonement as reconciliation, which was generally shared and widely expressed among Unitarians, should be borne in mind in interpreting Emerson's idea of the poet-priest as "reconciler" (*W*, III, 37; IV, 219.) "Time and nature yield us many gifts, but not yet the timely man, the new religion, the reconciler, whom all things await" (*W*, III, 37). Emerson's audience could not have failed to perceive a Christ-like connotation in this. Another idiosyncratic use of the term is in Brownson's

"Depravity" meant simply that the flesh is weak; "Regeneration" meant a progressive spiritual growth, not an immediate
transfiguration through a special interposition of grace; "Election" meant divine foreknowledge of what men will choose to
do. Countless examples of this same tactic recur throughout the
controversial writings of early Unitarianism. "Revivals" and
"Evangelical" were two other terms Unitarians delighted to
redefine in the same manner.

Such tactics naturally led, in the next generation, to a conviction of the relativity of all doctrinal truth. "To be at perfect
agreement with a man of most opposite conclusions," Emerson wrote in 1832, "you have only to translate your language
into his. The same thought which you call *God* in his nomen-
clature is called *Christ*. In the language of William Penn moral
sentiment is called *Christ*" (*JMN*, IV, 14). This was the birth
of comparative religion as a field of study in America. It also
gave rise to some intellectual gamesmanship. Two years later,
for instance, Emerson found that he could listen to a Calvinist
minister with admiration, "because though the whole is literally false, it is really true; only he speaks Parables which I translate as he goes. Thus, he says, 'the carnal mind hates God
continually': & I say, 'It is the instinct of the understanding to
contradict the reason.' One phrase translates the other" (*JMN*,
IV, 320).

Here we see Unitarian therapy beginning to be put to Transcendentalist uses. In the miracles controversy, the Transcendentalists turned the same weapon directly against the Unitarians. There again the strategy of the progressives was to read
the doctrine figuratively, as referring to nature rather than to
the supernatural, that is, to interpret "miracle" as meaning
something like "what is wonderful." What is so special about

New Views, where his vision of the future synthesis of Catholicism (or
spirituality) with Protestantism (materialism) is also called an atonement
(*Tr*, pp. 122–123).

miracles when all of life is itself a miracle?—that was the burden of their argument against the conservative definition.[22] The stakes in this dispute were unusually high, because the Unitarians had taken the position that the miracles of the Gospel are the one unshakable proof of the supernatural authority of Christianity. If they too were reduced to metaphor Unitarianism would no longer have solid ground for believing in anything. Hence the uproar; hence the importance of the episode in the history of religious liberalism in New England. The movement from Unitarianism to Transcendentalism is best seen, however, not in terms of one great crisis but as a relatively gradual transition from a dogmatics to a poetics of religion, in which the miracles controversy was simply the point of no return.

Emerson's sermons show the process of transition. Consider his idea of prayer, which is dealt with in three sermons, including the first he ever preached. Without ever quite abandoning the literal view of prayer as a devotional act, he stresses that "the right prayer is the habitual reference of the Soul of God." [23] From which position it is but one step to the definition of prayer in "Self-Reliance" as "the soliloquy of a beholding and jubilant soul" (*W*, II, 77). Similarly, in the sermons,

[22] The best account of the miracles controversy is William R. Hutchison, *The Transcendentalist Ministers* (New Haven: Yale University Press, 1959), pp. 52–97.

[23] Manuscript sermon 150, p. 9v, MS Am 1280.215, Houghton Library, Harvard University. See also manuscript sermon 86, and sermon 1, in *Young Emerson Speaks*, ed. Arthur McGiffert (Boston: Houghton Mifflin, 1938), p. 4. Prayer was a concept which other Transcendentalists also liked to define in a figurative way. See for example Cranch, "Prayer," *Western Messenger*, 6 (1839), 152; and Caleb Stetson, "Domestic Worship," *Christian Examiner*, 28 (1840), 203. For a traditional interpretation of prayer by a Transcendentalist, see Bartol, *Discourses on the Christian Spirit and Life*, pp. 137–138. Altogther it is impossible to judge the precise extent to which the Transcendentalists went in their redefinitions of religious terms except to say that as a group they did this more freely than other Unitarians.

Heaven "is not a place, but a state of the mind. *Hell* is a vice, the rebellion of the passions"; Divine Wrath means "the sufferings of man"; Christ is "continually spoken of in the Epistles almost as an abstract name for those virtues that shone in him"; indeed, "every commandment of religion truly considered is not so much God commanding man as it is a higher part of man contending against a lower part." Such statements read like Cyrus Bartol's anecdote of the Unitarian who declared that he spelled his "God" with two *o*'s and his "devil" without a *d*.[24]

But Emerson's definitions are not isolated examples. "A good essay might be written on the Unitarian Language," Edward Everett Hale once remarked.[25] To list some more items in the lexicon: death and damnation, Orville Dewey declared, "mean nothing else but that unavoidable misery which must spring from boundless wants unsatisfied." Salvation, wrote Bernard Whitman, "takes place whenever a person becomes a practical Christian." Of prayer, Charles Follen argued that "desire is the permanent essence, the particular requests or petitions are only the accidental and temporary directions or applications of prayer."[26] These figurative interpretations were not the only or even, for some ministers, the typical way of approaching religious subjects, but they were often to be met with, not just among Unitarian but Orthodox as well. James H. Perkins, for instance, complained about the Orthodox tendency "to talk of inability, when they mean unwillingness; and our sinning in Adam when they mean that we sin ourselves. Let these opponents of old Calvinism stand boldly out and denounce it, not

[24] The Emerson quotations are from manuscript sermons 37B, p. 5v; 89, p. 7; 123, p. 12v; and 141A, p. 1v, respectively. The Bartol anecdote is in *Radical Problems*, 3d ed. (Boston: Roberts, 1872), p. 103.

[25] Clarke, *Autobiography, Diary and Correspondence*, ed. Edward Everett Hale (Boston: Houghton Mifflin, 1891), p. 263n.

[26] Dewey, *Works*, p. 68; Whitman, *Christian Salvation* (Boston: American Unitarian Association, 1831), pp. 4–5; Follen, *The Works of Charles Follen, with a Memoir of His Life*, ed. Eliza Lee Follen (Boston: Hilliard, Gray, 1841), II, 261.

seek to creep under its skirts and stab it there; why fight so for a name?" [27] Clearly, the two camps were playing at the same game: trying to stay as long as possible under the old umbrella out of sentimental traditionalism or fear of public opinion.

Pushed far enough, the figurative approach is naturally going to lead a poetic temperament to poetry. Figurative language will seem a more appropriate way to convey one's insights than straightforward exposition. Channing lent credence to such thoughts in his praises of poetry; the leading theological reformer among the Orthodox, Horace Bushnell, went even further, declaring that since doctrines are always interpreted subjectively and language is never precise, "Poets, then, are the true metaphysicians, and if there be any complete science of man to come, they must bring it." [28] Like Emerson, Bushnell was led to this insight largely through his reading in Coleridge, and this plus the leading role he played in the church of his day testifies to the larger significance of the ferment within Transcendentalism, as Charles Feidelson has pointed out.[29] Of course the Divinity School Address makes the same point almost twenty years earlier, both in its argument and in its rhetoric. Such aphorisms as "[Miracle] is Monster" (*W*, I, 129) and "To aim to convert a man by miracles is a profanation of the soul" (*W*, I, 132) are attempts to act out in words Emerson's claim that doctrine can only be taught poetically. Notice that Emerson does not go so far as to deny that the Gospel miracles took place; his point is essentially the same as the argument expressed prosaically by Ripley and Hedge, that the locus of belief is in the consciousness and not in a historical event. Emerson's contribution, rather, is to show though his paradoxical style the inoperability of doctrine, to force the auditor

[27] James H. Perkins, *"Letters on the Difficulties of Religion," Western Messenger*, 1 (1836), 858.

[28] *God in Christ* (Hartford: Hammersley, 1849), p. 73.

[29] *Symbolism and American Literature* (Chicago: University of Chicago Press, 1953), pp. 151–157.

to read him figuratively, as he believes that scriptures should be read.

The figurative approach to doctrine did not always lead the Transcendentalists to a figurative style, as we have noted. Some lacked the talent and/or inclination to employ it. Some career ministers shied away from using Emersonian rhetoric if only to avoid confusing their flocks. For example, the poet-pastor Charles T. Brooks preached very Emersonian interpretations of prayer, resurrection, and the last judgment in very conventional language,[30] while Cyrus Bartol tended to transcendentalize in his essays but preach in a straightforward manner, at least until late in his career, when his sermons become more stylized and idiosyncratic.[31] Still, the reliance on metaphor as a substitute for doctrine can often be found in Transcendentalist preaching; the two categories set up earlier eventually break down, when applied to the preaching of Dwight, Cranch, Parker, the later Bartol, and a few others.[32] An interesting case in point is Thomas Treadwell Stone, an ex-Calvinist turned liberal who ministered in Salem and Bolton. Turning from his *Dial* essay, "Man in the Ages," one of the magazine's better contributions, to his published sermons, one finds the same rapt, oracular, and (at best) sensitive style. "Obedience to the Spirit," for example, starts from the text "He that hath an Ear, Let Him Hear" and unfolds the idea of obedience in terms of the metaphor of hearing:

---

[30] *The Simplicity of Christ's Teachings* (Boston: Crosby, Nichols, 1859), sermons 12, 14, 15.

[31] The difference in styles is apparent from contrasting Bartol's first two volumes of sermons, *Discourses on the Christian Spirit and Life* and *Discourses on the Christian Body and Form* (Boston: Crosby, Nichols, 1852), with his collection of essays, *Radical Problems*, and his eulogy, *Ralph Waldo Emerson: A Discourse in West Church* (Boston: Williams, 1882).

[32] For samples of Dwight's preaching, see "The Religion of Beauty," *Dial*, 1 (1840), 17-22; and "Ideals of Everyday Life," *ibid.*, pp. 307-311, 446-461.

As the eye brings its objects before us for the sight, type of mind in its conscious vision; so the ear opens the entrance to impulses of sound, symbol of the soul in the vividness of its quicker emotions. Obedience itself, as the very word traced to its origin indicates, is nothing else than a certain activity of hearing; the man hearkening to some higher voice which moves him, listening that he may drink from its influences, and going forth into deed, stern or gentle, as the welcome power impels.[33]

The passage is more florid and less succinct than Emerson, partly because Stone is trying to explain his paradox, the equivalence of obedience and hearing. But he does so by other figurative strategies: analogy and the appeal to etymology—Emersonian tactics both. Stone's message and approach are altogether very similar to Emerson's in "Spiritual Laws." Each discourse argues that the spirit is always calling us, if we would only listen; and in each case the author, desiring to stress the proximity and the naturalness of the spirit (and yet its specialness too), seizes on a concept with a double meaning. Stone's is hearing, which can either be passive or active, dull or perceiving; Emerson's more audaciously, is choice. The difference is that Stone unfolds his double sense at the outset, whereas Emerson teases the readers for almost ten pages with counsels of acquiescence and "do not choose" before explaining that he means choice only in the usual sense, that we *are* required to exercise the choice which is "a whole act of the man" and answer the "calling" in our "character" (*W*, II, 140).

As this comparison suggests, Transcendentalist exploitation of paradox and metaphor in general is carried to the fullest in Emerson's essays and those of Thoreau. Meant for reading, not listening, they are not restrained by the low threshold of understanding in oral communication, but have a density which

[33] *Sermons* (Boston: Crosby, Nichols, 1854), p. 2. A sketch of Stone's life and career is in George Willis Cooke, *A Historical and Biographical Introduction to Accompany "The Dial"* (Cleveland: Rowfant Club, 1902), II, 87–93.

makes all but a few of Emerson's lectures look thin by contrast. Nor are they bound by the occasion of the Sabbath. From Emerson to Thoreau, the use of metaphor is secularized. In Thoreau, religious terminology, when it appears, is usually divorced from its traditional contexts and used in startlingly innovative ways, not so much for its own sake as for a motif, for the purposes of atmosphere, wit, satire, or spiritualization of the subject, and sometimes all four at once. "Never again complain of a want of Power," he puns, referring to natural resources: "it is the grossest form of infidelity" (*Wr,* IV, 291). This remark is almost pure technical virtuousity. Elsewhere, however, his wit becomes more serious:

We are too inclined to go hence to a "better land," without lifting a finger, as our farmers are moving to the Ohio soil; but would it not be more heroic and faithful to till and redeem this New England soil of the world? . . . Every gazette brings accounts of the untutored freaks of the wind,—shipwrecks and hurricanes which the mariner and planter accept as special or general providences, but they touch our consciences, they remind us of our sins. Another deluge would disgrace mankind. [*Wr,* IV, 282–283]

Here again the subject is the need to harness natural energy. Thoreau's admonitions are deftly enhanced by the religious allusions, which remind us that this is not just a reviewer but a prophet who's speaking, and which add depth to his indictment. The "better land" spoofs both pious folks' views of heaven and the pie-in-the-sky attitude of those who migrate westward willy-nilly. What are called providences are simply symbols of our incompetence in dealing with nature, which is positively a "sin," in Thoreau's eyes. Altogether, the passage is "irreverent" but the underlying tone is quite serious: it conveys the impression that the speaker is a good deal more concerned about the "redemption" of the world than many people are about their souls. Religious language clearly interests Thoreau more as grist for his mill than for its original denotations; but he also feels the need for a religious connotation to add impact to his message.

For the most part, Thoreau assumes the homiletical role with a certain degree of comic exaggeration, or at least self-consciousness ("If I were to preach at all in this strain, I would say . . ." [*Wa*, p. 73]). But at times, notably in his antislavery writings, he throws himself into it fully and the result is a true jeremiad, as in his opinion of the constitutionality of the Fugitive Slave Law:

> Is virtue constitutional, or vice? Is equity constitutional, or iniquity? In important moral and vital questions, like this, it is just as important to ask whether a law is constitutional or not, as to ask whether it is profitable or not. ["Men of expediency"] persist in being the servants of the worst of men, and not the servants of humanity. The question is, not whether you or your grandfather, seventy years ago, did not enter into an agreement to serve the devil, and that service is not accordingly now due; but whether you will not now, for once and at last, serve God,—in spite of your own past recreancy, or that of your ancestor,—by obeying that eternal and only just CONSTITUTION, which He, and not any Jefferson or Adams, has written in your being. [*Wr*, IV, 401–402]

Thoreau and the Unitarian ministry would have been mutually outraged at the claim that they had a lot in common and that this passage proves it; but they did, and it does. Thoreau's religious vocabulary recalls the preaching of the seventeenth century rather than the nineteenth ("serve the Devil"; "in spite of your own past recreancy") and his stand on slavery is much more uncompromising than that of most of the ministry of his day.[34] But the homiletical cast of the passage is unmistakable—and undoubtedly intended, and the exposure of false legalism by interpreting the Constitution according to the spirit is squarely in the Unitarian tradition. It seems almost as if Transcendentalism has taken us full circle, that we are back

[34] The best discussion of the position of the Unitarian ministry on slavery is Daniel Howe, *The Unitarian Conscience,* pp. 270–305.

again listening to Channing's "Moral Argument against Calvinism." [35] Of course Channing would have seemed weak tea to a man who believed that "by far the greatest preacher of them all" was John Brown (*Wr*, IV, 443).

"His temperament is so moral, his least observation will breed a sermon," Ellery Channing said of Thoreau. [36] This is harsh but telling. The moment Thoreau departs from the purely descriptive level, it is instinctive with him to reach for some metaphor which can then be applied to the conduct of life—though he is not so crude as to beat the reader over the head with a moral except in case of emergencies like John Brown's arrest. Even in the most ephemeral piece Thoreau ever wrote, "The Landlord," he cannot resist turning his sketch into a parable: the tavern symbolizes the perfect house, and thus compares "favorably with the church"; the landlord is "a self-appointed brother of his race; called to his place . . . as truly as the preacher is called to preach" (*W*, V, 161–162, 154). The same propensity for elevating a secular situation by stressing its essentially sacred nature prevails throughout Transcendentalist writing. Emerson calls the lyceum his pulpit, often bursting into prophetic exhortation ("There will be a new church founded on moral science" [*W*, VI, 241], "O, my brothers, God exists" [*W*, II, 139], etc.); Alcott invokes Christ as a model for his pedagogy; Jones Very approaches literary history as a manifestation of spiritual evolution. [37]

These instances are a logical extension of the tendency in Unitarian preaching to broaden the range of pulpit subjects. It would be ridiculous to claim that Emerson's essays are simply warmed-over versions of his sermons; but there are some close parallels. "Self-Reliance," "Compensation," "Spiritual Laws,"

35 *Works*, 1, 217–241.
36 *Thoreau the Poet-Naturalist*, ed. F. B. Sanborn, new ed. (Boston: Goodspeed, 1902), p. 121.
37 See "Epic Poetry," *Poems and Essays*, ed. James Freeman Clarke (Boston: Houghton Mifflin, 1886), pp. 5–25.

"Manners," "Prudence," and "Wealth" are also treated in his sermons, where he comes to much the same conclusions on each subject. Another sermon spells out the four uses of *Nature* six years before the book itself.[38] And the characteristic movement of Emerson's mature essays from the level of commonsense to higher considerations is also a standard homiletical method. To a lesser extent, one finds echoes of this kind in Thoreau also. The theory of moral growth set forth in "Higher Laws" and the "Conclusion" to *Walden* is good Arminian doctrine, and the former chapter even uses the ascending structure (with a comic twist at the end). The instance in which a knowledge of sermon conventions is the most helpful to an understanding of Emerson and Thoreau is their essays on Friendship. Both are strikingly naive-sounding in some ways, and may justly be taken as evidence of personal failings in both writers; but they seem less pathological when one considers that their approach and theme are essentially homiletic—an analysis of actual friendship as judged against an ideal standard. According to religious convention (employed by Emerson in an early sermon on friendship, by the way) human relations always fall short; the celestial love is alone sufficient. So one should not be too much taken aback by Emerson's description of the friend as simply "the child of all my foregoing hours, . . . the harbinger of a greater friend" (*W*, II, 214).

Another stylistic resemblance between the Unitarian sermon and Transcendentalist discourse is the device of multiple statement or illustration. Unitarian preaching often shows a reiterative quality similar to that of Transcendentalist prose. Buckminister feels obliged to throw out five parallel aphorisms on approbation versus admiration; Thoreau cannot rest his case against avarice in "Life Without Principle" until he has brought in popular literature, wood-measuring, gold-digging in California and Australia, grave-robbing, and high-society preachers.

[38] For this insight I am indebted to Richard P. Adams, "Emerson and the Organic Metaphor," *PMLA*, 69 (1954), 121.

On the most basic level, the purpose of reiteration is to make sure that the audience gets the point. Any speech is thus bound to contain a fair amount of repetition. But beyond this, the Unitarians' unusual fondness for the device had to do with their idea that the truths of religion were simple and the job of preaching was to impress them on the minds of men. From this it followed that their sermons were often thin on the level of argument and copious on the level of demonstration. Take for instance Dewey's "The Religion of Life." Here the doctrine is simply "that everything is beautiful in its time, in its place, in its appointed office; that everything which man is put to do, naturally helps to work out his salvation." [39] The rest of the sermon simply applies this platitude to medicine, law, several of the arts, recreation, and social intercourse. It is not one of Dewey's better efforts. The categories are very general, the explanations are prolix, the ideas are trite, and the rhetoric is inflated. But the performance is quite Emersonian in its accretion of a great diversity of examples around a single, simple, spiritual idea. As in an Emerson essay, the originality and effect of the sermon, such as they are, consist not in the doctrine, not in the argument, but in the variety and newness of the examples, the last two particularly. It was just this characteristic, significantly, which led one of the last Transcendentalists, O. B. Frothingham, to call Dewey "perhaps the greatest" preacher "that the Unitarian communion has produced." To Frothingham, Dewey rated higher even than Channing because he applied Channing's doctrine of the dignity of human nature to all walks of life.[40]

Even in preachers too fastidious to descend to social references in the pulpit, like the senior Frothingham, one finds parallel examples. In his sermon on "The Measures of Time," for example, Frothingham has a message as simplistic as Dewey's, namely that our lives are measured by the good works we do. But he leads up to this point in cleverly devious fashion,

[39] *Works,* p. 123.
[40] O. B. Frothingham, *Recollections and Impressions,* p. 186.

by distinguishing four lesser ways of measuring time: by our moods, by our minds, by the stars, and by artificial instruments.[41]

From Frothingham and Dewey it was but a step to the range of reference and imagery exhibited by the best Transcendentalist writers. The simplification and humanizing of doctrine which produced such sermons as the two just discussed were extended to their limit, and more emphasis was placed on variety of application than ever before. Parker said he had only three doctrines—the infinite perfection of God, the adequacy of man for all his functions, and absolute or natural religion; [42] Emerson claimed to have only one, "the infinitude of the private man" (*JMN*, VII, 342). Knowing these ideas one can usually anticipate their drift of thought; its chief attraction lies in the variety of shapes it assumes. Parker's style is especially interesting for the way it takes the sermon form as far as it can go without ceasing to be sermon. His subjects ranged "from those of the soul to those of the kitchen," as O. B. Frothingham said.[43] Many of his discourses resemble sociological and historical essays, including lengthy circumstantial accounts and even statistics; to some hearers, they seemed no different from lectures. His points are illustrated in every conceivable way. In "Conventional and Natural Sacraments," for example, he argues that the observances of all religions are equally arbitrary by lumping the rites of various religious traditions together:

If you ask a New England Powwow for proof of the religious character of a red man, he would have cited the offering of tobacco to the Great Spirit; a Teutonic priest would refer to the reverence of his countrymen for the ceremony just spoken of [idol-worship]; a New-Hollander would dwell on the devotion of his neighbors, and

[41] *Sermons, in the Order of a Twelvemonth,* pp. 14–26.

[42] *Autobiography, Poems and Prayers,* ed. Rufus Leighton (Boston: American Unitarian Association, 1911), p. 349.

[43] *Theodore Parker: A Biography* (Boston: Osgood, 1874), p. 338.

show the little fingers cut off; a Hebrew would expatiate on the sacrament of circumcision . . . ; the Christian dwells on his distinctive sacramental opinion, that Jesus is the Son of Jehovah.

Later on, Parker compares the unnaturalness of trying to perpetuate such rituals beyond their day to putting a wig on a person with hair, asking a grown man to ride a hobby-horse, and galvanizing a corpse.[44]

In such passages as the above we can see the link between Unitarian preaching and the catalogues of Emerson and Whitman. Parker's piling up of multiple and far-ranging examples is a logical consequence of the Unitarian tendency to view earlier forms of worship as imperfect though genuine expressions of the religious sentiment, analogous though inferior to liberal Christianity. Following Unitarian precedent, Parker traces a progressive development from primitive religion to Protestantism, but he does not admit the specialness of Christian revelation. Instead of analogy he sees identity. In this respect his vision is the same as that of Emerson and Whitman, who hold to the notion of unity of spirit in variety of form. But unlike their catalogues, Parker's is not an exuberant affirmation of the principle but a negation, an attempt to make modern religious forms seem absurd by linking them with ancient custom, and ridiculous hypothetical situations. Though this sermon was written later than "Song of Myself" its reductionism belongs to an earlier state of religious thought, to the struggle that Emerson went through in the early 1830s and which Whitman, who got his religion by osmosis and later than they, never went through at all.

Another difference between Parker's rhetoric and that of Emerson and Whitman is its structure. Parker's is much tighter. However lyrical he gets—and he can be very eloquent, as we shall see—his writing always has a distinct linear movement.

---

[44] *Sermons of Religion,* ed. Samuel A. Eliot (Boston: American Unitarian Association, 1908), p. 251.

This is true of all Unitarian preaching. Emerson as essayist, by contrast, seems almost to go out of his way to weaken his transitions, although in his early sermons he was as coherent as Parker. Emerson's idea of the structure of truth changed as radically as his idea about the language of truth. The measure of how far he eventually deviated from his origins is his amazing reply to Henry Ware, Jr.'s request for proofs of his position in the Divinity School Address: "I do not know . . . what arguments mean in reference to any expression of a thought." [45]

This statement must have surprised his former mentor, to say the least; but even it had its origins in Unitarianism. Ware himself, as recent scholars have pointed out, was a deeply pious man (as well as a frustrated poet) who held the religious emotions in much higher esteem than doctrinal niceties, even though he was appalled by revivalism.[46] The passages from Channing and Greenwood quoted above show too that Unitarian sermons often tended to be loosely-organized effusions upon a given theme. Another case of special interest, since Emerson copied it into an early journal, is this excerpt from Nathaniel Frothingham.

"And the Word was made flesh & dwelt among us—full of grace & truth." The word is the utterance or manifestation of the divine presence perfections & will. It is nothing distinct from God. It is God himself considered as displayed in what he is, does, commands, purposes. This word has been limited to no age of the world to no generation of men. "It was in beginning" & has never left itself without witness. It is not confined to any place. It has gone out into all the earth & sent its speech to the end of the world. It is not heard only in one form through one organ or thro' a few organs of communication; but from the whole order of nature, & harmony of the universe; from the sun declaring as he rises the

[45] *The Letters of Ralph Waldo Emerson,* ed. Ralph L. Rusk (New York: Columbia University Press, 1939), II, 167.
[46] See Chapter 1, note 25, above.

glorious work of the Most High from the moon walking in brightness, from the stars as they sing together;—from the restless elements & the sounding sea, for the Spirit of God is breathed thro' the air & moves over the face of the waters. It has been heard from among the enjoyments of merely sentient beings, the sympathies & charities of social life the plain laws of a moral govt.; the distinctions capacities obligations hopes of a moral nature & from the whole eventful history of man. The word was made order & design in the visible Creation. The word was made Flesh. [*JMN*, III, 141]

Frothingham's language and syntax are clearer and more convential than in Transcendentalist rhetoric; otherwise the passage strongly resembles, say, Emerson's "Method of Nature" or Thoreau's celebration of "reality" at the end of "Where I Lived and What I Lived for." It is very reiterative; the sentences are self-contained units of thought related like a series of concentric circles, encompassing more and more in their imagery until they have taken in the whole creation from the beginning of time. The passage is not at all an appeal to the understanding but to the sensibility. It inspires awe and wonder. As an explication it is muddled, even dangerously misleading: to claim that the manifestation of God in the creation "is nothing distinct from God," is "God himself considered as displayed in what he is," opens the door to a Parkerist or even a pantheist interpretation which the later references to Christ do nothing to refute. The passage, in short, has to be taken as a lyric celebration upon the metaphor of word and flesh as matter and spirit.

It is possible that Emerson transcribed the Frothingham passage from memory and altered it somewhat in his imagination. But in any case, such passages occur fairly often in Unitarian preaching, especially in perorations and when the preacher dwells on the themes of the omnipresence of divine benevolence and the dignity of human nature. This is to be expected. First, divine benevolence and the dignity of human nature were doctrines to celebrate about; they were what the Unitarians had as a substitute for the Calvinist doctrines of grace and omnip-

otence. And secondly, as to the mode of utterance, the chain
of aphorisms or concentric circles method is well adapted to
oral delivery calculated to impress. Oratory, like conversation,
lends itself to nutshell manifestos: speaking is slower than reading, so that terseness and restatement are more helpful; and a
barrage of quick formulations is likely to be more effective than
a complicated argument.

It may seem perverse to insist on the nonlogical elements of
Unitarian preaching as foreshadowing the Transcendentalists,
when the latter were notoriously in revolt against Unitarian
rationalism. But the incongruity disappears when we recall
that the Unitarians themselves were, in a sense, trying to escape
from their own rationalism. Preachers like Frothingham,
Greenwood, Dewey, and Channing accepted the conclusions of
rational theology as formulated by Andrews Norton, but ignored
the rigors of their method by turning their sermons into beautiful tributes to its general principles. Hence the paradoxical
influence of Channing, the avowed exponent of "rational religion" but acclaimed—justly—much more for inspirational
power than for his reasoning ability. For that matter, anyone
who reads *The Latest Form of Infidelity* cannot fail to recognize that the "arguments" of Andrews Norton himself rested
heavily on appeals to emotion:

There are many who avow their disbelief of all that is miraculous
in Christianity, and still affect to call themselves Christians. But
Christianity was a revelation from God; and, in being so, it was
itself a miracle. Christ was commissioned by God to speak to us in
his name, and this is a miracle. No proof of his divine commission
could be afforded, but through miraculous displays of God's power.
Nothing is left that can be called Christianity, if its miraculous
character be denied. Its essence is gone; its evidence is annihilated.[47]

[47] *A Discourse on the Latest Form of Infidelity* (Cambridge: Owen,
1839), p. 22.

The sentences come in short, impassioned bursts; the repetition of "miracle" and "miraculous" has a mesmerizing effect. Passages like this suggest that Joseph Allen's description of Theodore Parker's system could be applied to all of Unitarianism: "dogmatism resting on sentiment." [48]

On the other hand, Transcendentalist writing also partook of the rationalism it professed to react against. Its cast is also markedly abstract and intellectual. The passage from Frothingham is in fact a much more obviously inspired performance, in the sense of seeming improvised, than a typical Emerson paragraph, which is a careful condensation of thought—half a dozen bricks baked and stacked. One might even go so far as to say that Emerson *fulfils* the Unitarian ideal of preaching. Taking his essays as they have most often been taken, as a conglomeration of wise sentences, they approach more closely than even Buckminister to the Unitarian ideal of moral inspiration. [49]

The risk of abandoning logic for the sake of inspired utterance is that when inspiration fails one becomes maudlin and flabby. Worse, one forfeits his critical sense and runs into self-deception. Unfortunately this too was a legacy of the Unitarians to Transcendentalism. They used rhetoric partly to fill the vacuum created by the erosion of traditional theology. Logic gave way to leitmotif; sentimentality and bombast sometimes replaced creeds and hard thinking. "Every pulsation of our hearts is a prayer-bell," says Greenwood; Christianity is like "a truly angelic heart, whose thousand strings of feeling, attuned to sweetest harmony, are making melody at every

---

[48] *Our Liberal Movement in Theology* (Boston: Roberts, 1882), p. 77.

[49] Emerson's statement in the Divinity School Address that "a true conversion" comes through "the reception of beautiful sentiments" (*W*, I, 132) calls to mind his youthful perception that "the highest species of reasoning upon divine subjects" is "the fruit of a sort of moral imagination," of which Channing's preaching seems a model (*JMN*, II, 238).

touch," another minister exudes.[50] "The religious sentiment . . . is myrrh and storax, and chlorine and rosemary,"
says the Divinity School Address, in exactly the same vein
(*W*, I, 124–125). The saccharine piety of such formulations
seems like a wilful evasion of fact. It becomes most unpleasant
indeed when the subject seems to call out for a straightforward
statement. A case in point is Cyrus Bartol's response when his
parishioners requested him to define his beliefs:

I believe that not only God is, but that God hath spoken. I believe
in His word. I believe in the Bible. We do not worship this infinite
spirit in veiled and speechless majesty alone. We do not worship
Him in the silent wonders of His hand alone. Lo! His face is revealed, and his mouth hath spoken. Language, human language,
that our ear can hear and our soul understand, tells us more of the
Supreme Being than all the grandeurs of creation can distinctly
attain to. The engraven tables of stone open a meaning clearer
than the thunders of Sinai can pronounce, though they emphat-
ically authenticate. And those words respecting Jesus,—"He opened
his lips and taught them, saying,"—are a deeper introduction into
the mind of God, than miracle and prophecy, which yet seal his
commission to teach. I believe then in the Bible as God's spoken
word.[51]

Oh? One wonders. From beginning to end the language of this
sermon is inflated, unctuous, santimonious, creating the impression of a verbal smokescreen. Bartol seems to be saying as little
as possible about what in the Bible he believes, taking refuge—
like Frothingham—in ringing changes on the meanings of "the
word." Does he believe in the priority of revelation to reason,
like a good orthodox Unitarian, or does he hold with Ripley
that internal evidence outweighs that of revelation? The penultimate sentence implies the second; the nominal argument of
the passage implies the first; the remark about the "engraven

[50] George F. Briggs, *The Bow in the Cloud* (Boston: Dowe, 1846), p. 19;
Greenwood, *Sermons* (Boston: Little, Brown 1844), II, 93.
[51] *Confession of Faith: A Sermon* (Boston: Greene, 1844), pp. 9–10.

tablets of stone" is hopelessly vague. This is the sort of intellectual evasiveness—or dishonesty—which Martin Green rightly singles out as a primary reason why the flowering of New England turned into the Genteel Tradition within little more than a generation.[52]

Fortunately, Bartol in his later years was man enough to withstand the pressure to make wishy-washy confessions of faith. After 1850 he resisted the growth of sectarian feelings within Unitarianism, even at the cost of ostracism by his colleagues.[53] But it may be unfair to charge him with insincerity even in his early years. In the foregoing passage and throughout his sermon, Bartol is grappling with a problem which continually led Unitarians, and the Transcendentalists after them, into equivocations. This was the epistemological dilemma of how to reconcile inner and outer evidence as to the nature of the universe. In Unitarian terms, the question was how to reconcile the conclusions of the reason with the content of revelation. In Transcendentalist terms, the question became how to square the intuitions of Reason with the facts of experience. One might insist in theory that there was no essential contradiction, but in practice the Unitarians were always questioning the authority of the scripture on which they professedly based their faith, while the Transcendentalists, who celebrated the god within, were acutely aware of the flickeringness of their inspiration. In both cases the sensibility oscillated between a pietistic anaesthesia and a pseudo-scientific rigor, as seen for instance in Norton's research into the Gospels and Thoreau's study of nature, which sooner or later led to a skepticism or exhaustion which drove the individual back to the opposite pole again. Hence one finds the spectacle of Emerson's address,

[52] *The Problem of Boston: Some Readings in Cultural History* (New York: Norton, 1966), chaps. v–ix.

[53] See William Hutchison, "To Heaven in a Swing: The Transcendentalism of Cyrus Bartol," *Harvard Theological Review*, 56 (1963), 275–295.

which he refused to defend and about which he had his own
doubts, being countered in the *Christian Examiner* by an
equally hazy rebuttal from Greenwood which begins bravely as
a refutation of Transcendentalism and defense of historical
Christianity but then abruptly breaks down, unable to go on:
"I will not enter into an argument with a theory which would
separate Christianity from Christ, or divorce religion from the
Bible. . . . My strongest, dearest, and liveliest faith is in the
revelation of God by his Son Jesus; my chief hope is in the
mercy of God through Christ; and God forbid that I should
glory save in his cross." [54]

Here as in the other cases of fuzzy thinking just discussed, the
root cause of the fuzziness seems to be the speaker's intoxication
with the sublimity of his idea as opposed to its accuracy. This
is to be expected from preachers who made so much of the role
of "moral impression," and it is implicit in all the other points
at which we have noted Unitarian rhetoric as anticipating
Transcendentalist prose: the figurative approach to doctrine
and (occasionally) language; multiplicity of demonstration,
verging on catalogue rhetoric; and intermittent use of rhapsodic
as opposed to logical ordering. All of these techniques betray
an impulse to go beyond truth unadorned to celebrate the
beauty of truth, an impulse which tends to accelerate as the subject gets more secular, the theological content gets more tenu-
ous, and the writer concentrates more on the appearances or
manifestations of his principle than the articulation of the principle itself. The principle is never lost sight of, but it tends to
become the muse, so to speak, rather than the subject of the discourse. The high seriousness which one expects from sermons
remains, but it is mingled with a sense of euphoria, vagueness,
and evanescence. Where it is retained, as in Parker, the credit
often seems due to some extrinsic factor, such as the gravity of
the situation or the speaker's compulsion to be encyclopedically
thorough.

[54] "Historical Christianity," *Christian Examiner,* 28 (1840), 170.

More than any of the specific techniques described earlier, this general quality of interfusion of the interests of beauty and the interests of truth, which underlies almost every excerpt quoted here, is the chief line of connection between Unitarian preaching and Transcendentalist prose style. In the former, beauty is usually secondary; in the latter it is dominant. Beyond a certain point, the conventions of the sermon are too restrictive to hold it. As John Sullivan Dwight found out, one can preach only so long on "The Religion of Beauty" before one's parishioners become restless. Ultimately the preacher's end has to be didactic; the moral artist can be more lyrical.

Perhaps the best way to describe the shift from Unitarian preaching to Transcendentalist prose is to call it a movement from sermon to scripture. All the salient points of resemblance described above are also characteristic of the ancient scripture: figurative expression, reiteration, rhapsodic flow and vagueness, interfusion of poetic feeling and moral tone. One thinks of the book of Psalms or the Upanishads; and, closely related, bardic poetry. Once it had turned its back on the ministry, literary Transcendentalism did not look to the sermon as a literary ideal but to these. Emerson called upon the divinity students to write the new Bible. Thoreau collected sayings from the "ethnical scriptures" of all nations—which he declared were his favorite reading—and liked to imitate their style. Very and Whitman assumed the role of latter-day messiahs.

Trusting as all these writers did in the possibility of an original relation to the universe, it was natural that they should have set their sights so high. Sermons, however creative, must basically address themselves to the inculcation, in orderly and intelligible form, of dogma or precepts shared in common by speaker and audience. Scripture, on the other hand, is not the formulation of accepted truth but (in the opinion of the Transcendentalists, anyhow) the record of the scribe's spiritual experience, of the Word speaking through him. It is first-hand

and not derivative. Nor, since it is a communication of the ineffable, is it under an obligation to be precise, or coherent, or codified. The only crucial requisite of the prophet or poet is that he speak from direct experience, "from within," in "the tone of having," as Emerson put it (*W*, II, 287).

The ultimate limitations of the sermon as a vehicle for Transcendentalist prophetic vision is well illustrated by the case of Theodore Parker. Parker was a man of considerable poetic gifts (though his verse is even more mediocre than most Transcendentalists') and a strong mystical bent. Critics who accept Emerson's opinion that his bluntness showed a lack of poetic feeling, or who deduce from Parker's methodical structures that he was a rationalist, are, I think, mistaken.[55] Rather, Parker was an ardent and sensitive person who was driven by his sense of mission into a rigor which he simultaneously distrusted. His writings are invariably polemical, but his central message was that religion is a matter of feeling, not argument. Perhaps he fell into this inconsistency because he believed that he had to master the approach he opposed in order to confute it, or rather to put it in the secondary position where it belonged. This is suggested by one sermon on Immortality in which he says at the outset that the doctrine is not subject to

[55] All commentators acknowledge what Commager calls "The Dilemma of Theodore Parker," *New England Quarterly*, 6 (1933), 257–77—i.e., a wavering between piety and rationalism; some, however, have overemphasized the latter side. Herbert Schneider flatly asserts, for instance, that Parker "did not indulge in, and probably did not believe in, the reason that passeth understanding" (*A History of American Philosophy* [New York: Columbia University Press, 1946], p. 268). Schneider's student, John Edward Dirks, taking a more balanced view, pictures Parker as "transitional" between "the extreme orthodoxy of Norton, based on empiricism, and Emerson's equally extreme emphasis on the individual reason and the 'authentic' insights of the individual soul." But Dirks is still inclined to disassociate Parker from Emerson and see him as a child of the Enlightenment (*The Critical Theology of Theodore Parker* [New York: Columbia University Press, 1948] p. 132 and chaps. i, iii, iv passim.)

proof, that you must experience its truth for yourself (as he has), but for those who want them he is prepared to give some evidences, which he then does.[56]

"When I was a boy," Parker confided to George Ripley, his best friend, "I had an intense passion for beauty in every form. I knew all the rare flowers, wild or cultivated. . . . Beauty of sound (not artificial, of music) filled me with ravishment. The winds in the leaves, and the rushing brooks, were a delight from the earliest boyhood till now. I am much less of a practical man than men think!" [57] As a young schoolteacher, he liked to take students into the fields, cultivate their powers of observation, and moralize from natural objects; and he did much the same in his preaching too. "In all my sermons," he told Elizabeth Peabody, "there is an excess of metaphors, similes, and all sorts of figures of speech. But this is my nature—I could not help it if I would." [58] The most striking expression of this side of Parker occurs not in his sermons, however, but in a letter which he wrote to his congregation from the West Indies, shortly before his death. In this letter he reviews his ministry at length and tries to convey the sense of delight he took in writing sermons on common things: "To compose sermons, and preach them to multitudes of men of one sort but many conditions, thereto setting forth the great truths of absolute religion, and applying them to the various events of this wondrous human life, . . . this has been my great delight. Your pulpit has been my joy and my throne." Even though he is sick, Parker insists, "sermons are never out of [his] mind":

Still by long habit all things will take this form; and the gorgeous vegetation of the tropics, their fiery skies so brilliant all the day, and star-lit too with such exceeding beauty all the night; the flittering fishes in the market, as many colored as a gardener's show, these

[56] *Sermons of Religion,* pp. 320–325.
[57] Quoted in Frothingham, *Theodore Parker,* pp. 330, 331.
[58] Quoted in John Weiss, *Life and Correspondence of Theodore Parker* (New York: Appleton, 1864), I, 340.

Josephs of the sea; the silent pelicans, flying forth at morning and back again at night, the strange fantastic trees, the dry pods rattling their historic bones all day, while the new bloom comes fragrant out beside, a noiseless prophecy; the ducks rejoicing in the long-expected rain; a negro on an ambling pad; the slender long-legged, half-naked negro children in the street, playing their languid games, or oftener screaming 'neath their mother's blows, amid black swine, hens, and uncounted dogs; the never-ceasing clack of women's tongues, more shrewd than female in their shrill violence; the unceasing, multifarious kindness of our hostess; and, over-towering all, the self-sufficient, West Indian Creole pride, alike contemptuous of toil, and ignorant and impotent of thought—all these common things turn into poetry as I look on or am compelled to hear, and then transfigure into sermons.[59]

In this striking and remarkably vivid passage, worthy of anything in Whitman, Parker's sense of beauty is given full play, quickened by the awareness of approaching death, before it can be "transfigured" into the sermons he never lived to write. It is clear both that Parker was a true Poet, in the Emersonian sense, and that his poetry could never have been written, except rare instances like this, even had he survived. The prose poetry of this passage he values not for itself but as the raw material for sermons. In the process of transmutation, it would all have been subsumed within the framework of argument, as exampla. Even then it can be impressive at its best, but the feeling of free play, of unmediated vision, is diminished or lost, even in such an exuberant sermon as "The Delights of Piety":

The aspect of beauty in every form is always a joy—in the shape and color of a blade of grass, a nut, a fly's wing, a pearl found in a mussel of a New Hampshire brook. What higher delight is there in the beauty of the human form! [60]

[59] *Autobiography, Poems and Prayers,* p. 407.
[60] *The World of Matter and the Spirit of Man,* ed. George W. Cooke (Boston: American Unitarian Association, 1907), p. 200.

Each of the four images here may once have come to Parker as a particular epiphany but their beauty is dulled by the homiletical context. Like Dr. Channing, Parker developed a clerical distrust for dreaminess and aestheticism, identifying himself first of all with the roles of minister and social activist. In the area of literary expression it was indeed the *sermon* which was his joy and his delight. Though he used it more flexibly than any of his colleagues, his sensibilities were channeled by the didactic form.

For those who escaped the limitations of this form, the question was what to substitute for it. The concept of scripture alone was not a sufficient guide, for as Emerson had said in the Divinity School Address, ancient scripture was in itself a fragmentary form. The Transcendentalists' nearest attempt to it was a disaster: Alcott's Orphic Sayings. Like Parker in his off-hours, therefore, they turned instinctively to that which had gradually replaced historical Christianity as the chief locus of God's word, Nature. As prophets, their responsibility was to rediscover the world for themselves and to utter or "build" it anew, as Emerson urged in *Nature* (*W*, I, 76). In the next section we shall see the literary results.

PART III

WORD AND WORLD: NATURE AS A MODEL FOR LITERARY FORM

The infinite diffuseness refuses to be epigrammatized, the world to be shut in a word.

—Emerson

Students of American literature have often commented on its solipsistic tendency. Following Emerson's advice, many of our authors seem to have built their own fictional universes. Well before Yeats and Joyce invented private mythologies as a substitute for orthodox Christianity, Melville, Whitman, and Emily Dickinson had begun to devise for themselves esoteric vocabularies and symbolic systems. One scholar has even sought to trace this practice back to the Puritans.[1] Carried to its fulfilment, it has led to such works as *Eureka, Moby-Dick, The Bridge, Paterson,* and *Giles Goat-Boy,* which A. D. Van Nostrand aptly calls "cosmologies," or attempts to reconstruct the universe according to one's own vision.[2]

[1] Roy Harvey Pearce, *The Continuity of American Poetry* (Princeton: Princeton University Press, 1961), chap. ii. Cf. Tony Tanner, "Notes for a Comparison between American and European Romanticism," *Journal of American Studies,* 2 (1968), 92–94.

[2] *Everyman His Own Poet: Romantic Gospels in American Literature* (New York: McGraw-Hill, 1968). This work distinguishes several different

One thinks of this tradition of literary world-building as originating in the sense of America as a new world and the American as the new Adam.[3] Before these myths could achieve full expression in literature, however, the neoclassical aesthetics that prevailed in the early national period needed to be infused with the romantic vision of the poet as a liberating god and the poem as a heterocosm, or second creation. This development was brought about, in good part, through the impact of such cultural middlemen as Coleridge, Carlyle, and Emerson upon the next generation of American writers, particularly Thoreau, Whitman, Melville, and Emily Dickinson.

In the writings of the Transcendentalists, we find the first instance in American literature of anything like an organized effort to articulate and act out the idea of the poet as world-creator. This attempt was a natural consequence of their ambivalent relationship to the theological tradition, as described above. They departed from historical Christianity but remained fervent natural believers. They were impatient with traditional sermons but prized the living word. Their respect for the office of the preacher was fast-waning, but they desired to preserve its substance by redefining him as a poet-priest.

I want now to examine at length how the idea of the work as commensurate with the world underlies Transcendentalist criticism and literary practice. Though the subject has been treated before, it still deserves extended consideration, not only because of its historical importance as the basis of the Transcendentalist aesthetics of form and as the first full-fledged ap-

---

types of cosmologies, according to the degree to which the author makes himself central in or aloof from his work. A related work is Richard Poirier, *A World Elsewhere: The Place of Style in American Literature* (New York: Oxford University Press, 1966), which confines itself largely, however, to discussion of linguistic innovativeness in particular passages.

[3] R. W. B. Lewis, *The American Adam: Innocence, Tragedy and Tradition in the Nineteenth Century* (Chicago: University of Chicago Press, 1955), discusses the importance of this myth for Emerson and his contemporaries.

pearance of the cosmology motif in American literature, but also because it is easily misrepresented. For one thing, it is hard to take seriously what the Transcendentalists have to say about form, because their criticism on the subject is always desultory and sometimes jejune, and the idea of the work as world is itself exceedingly nebulous, as a general proposition. Second and more important, it is hard to avoid the modernist temptation to view their idea of the cosmology as *purely* metaphorical. But they were not like Yeats, who, when he backed himself into a corner in the preface to *A Vision,* had to admit that his theories about the phases of the moon were "plainly symbolical" and his gyres were "stylistic arrangements of experience." [4] On the contrary, the Transcendentalist literati were not merely committed as Yeats was to the principle that the secrets of the universe could be discovered and expressed through poetry; they also believed it. They believed, that is, that the poet's approach was (or could be) metaphysically as well as metaphorically true. Partly this was because they lived at the tail end of the age of traditional faith. An equally important reason, however, was that they defined the poet not so much in terms of his role of craftsman (which inevitably leads to the consciousness of solipsism in the artist's reordering of experience) but in terms of his character, in terms of his roles as visionary, thinker, social animal, and observer of nature. Thus *Nature* is a more serious work than *A Vision,* to the degree that Emerson believes his ideas actually to be true, just as *Walden* is a more serious work than "The Lake Isle of Innisfree."

On the other hand, the Transcendentalists were by no means unaware that the creative artist imposes his vision on his universe. "Poetry," Emerson recognized, "begins . . . when we look from the centre outward, and are using all as if the mind made it" (*W,* VII, 41). Usually Emerson took pleasure in this fact, as a sign of the mind's supremacy over nature, but in his

[4] *A Vision* (New York: Macmillan, 1961), pp. 24, 25.

more sober moments he had to admit that "though the world exist from thought, thought is daunted in presence of the world" (*W*, VI, 320). In the Transcendentalists' handling of the relationship between nature and the creative imagination, this awareness leads to a very provocative dilemma, the complexity of which may easily be missed because we have largely resolved it for ourselves. Transcendentalist literature refuses to commit itself either to a straightforwardly literal or an out-and-out metaphorical approach to the subject at hand. It is constantly trying, failing, and trying again to balance and reconcile the external world with the world of the imagination. Because we no longer believe in the divine authority of the imagination, or because Yeats and Joyce have taught us to suspend our disbelief as we read their work, the Transcendentalists' vacillations may at first seem annoying, merely a psychological barrier that keeps them harping obsessively on the same issue and prevents them from ever finishing anything. But in the long run the best of their writing gains from this stimulus in richness and suggestiveness far more than it loses in indecision.

Of the following five chapters, the first gives a general outline of the Transcendentalists' idea of nature as a literary model and how it applies in practice, as exemplified chiefly by Emerson's criticism and style. The next two discuss in more detail two particular types of expression encouraged by the identification of art with nature: the literary catalogue and the symbolic excursion. Thoreau's *A Week on the Concord and Merrimack Rivers* is treated at length in Chapter 8, partly as an example of the excursion form, partly because I regard it as the most ambitious literary work—in scope if not in accomplishment—that the Transcendentalist movement produced. Finally, Chapter 9, in presenting an overview of the poetry of Ellery Channing, calls attention to a writer who has suffered more than his share of obloquy and dramatizes the irreconcilability of the problem that confronted all those Transcendentalists who placed too much trust in nature.

5 Emerson and the Idea of Microcosmic Form

Nature as a literary pursuit was an acquired taste for the Transcendentalists, sometimes never acquired at all. The majority of Transcendentalist ministers, for example, were content to celebrate "nature" and "cosmic unity" as splendid abstractions and perhaps dash off a few poems in their spare time on the "tender flush of vernal dawn" or the sublimity of Niagara Falls.[1] The prestige of *Walden* has taught us to associate Transcendentalism with a "return to nature," but in fact Thoreau was a less typical figure in this respect than Margaret Fuller, who "delighted in short country rambles" (*Ossoli,* I, 263) but was too nearsighted, unhealthy, and citified to convey much more than a tourist's enthusiasm for what she saw. She did write some interesting verse and prose-poetry on natural subjects, and some patches of good descriptive prose; but on the whole nature plays a minor role in her writing, and in her liter-

[1] Quotation from Charles T. Brooks, "Spring," in *Poems, Original and Translated,* ed. W. P. Andrews (Boston: Roberts, 1885), p. 125. Like most of their contemporaries, the Transcendentalists used the term "nature" ambiguously. Sometimes it denotes the entire empirical world or Not-me (as in Emerson's *Nature*); sometimes it denotes the spiritual law working through the Not-me; sometimes it simply means "the outdoors." At times the term is used in other senses as well. Nevertheless Transcendentalist usage is fairly predictable and easy to convey if one is careful in his phrasing. As a philosophical and literary concept in Transcendentalism, nature means primarily the physical universe as an expression of Spirit.

ary criticism she has almost nothing to ssay on the subject. Her love of nature was strong, but it did not much affect her literary personality.

Most of her fellow Transcendentalists also have more to say about Genius, Beauty, and Truth than about Nature. Even those who wrote most about nature arrived at their subject only after a preliminary period of meditation on religion, the conduct of life, and other matters similarly abstruse. Although James Russell Lowell was pig-headed in refusing to concede Thoreau much knowledge of nature, he was right that Thoreau had relatively little at the start of his career.[2] Indeed, almost all the Transcendentalists, perhaps even Thoreau, were closer to being humanists than naturalists. At bottom they were more interested in man than nature, more interested in thought than observation. "What is Nature unless there is an eventful human life passing within her?" Thoreau asks (*JT*, V, 472). "A single good man, at one with God," says Parker, "makes the morning and evening sun seem little and very low."[3] The deliberate appraisals of nature made by all the Transcendentalists fall between these two degrees of qualification. The central preoccupation of the movement was the relationship between self and God; compared to this, nature was of secondary importance.

But though the Transcendentalists were primarily children of the Puritans rather than children of nature, their reverence for the natural creation surpassed their ancestors', and with reason. To begin with, nature was no longer a threat or obstacle to survival. Whereas for the Puritans the "howling wilderness" was a hostile force, for the Transcendentalists it could serve as a sentimentally attractive image of the vigor and spontaneity lacking in their more comfortable existence. Beyond this, their distrust of historical Christianity made them attach an un-

[2] Lowell, "Thoreau," in *The Recognition of Henry David Thoreau*, ed. Wendell Glick (Ann Arbor: University of Michigan Press, 1969), p. 39.

[3] *A Discourse of Matters Pertaining to Religion*, ed. Thomas Wentworth Higginson (Boston: American Unitarian Association, 1907), p. 200.

usually high theoretical value to nature as evidence and analogue of man's relation to God. This attitude, in turn, was reinforced by the romanticist cult of nature, particularly the vision of an organic universe,[4] and by the nationalist cliché of America as nature's nation, which seemed to make romanticist ideology all the more relevant to their situation.[5] As a result, nature tended to become a crucial touchstone in matters of religion, as when Emerson condemned the doctrine of miracles as monstrous because "it is not one with the blowing clover and the falling rain (*W*, I, 129). Some Transcendentalists thought this too radical, but the general drift of the movement was from the rational supernaturalism of the Unitarians to natural religion to the religion of nature.

In their aesthetics, likewise, the Transcendentalists relied heavily upon the analogy of nature whenever they went further than simple celebrations of inspiration and genius and undertook to discuss style and form. As scholarship has conclusively and repeatedly established, they accepted the romantic-expressivist principle of organic form,[6] believing that the work of art, rather than adopt an arbitrary pattern, should take shape like an organism according to the nature of the thing expressed. The *locus classicus* of this motif in Transcendentalist thought is Emerson's declaration in "The Poet" that "it is not metres,

[4] For some good general discussions, see Joseph Warren Beach, *The Concept of Nature in Nineteenth-Century English Poetry* (New York: Macmillan, 1936), pp. 301–394; Richard P. Adams, "Emerson and the Organic Metaphor," *PMLA*, 69 (1954), 117–130; and Perry Miller, "Thoreau in the Context of International Romanticism," *Nature's Nation* (Cambridge: Harvard University Press, 1967), pp. 175–183.

[5] A concise treatment of the way nationalism influenced American thought about nature is Roderick Nash, *Wilderness and the American Mind* (New Haven: Yale University Press, 1967), pp. 67–83.

[6] See for example Vivian Hopkins, *Spires of Form: A Study of Emerson's Aesthetic Theory* (Cambridge: Harvard University Press, 1951), pp. 63–146; and Fred Lorch, "Thoreau and the Organic Principle in Poetry," *PMLA*, 53 (1938), 286–302.

but a metre-making argument that makes a poem,—a thought
so passionate and alive that like the spirit of a plant or an animal it has an architecture of its own, and adorns nature with
a new thing" (*W*, III, 9–10).

To attempt to explore the implications of this analogy for
Transcendentalist literary form may at first seem quixotic, in
light of the apparent formlessness of much Transcendentalist
writing and the notorious vagueness of the idea of nature as an
aesthetic model, especially when it comes to the concept of
structure. Morse Peckham has even gone so far as to claim
that "no one to this day has been able to define organic unity
in any useful manner." [7] Certainly the Transcendentalists did
not. Vivian Hopkins rightly concludes that "Emerson's discussion of form shows little recognition of architectonic
sense." [8] As for Thoreau, Fred Lorch is equally decisive: "In
deriving intuition from the divine, [he] was quite explicit; concerning the relation between intuition and form he was
vague." [9] The organic analogy generally enters Transcendentalist criticism as a metaphor for the idea of inspiration rather
than as a basis for hard thinking about structure.

Nevertheless, Thoreau's use of seasonal myth in *Walden* suggests that he at least had a practical awareness of what organic
form might be; and the same is true, I think, of the other
writers discussed in this section. Just as such scholars as M. H.
Abrams and Albert S. Gérard have shown how some of the
characteristic patterns of romantic consciousness function as
formal principles in certain British lyrics, so criticism of Transcendentalist literature—notably *Walden*—has begun to identify some ways in which the vision of nature gives shape to the
writings of Emerson and Thoreau.[10]

---

[7] *Victorian Revolutionaries* (New York: Braziller, 1970), p. 265.

[8] Hopkins, pp. 68–89.   [9] Lorch, p. 290.

[10] See M. H. Abrams, "Structure and Style in the Greater Romantic
Lyric," in *From Sensibility to Romanticism: Essays Presented to Frederick A. Pottle,* ed. Frederick W. Hilles and Harold Bloom (New York:

The basis of Transcendentalist thinking as to the role of nature in art is the idea of a metaphysical correspondence between nature and spirit, as expressed chiefly by Emerson. Man and the physical universe, Emerson says, are parallel creations of the same divine spirit; therefore natural and moral law are the same and everything in nature, rightly seen, has spiritual significance for man. The universe is thus a vast network of symbols—a Bible or revelation purer than any written scripture—which it is the chief task of the poet to study, master, and articulate. He above all others is qualified for this task because, unlike the theologian and the scientist, who attempt to reduce the meaning of nature to a rationalistic system, the poet follows the method of nature herself: he is guided by inspiration rather than logic, and expresses his thoughts in the form of images, in the same way that nature expresses spirit. A good literary work is therefore not an artificial construct, but a "second nature," growing out of the poet's mind as naturally as the leaf of a tree.[11]

Historically speaking, Emerson's theory might be described as one latter-day version of the tradition of Christian typology in western thought, leavened by pantheistic influences. He imbibed these traditions from a variety of sources, including the neoplatonic tradition from Plotinus to Cudworth; more recent German, French, and English Unitarian pantheisms as digested and transmitted by Coleridge; Swedenborgianism; seventeenth-century metaphysical poetry; and Goethe's idea of the metamorphosis of plants. But rather than insist on specific sources, it

---

Oxford University Press, 1965), pp. 527–560; and Albert S. Gérard, *English Romantic Poetry: Ethos, Structure, and Symbol in Coleridge, Wordsworth, Shelley, and Keats* (Berkeley: University of California Press, 1968).

[11] For Emerson's most significant discussions of correspondence, see *W*, I, 25–60; III, 3–37; IV, 93–146; and VIII, 3–57. The most thorough scholarly study of Emerson's idea is Sherman Paul, *Emerson's Angle of Vision* (Cambridge: Harvard University Press, 1952).

is fairer to say that the idea of correspondence was generally in the air; Coleridge, Swedenborg, Goethe, and the others served primarily as catalysts.[12] As early as his seventeenth year, Emerson was journalizing about "that eternal analogy which subsists between the external changes of nature & scenes of good & ill that chequer human life" (*JMN*, I, 19). And a century before this, typology was a significant motif in Puritan thought, though it seems not to have descended directly to Emerson and his circle, except in the very general sense in which their heritage conditioned them to see nature in a spiritual light.[13]

Other Transcendentalists, less interested than Emerson in philosophizing about correspondence, generally accepted the principle of nature as a spiritual analogue to man, as well as the main conclusions about poetic style to which this analogy led Emerson, whether or not they tried to put these conclusions into practice for themselves.[14] This is understandable. Natural

[12] On Emerson's sources see, for example, Paul, pp. 28–70; and Kenneth W. Cameron, *Emerson the Essayist* (Hartford: Transcendental Books, 1945), I, 17–336.

[13] Ursula Brumm points out that the parallels between Edwards' and Emerson's thinking about nature and typology are "due to the continuous development of modes of thought of a single cultural tradition rather than to direct borrowing" (*American Thought and Religious Typology*, trans. John Hoaglund [New Brunswick, N.J.: Rutgers University Press, 1970], p. 102). This work provides the best available overview of the development of typology in American thought.

[14] See for example Odell Shepard, *Pedlar's Progress* (Boston: Little, Brown, 1937), pp. 156–157; Sherman Paul, *The Shores of America* (Urbana: University of Illinois Press, 1958), pp. 195–196, 257–258; Anthony Herbold, "Nature as Concept and Technique in the Poetry of Jones Very," *New England Quarterly*, 40 (1967), 244–259; and Cyrus Bartol, *Pictures of Europe* (Boston: Crosby, Nichols, 1855), pp. 140–141. Paul and Herbold also point out the limitations of their subjects' interest in correspondence: Thoreau found it more difficult to relate to nature in his later years; Very's belief was strongly qualified by his religious orthodoxy. Actually, similar qualifications can be found in Emerson also, especially of the Thoreauvian sort. It is better to think of correspondence as a characteristic theme in Transcendentalist thought than as an article of fixed and

religion, which Transcendentalism essentially was, has strong pantheistic tendencies, which inevitably come to the fore when the devotee turns to nature in a reverential mood. Pantheism, in turn, is a highly poetic religion. Its central principle, that God is everywhere, is allied to the symbolic perception in poetry; and both share a strong mystical bent.

The idea of correspondence as Emerson inherited it was particularly well calculated to reinforce his vision of the poet-priest. It seemed to possess both the authority of doctrine and the flexibility of a poetics. For the Swedenborgians, on the one hand, the significances of nature were fixed by divine ordinance and susceptible to dogmatic formulation. The metaphysical poets, at the opposite extreme, used nature symbolism rather for its beauty, subtlety, and figurative validity than for its literal truth. In Emerson's thought, these two interests fuse. His reverence for nature as the primary revelation of God makes him take the business of typology very seriously, but his emancipated view of traditional theology keeps him from seeing more than poetry in Swedenborg.

From this ambiguous perspective, Emerson examines the nature of literature in a series of lectures, essays, and ex cathedra remarks, of which *Nature,* "The Poet," and "Poetry and Imagination" are the most important documents. His method is unsystematic but his results are fairly consistent and, in their own way, hang together.[15]

---

literal belief, and to interpret its meaning loosely, as connoting a general preoccupation with spiritual analogies between nature and man.

[15] As René Wellek remarks, Emerson's poetic "is on the whole open to the charge rather of monotony, repetitiveness, and inflexibility" than the usual allegation of "random eclecticism" ("Ralph Waldo Emerson," in *A History of Modern Criticism, 1750–1950: The Age of Transition* [New Haven: Yale University Press, 1965], p. 165). Wellek's chapter on Emerson's poetic is probably the best short account, though it exaggerates both the "one important inconsistency" in Emerson's poetic and its prevailing "monotony." The most thorough studies of Emerson's aesthetic theories, generally reliable, are Hopkins, *Spires of Form,* and Emerson Grant

On the one hand, Emerson develops the notion of a poetics based on nature, attempting to deduce particular critical principals from particular natural laws. His key rhetorical terms have a double reference, both to aesthetics and to natural processes. To take a simple example, "Rhyme" is identified with the principle of iteration in nature, in shadows and reflections in water (*W*, VIII, 45); rhyming couplets, in "Merlin II," are linked with the principle of polarity: "Balance-loving Nature / Made all things in pairs. / To every foot its antipode" (*W*, IX, 123). Through such comparisons, Emerson interprets poetry and nature in terms of each other, thereby also "proving" the correspondence between matter and mind. Poetry is judged according to nature: "A rhyme in one of our sonnets should not be less pleasing than the iterated nodes of a seashell" (*W*, III, 25). Conversely, nature is comprehended poetically, in terms of rhyme: "Astronomy, Botany, Chemistry, Hydraulics and the elemental forces have their own periods and returns" (*W*, VIII, 49). The method of poetry is nature; the method of nature is poetry. The rhymes of poetry are therefore seen to have a significance beyond the mere pleasure of their music, to the extent that they govern in nature also; so that Emerson can affirm at least metaphorically that "The rhyme of the poet / Modulates the king's affairs" (*W*, IX, 123).

On the other hand, however, Emerson's "argument" here is itself a metaphor, rather than an inquiry in the usual sense. What excites him is the general sense of reciprocity between poetry and nature rather than any precise deductions about prosody or science. He is neither a theologian nor a critic on

---

Sutcliffe, *Emerson's Theories of Literary Expression* (Urbana: University of Illinois, 1923). The most intensive study of Emerson's interest in poetic symbolism is Charles Feidelson, *Symbolism and American Literature* (Chicago: University of Chicago Press, 1953), pp. 119–161. See also Jonathan Bishop, *Emerson on the Soul* (Cambridge: Harvard University Press, 1964), pp. 101–143, a brilliant short discussion of several aspects of Emersonian style and their basis in Emersonian thought.

such occasions but rather "an artist in the medium of theory," in Charles Feidelson's admirable phrase.[16] His "poetic" is a poem or myth in itself—a series of desultory celebrations, full of wit and lyricism and sometimes whimsy. One doubts whether Emerson set great store by his "theory of rhyme," for example. Indeed, the passages quoted above are less characteristic of him than disparagements of rhyme as a minor and artificial grace.

That Emerson is not as hard-nosed a critic as Johnson or Coleridge does not mean, however, that he should be taken lightly. On the contrary, his peculiar combination of sensitivity and insouciance enabled him to get much better results from the correspondential theory than one would expect from Coleridge even if Coleridge had taken the trouble to develop it in detail. Coleridge wanted to see correspondence adumbrated as a metaphysic, which would have removed a good deal of its poetic suppleness. Precisely because Emerson did not care as much about methodological rigor, he was better suited to pursue the poetic implications of correspondence. René Wellek rightly calls him "the outstanding representative of romantic symbolism in the English-speaking world." [17] We will best appreciate this if we read him in the same spirit that he read Swedenborg, interpreting much of what he says as figurative but taking very seriously his principle of nature as a model for art.

The core of Emerson's poetic is the idea of the symbolic image, which is also the basis of the principle of correspondence itself. Largely because Emerson's thought on this point anticipates modern theories of symbolism, a great amount of attention has been devoted to it.

Emerson sums up the matter beautifully in "Poetry and Imagination":

As a power [poetry] is the perception of the symbolic character of things, and the treating them as representative: as a talent it is a magnetic tenaciousness of an image, and by the treatment demon-

[16] *Symbolism*, p. 158.   [17] *History of Modern Criticism*, p. 176.

strating that this pigment of thought is as palpable and objective to the poet as is the ground on which he stands, or the walls of houses about him. [*W,* VIII, 27]

In making images, that is, the poet participates in the natural law of spirit "to manifest itself in material forms" (*W,* I, 34). In the process, Emerson claims elsewhere, the poet restores language to its original state of purity, inasmuch as words themselves are originally derived from nature (or so Emerson and many of his contemporaries believed). In a double sense, therefore, "picturesque language" is of metaphysical value and certifies "that he who employs it is a man in alliance with truth and God" (*W,* I, 30). The language of poetry should be imagery because imagery is the language of nature and also the nature of language.

Emerson did not exalt the image simply for metaphysical reasons; it was also a matter of instinct with him. In his own experience the feeling of inspiration was linked with the image-making power,[18] and in his reading he relished language which was pungent and concrete. Even if he had never heard of the theory of correspondence he would have been an imagist in temperament. Likewise the modern reader may reject the metaphysical basis of his aesthetic and still profit from his criticism. Emerson's naive ideas about typology and the origin of language led him to some fruitful conclusions about poetic language, just as in our century Ezra Pound was stimulated by Ernest Fenollosa's equally inaccurate theory of the Chinese character (which owed something to Emerson, by the way).[19] If Emerson was wrong in thinking that savages converse in tropes, he was right that there is a fossil poetry in words. If he was wrong in saying that cunning people correspond to foxes and spiteful ones to snakes, he was right about the imaginative fitness and

[18] See *W,* I, 31; and *JMN,* V, 77, 106. I owe this insight to Bishop, pp. 119–120.

[19] Donald M. Murray, "Emerson's 'Language as Fossil Poetry': An Analogy from Chinese," *New England Quarterly,* 29 (1956), 204–215.

force of such analogies. A happy symbol *is* "a sort of evidence that your thought is just" (*W*, VIII, 13).

What raised Emerson's devotion to poetry from a personal pleasure to the level of something like reverence, however, was not his aesthetic preferences so much as the conviction that the method of the poet is metaphysically true. The power of the image derives from the nature of nature. "The value of a trope is that the hearer is one: and indeed Nature itself is a vast trope, and all particular natures are tropes" (*W*, VIII, 15). Tying art to metaphysics in this way was both a limitation and a strength. It limited Emerson as a critical theorist, not so much because it prevented him from going into the analytical detail of an Edgar Allan Poe, as because of a vagueness in his idea of correspondence itself. On the one hand, as in the "Language" chapter of *Nature*, Emerson seems to take the Swedenborgian position that there is an exact system of one-to-one correspondences between natural and spiritual facts. Elsewhere, however, he explicitly rejects this view, stressing that "in nature, each individual symbol plays innumerable parts" (*W*, IV, 121). This latter position is far more characteristic of Emerson, yet to the last he never entirely abandons the idea that natural objects "are really parts of a symmetrical universe, like words of a sentence; and if their true order is found, the poet can read their divine significance orderly as in a Bible" (*W*, VIII, 8). Even as he discounts all existing symbolic systems as merely metaphoric, Emerson clings to the belief that there must be a fixed universal order for the poet to perceive.

This leads to a corresponding ambiguousness in Emerson's poetic. At times poetry is seen as pre-existing in nature and merely discovered by the poet ("poetry was all written before time was"; "poems are a corrupt version of some text in nature with which they ought to be made to tally" [*W*, III, 8, 25]), while elsewhere the poet is seen as using nature creatively for his own purposes ("He unfixes the land and the sea, makes them revolve around the axis of his primary thought, and disposes

them anew" [*W*, I, 51–52]). Emerson the neoplatonist was at
odds with Emerson the romantic, one might say. In the abstract
this contradiction can of course be resolved by invoking the
theory of inspiration. The ideal bard will be so sensitive a conductor of the Oversoul that even "when he seems to vent a mere
caprice and wild romance, the issue is an exact allegory" (*W*,
II, 34). But in actuality Emerson could find no such poet, nor
could he advance as definite a notion of cosmic or poetic form
as he seems, in his more optimistic moments, to think exists.
To have done so, indeed, would have been to risk the kind of
pedantry he disliked in Swedenborg. What excites Emerson in
his discussions of nature and the creative imagination, rather,
is their fecundity and many-sidedness. His instinct is simply to
affirm the principle of cosmic unity-in-diversity on the one
hand, and to celebrate the sheer image-making power of the
poet on the other. Every particle is a microcosm of the universe;
every creature is a modification of every other; "in the transmission of the heavenly waters, every hose fits every hydrant" (*W*,
IV, 121). "The feat of the imagination," therefore, "is in showing the convertibility of every thing into every other thing"
(*W*, VI, 304), in capturing the sense of cosmic opulence and
rapidity of metamorphosis by displaying "in every word instant
activity of mind, shown in new uses of every fact and image, in
preternatural quickness or perception of relations" (*W*, VIII,
17). That in two sentences is the emotional center of Emerson's
poetic, and its metaphysical foundation. "The whole fascination
of life for him," as O. W. Firkins says without much exaggeration, "lay in the disclosure of identity in variety, that is, in the
concurrence, the *running together,* of several distinct images or
ideas." [20]

Emerson's fascination with metamorphosis, combined with
his rather blithe assurance that order must exist somewhere, runs
him into difficulty on the question of literary form, as his critics
have always been quick to point out. Whereas Coleridge sees the

[20] *Ralph Waldo Emerson* (Boston: Houghton Mifflin, 1915), p. 237.

imagination as a synthesizer, Emerson sees it primarily as a multiplier of images.[21] Carried to its logical conclusion, this view deprives him of "any brake on the transmutation of form," as Feidelson says.[22] Emerson's own prose style has often been cited as a perfect instance of such formlessness. Its most familiar pattern is a staccato movement through a succession of analogies, a continuous process of statement and restatement until the topic seems finally exhausted. "Circles" is a (seemingly) clear case of structural miscellaneousness. At the outset Emerson says flatly that the concept of the circle "may conveniently serve us to connect many illustrations of human power in every department" (*W*, II, 301), and then proceeds to ancient Greek art, engineering, architecture, farming, psychology, friendship, philosophy, war, conversation, literature, religion, ethics, natural science, and other fields as well. At least upon first inspection, it is as if Orville Dewey's sermon "Everything in Life is Moral" had been rewritten in prose run mad. The conception seems excessively simple, the point-by-point movement excessively capricious.

Emerson himself also conceded weakness in the area of form. To Carlyle he admitted regretfully that his sentences were "infinitely repellent particles";[23] in his journal he frequently speaks with a kind of ruefulness of the importance of form to the writer. "Diamond & lampblack . . . are the same substance differently arranged. Let it teach the importance of Composition," says one journal entry (*JMN*, V, 233). Like rhyme and language and image, "composition" is another rhetorical term which Emerson defined correspondentially. It means the arrangement of parts either in a work of art or in a landscape. In both cases, the "Each and All" principle should apply: "All are needed by each one; / Nothing is fair or good alone" (*W*, IX, 4). Just as objects gain in beauty through composition, so too

[21] Cf. Hopkins, pp. 38 ff.   [22] *Symbolism*, p. 150.
[23] *The Correspondence of Emerson and Carlyle*, ed. Joseph Slater (New York: Columbia University Press, 1964), p. 185.

do our thoughts, "when put together by their natural affinities." [24] Or as the journal puts it: "It is much to write sentences;
it is more to add method, & write out 'the spirit of your life
symmetrically. . . . To arrange many general reflections in
their natural order so that I shall have one homogeneous piece,
. . . this continuity is for the great" (*JMN*, VIII, 49). But here,
as in the previous quotation, the key word is "natural." The
arrangement must be a "natural order," the thoughts must be
tied by "natural affinities," and they must express the "spirit of
your life"—nothing insincere will do. Hence we find Emerson
saying elsewhere, quite cheerfully, that though it is desirable to
be more methodical than he has been able to be, "the truth
speaker may dismiss all solicitude as to the proportion & con-
gruency of the aggregate of his thoughts so long as he is a faithful reporter of particular impressions" (*JMN*, VII, 303). Honesty is the first requisite of authorship; form is important also,
but only as honesty permits.

Such declarations, in the context of Emerson's seemingly
haphazard prose, have generally kept his readers from taking
his philosophy of composition any more seriously than Poe's,
except as a confession of personal failure. He has been taken as
the philosopher and poet of the aphorism and the image. In
varying degrees, the same judgment has been passed on those
other Transcendentalists whose rhetoric resembles his, as well
as Walt Whitman. The critical consensus has traditionally been
that both in theory and in practice these writers were weak in
respect to structure—with certain honorable exceptions, of
which *Walden,* "Crossing Brooklyn Ferry," "Out of the Cradle," and "When Lilacs Last" are the most prominent.

Actually, the assumption that correspondence implies no
theory of form is simplistic. Although Emerson has little to say
directly about the matter, his implied model is surely the microcosm, or "miniature universe" as Richard Tuerk calls it in his

[24] *The Early Lectures of Ralph Waldo Emerson,* ed. Robert E. Spiller
et al. (Cambridge: Harvard University Press, 1959–), I, 317.

explication of the structure of *Nature*.[25] Just as each object in nature, in Emerson's most characteristic view of correspondence, epitomizes the whole order of nature, so must the work of art. As both Emerson and Thoreau liked to put the matter, the poet is he who sees the "integrity" of the landscape which other people see part by part. They own their separate tracts; the poet has his "property" in the horizon, in the whole.[26] To the perfect perception, "all nature will be *fable,* and every natural phenomenon be a myth," Thoreau says (*JT,* V, 135). The poet's individual images should take on universal significance and his work as a whole should reticulate them together so that they "fall within the great Order not less than the beehive or the spider's geometrical web," as Emerson puts it in "The Poet" (*W,* III, 19). The kind of literary structure to which these metaphors point would seem to be close to what Frye calls "encyclopedic form"—namely a structure which will be atomistic, discontinuous, yet comprehensive and essentially unified by the artist's vision of the cosmic order.[27]

Given Emerson's emphasis on the fluidity of nature, this formulation may seem practically useless, just another way of saying that the Transcendentalist concept of form amounts to formlessness. Emerson does, however, present models of universal order in between the extremes of the radically open-ended view of Nature as flux and the uncharacteristically rigid Swedenborgian idea of Nature as a book of types. The most important of these are polarity (as in "Compensation") and spiritual hierarchy, or scale-of-being order (as in *Nature*). Although Emerson rarely advances these concepts as aesthetic paradigms

[25] "Emerson's *Nature*—Miniature Universe," *American Transcendental Quarterly,* No. 1 (1969), 110–113.

[26] E.g., *W,* I, 8; *Wa,* p. 81.

[27] Northrop Frye, *Anatomy of Criticism* (New York: Atheneum, 1967), pp. 55 ff, 315 ff, and passim. To the extent that Frye retains the epic as a prototype for this mode, the analogy does not hold. Perhaps the more overworked "microcosm" is the more satisfactory term after all.

("Merlin II," on polarity and rhyme, is an exception), they frequently serve that purpose in his essays, as in the two just cited. Notwithstanding the cliché Alcott perpetrated about Emerson's prose, "You may begin at the last paragraph and read backwards," [28] it has been shown that Emerson was very successful at his best in ordering his diverse materials into polar and dialectical patterns. The best examples of this are probably *Nature,* where a six-fold layering of approaches to nature are dovetailed into one another, and "Experience," where the seven lords of life are unfolded in such a way as to move from the most superficial level of experience ("Illusion") to the most interior ('Subjectiveness").[29]

Even the seemingly amorphous "Circles" discloses a hierarchical structuring of sorts upon inspection. The apparent miscellany of examples falls under two heads, nature and man, introduced in parallel phraseology: "There are no fixtures in nature" (*W,* II, 302); "There are no fixtures to men" (306). The categories seem confusing because Emerson also talks about man in the first part and nature in the second. The essay becomes clearer, however, when one sees that mankind is discussed as an aspect of the course of nature and history in the first section, while nature is seen as a field of human endeavor in the second. In each section, furthermore, Emerson treats his subjects in roughly ascending order of importance, which is consonant with his main theme that "every action admits of being outdone" (301). Illustrating his first point, he begins with a historical sketch of the impermanence and perpetual advancement of various cultural forms and achievements from Greece

[28] *Concord Days* (Boston: Roberts, 1872), p. 33.

[29] For previous scholarship on the structure of Emerson's essays, see especially Tuerk, "Emerson's *Nature*"; Walter Blair and Clarence Faust, "Emerson's Literary Method," *Modern Philology,* 42 (1944), 79–95; Richard Francis, "The Architectonics of Emerson's *Nature,*" *American Quarterly,* 19 (1967), 39–53; and Lawrence Buell, "Reading Emerson for the Structures: The Coherence of the Essays," *Quarterly Journal of Speech,* 58 (1972), 58–69.

to the present (302–303), then gives a general overview of man as a creature whose efforts of the moment are continually being superseded by himself and others (304–305). Now, proceeding to his second point, he notes this principle at work in a number of different areas of human behavior, which are again arranged in roughly ascending order of importance: emotional moods (306–307), relations with other people (307–308), philosophy (308–310), conversation (310–311), literature (311–312), religious institutions (313), natural religion (313–314), moral and spiritual growth (314–317).

This outline exaggerates the impression of coherence which "Circles" conveys, of course. Emerson is almost perversely casual about transitions, key words, topic sentences, and other such rhetorical signals. And to a large extent he converts this casualness into a stylistic virtue, too. The précis is sterile compared to the prose itself; one of the most distinctive and impressive features of Emersonian style in general is its unpredictable, vigorous fecundity. The point is simply that this quality is controlled in his writing, at least through 1860. Just as in good poetry there is an interplay between an implied metrical pattern and continual deviations from the norm in particular lines, so in Emerson's essays there is generally an implicit framework, which is continually being blurred and defied by improvisation and diffuseness. This tension expresses both Emerson's metaphysical belief in a universe which is essentially purposeful but continuously in the process of change, and also his aesthetic sophistication. "If you desire to arrest attention," he writes in his journal, "do not give me facts in the order of cause & effect, but drop one or two links in the chain, & give me with a cause, an effect two or three times removed" (*JMN*, VII, 90). This is a beautiful description of the method of his best essays.

Emerson's arrangements of essays within collections also show an eye for order, especially in *Essays, First Series* and *Conduct of Life*, as Sherman Paul has pointed out.[30] The former relies

30 *Emerson's Angle of Vision*, pp. 117–118.

on the principle of polarity: "History" and "Self-Reliance" (the
Not-me and the Me); "Compensation" and "Spiritual Laws"
(nature's law of opposites and the law of the soul which underlies it); "Love" and "Friendship" (relationships with the female
and the male); "Prudence" and "Heroism" (mundane and great
action); "The Over-Soul" and "Circles" (the fountainhead of
the spirit and the activity which it inspires); "Intellect" and
"Art" (the mind and its creation). *Conduct of Life,* Emerson's
most sophisticated book in terms of literary structure, ascends
in a three-fold series of triads, in accordance with Emerson's
idea that "there is a climbing scale of culture" from the material
to the human to the intellectual levels (*W,* VI, 306). Emerson
surveys his subject first primarily on the material or prudential
level, then in terms of the formation of character, and finally
on the level of intellectual law. In the first part of the book,
"Fate" and "Power" are juxtaposed as opposites (and in each
essay a further polarity is drawn between the users and the
used); "Wealth"—by which Emerson means broadly the art of
controlling nature, not just making money (86)—encompasses
the first two approaches by showing the ways in which power
overcomes fate. The next trio of essays also presents a polarity,
"Culture" and "Behavior" (the education of the mind and of
manners) subsumed by the third chapter, "Worship," which is
defined as the "flowering and completion of culture (204). The
three final essays reverse this pattern somewhat. The last two,
"Beauty" and "Illusions," examine the cosmic paradox of flux
versus permanence from the perspectives of beauty and truth,
while "Considerations by the Way," the antepenultimate chapter, is an attempt at a comprehensive description of the ideal
life-style. The reason that it is not given the last word in the
book, in addition to the fact that it is a mediocre performance,
would seem to be that it is ethical rather than philosophical as
the last two pieces are. It is both striking and symbolically appropriate for Emerson to end a book which begins by describing
the "laws of the world" (4) with the image in "Illusions" of the

transfigured scholar catching a glimpse of "the gods . . . sitting around him on their thrones,—they alone with him alone" (325).

It might be said in objection to the preceding examples that polar, triadic, and hierarchical methods of organization may often be after-the-fact rationalizations rather than integral to the process of composition. To the extent that Emerson seems to bind himself merely on general principles to recapitulating a given pattern, it might indeed be argued that he is not a true literary organicist, even though the pattern in question happens to be derived from nature. But the fact remains that it was instinctive for Emerson to think and order his perceptions in terms of such patterns, and therefore his essays tended naturally to take shape around them. That is the essential point to notice here: the tendency for Emerson's writing to rely on concepts of natural order as structural principles, albeit with varying degrees of success. The same holds true also for a number of works by other Transcendentalist authors. Thoreau's two major books are organized around cycles of nature, which also symbolize the process of spiritual growth; and almost all his other nature writings delineate excursions into nature which fulfil, in some measure, a mythic pattern of quest and return. Ellery Channing builds his major pastorals largely around seasonal cycles; Bronson Alcott uses a scale-of-being arrangement in *Tablets* and a seasonal order in *Concord Days*. The structural pretensions of all of these works deserve to be taken as seriously as *Walden*'s have been taken, though they do not come nearly so close to realizing the possibilities of their design. Do not believe Bronson Alcott's motto in *Tablets:* "For curious method expect none, essays for the most part not being placed as at a feast, but placing themselves as at an ordinary." Alcott tried a lot harder than that, but it was in the transcendental interest to give the impression of thoughts naturally taking shape, rather than being ordered by the impresario.

Perhaps the most striking example of the kind of structure

implied by the idea of correspondence was a work Thoreau
planned but never quite wrote, though *Walden* came close. "I
think I could write a poem to be called 'Concord,' " he says in a
well known early journal entry. "For argument I should have
the River, the Woods, the Ponds, the Hills, the Fields, the
Swamps and Meadows, the Streets and Buildings, and the Vil-
lagers. Then Morning, Noon, and Evening, Spring, Summer,
Autumn, and Winter, Night, Indian Summer, and the Mountains in the Horizon" (*JT*, I, 282). This truly would have been
the poem of the universe, at least the local universe.[31] Of course
a perfect realization was impossible. Ideally, each page "should
be written in its own season and out-of-doors, or in its own
locality wherever it may be" (II, 239). Even if this could be
done, "the seasons admit of infinite degrees in their revolu-
tions" (IV, 117); their order cannot be fixed. Or even if they
could be, it would be impossible to represent every gradation of
feeling which an environment inspires. Though men may have
"detected every kind of flower that grows in this township,"
Thoreau remarks, "have they with proportionate thoroughness
plucked every flower of thought which it is possible for a man
to entertain, proved every sentiment which it is possible for a
man to experience, here?" (IV, 289). Understandably, the true
poem of Concord remained an elusive ideal for Thoreau, but
a compelling one, against which to measure what he actually
did write.[32]

In line with Bronson Alcott's gentle duplicity, Thoreau's
remarks, as well as the other Transcendentalist attempts to represent the natural order in the works mentioned above, seem

[31] Thoreau's plan for a literary book of the seasons was of course not in
itself original but a common motif in English literature of nature, e.g.,
James Thomson's *The Seasons* and William Howitt's *The Book of the
Seasons,* not to mention Spenser's *Shepheards Calender.* Emerson toyed
with the idea also (*JMN*, V, 25).

[32] Ellery Channing notes, however, that the literary calendar idea was
"only one of the various plans" Thoreau had in mind (*Thoreau the Poet-
Naturalist,* ed. F. B. Sanborn, new ed. [Boston: Goodspeed, 1902], p. 67).

to cherish simultaneously a desire for total imaginative freedom and a desire for metaphysical coherence. Any just appreciation of the quality of their vision must therefore be somewhat double-minded also. It is necessary to do justice both to the extreme care with which they were capable of arranging that vision, and to their moments of exhilaration in the sheer power and spontaneity of natural processes, at which time coherence is purposely undercut or abandoned for lyric flights. At the same time, their very moments of abandonment need to be examined for elements of escapism and concealed self-doubt, for as we have seen from Emerson's own modest appraisal of his achievements he was far from satisfied with his own performance. The same sense of frustrating indefiniteness which inevitably makes up a part of one's response to his writing was, furthermore, an aspect of his own response to nature. "I have intimations of my riches much more than possession," a typical entry in his journal reads. "Every object suggests to me in certain moods a dim anticipation of profound meaning, as if by & by it would appear to me why the apple-tree, why the meadow, why the stump, stand there, & what they signify to me" (*JMN*, VII, 98–99). The structure, tone and themes of Transcendentalist writing all convey a strong but precarious sense of imminent fulfilment. The possibilities are boundless, but nothing may come of them; the world is full of meaning, but that meaning is yet to be disclosed. Ellery Channing is the end of the Transcendentalist line in this respect, so I have reserved him for last in this section. But some of the sombre, as well as the ecstatic, can be seen even in the early Thoreau and in the most seemingly exuberant of all Transcendentalist forms of expression, the rhetoric of the catalogue, which we shall examine next.

6 Catalogue Rhetoric

No element in Transcendentalist style is more responsible for its appearence of anarchy than what is generally called enumerative or catalogue rhetoric—that is, the reiteration of analogous images or statements in paratactic form, in prose or verse. Emerson, Thoreau, Alcott, Fuller, Parker, and Bartol all habitually express themselves in a barrage of aphorisms. This creates an impression of vigor and excitement, but also of rambling and redundancy. It seems that everything moves parallel, nothing moves forward. This suspicion is raised even more strongly by the poetry of Whitman, who cannot sing his "Song of Occupations" without naming them all:

> House-building, measuring, sawing the boards,
> Blacksmithing, glass-blowing, nail making, coopering, tin-roofing, shingle-dressing . . . [ll. 103–104]

Faced with such outpourings one may well conclude with Harold Bloom that "the American Muse is a *daimon* of disorder, whose whispered counsel in the dark is: 'Evade and multiply.' " [1]

Because multiplication is in itself a rudimentary device, and easily abused, catalogue rhetoric has not often been studied as a literary form.[2] After all, since even Emerson considered Whit-

[1] "Bacchus and Merlin: The Dialectic of Romantic Poetry in America," *Southern Review*, n.s., 7 (1971), 152.

[2] For previous scholarship on Transcendentalist catalogue rhetoric, see especially Mattie Swayne, "Whitman's Catalogue Rhetoric," *University of Texas Studies in English*, 21 (1941), 162–178; Stanley K. Coffman, Jr.,

man's use of it simple-minded [3] and was embarrassed at his own fragmentariness besides, why should we rise to the Tran-scendentalists' defense? Still, catalogue rhetoric at its best does, I think, deserve close critical attention, both for historical and intrinsic reasons. Historically, the catalogue is that aspect of the grammar of Transcendentalism which most differentiates it from all the British romantics except Blake; and thanks to the imitators of Whitman, the catalogue has since also become a staple technique in twentieth-century American poetry from Hart Crane to Roethke and Ginsberg. A similar motif runs through our fiction, as in Melville's encyclopedic treatment of sea subjects and the exhaustiveness of detail in the naturalist novel, which has been more popular in this country than in Europe.

One reason for its American popularity is that catalogue rhetoric seems an inherently "democratic" technique. It has vista, as Whitman would say. It suggests the vast, sprawling, loose-knit country which America is. It also adheres to a sort of prosodic equalitarianism: each line or image is of equal weight in the ensemble; each is a unit unto itself. The fact that these associations were first fully exploited by Whitman, the recognized poet of democracy, adds authority to the notion of catalogue poetry as political action. Of course the technique actually antedates Whitman, by more than two thousand years.

" 'Crossing Brooklyn Ferry': A Note on the Catalogue Technique in Whitman's Poetry," *Modern Philology*, 51 (1954), 225–232; Harry R. Warfel, "Whitman's Structural Principles in 'Spontaneous Me,' " *College English*, 18 (1957), 190–195; and Lawrence Buell, "Transcendentalist Catalogue Rhetoric: Vision versus Form," *American Literature*, 40 (1968), 325–339. My views on the subject have altered considerably since that essay was written, as the following discussion shows. An essay which succeeds beautifully in conveying the spirit of catalogue rhetoric is Randall Jarrell's partial imitation of the form in "Some Lines From Whitman," in *Poetry and the Age* (New York: Knopf, 1953), pp. 112–132.

[3] Edward Emerson, *Emerson in Concord* (Boston: Houghton Mifflin, 1889), p. 228n.

Homer used it for scope; the Book of Psalms used it for praise. Since then, the epic and liturgical traditions have followed their examples. In nineteenth-century America, we have seen that preachers also used something like the catalogue for both these purposes, as well as for exhortation. Malcolm Cowley, V. K. Chari and others who approach Whitman as a religious poet are altogether right in tracing his prosody back to the Bible and placing him in the same literary-scriptural genre that produced the sacred books of India and the poetry of Blake and Smart.[4] But the catalogue was never much more than a stylized form of incantation, now and then turned into first-rate poetry by isolated geniuses, until it was absorbed, transmuted, and perpetuated by the Transcendentalist world-view.

Transcendentalism, in a sense, is the natural religion of democracy, by virtue of its claim that divinity inheres in every human being and indeed in every particle of the universe.[5] Of course it can become the religion of aristocracy also, when one adds riders to the effect that some are more inspired than others, or that sometimes the divinity is present and sometimes not.[6] But in its original state, as enunciated by Emerson and Whitman before they grew old and cautious, it is purely democratic. "Each particle is a microcosm," says Emerson (*W,* I, 43); "I swear I see now that every thing has an eternal soul!" Whitman cries.[7] Simply to speak of these utterances in relation to democracy is too restrictive, however. They are not merely political,

---

[4] Malcolm Cowley, Introduction to *Walt Whitman's Leaves of Grass: The First (1855) Edition* (New York: Viking, 1959), pp. x–xxxvii; V. K. Chari, *Whitman in the Light of Vedantic Mysticism* (Lincoln: University of Nebraska Press, 1964), pp. 3–8 and passim.

[5] Not all so-called Transcendentalists made claims so radical as these, but they may be considered as the quintessence of Transcendentalism.

[6] For a provocative account of the elitist tendency in Emerson's thought, and the success with which he resisted it, see Perry Miller, "Emersonian Genius and the American Democracy," *New England Quarterly,* 26 (1953), 27–44.

[7] "To Think of Time," l. 131, *Leaves of Grass,* 1855 ed. Later, Whitman changed "see" to "think."

or ideological, but visionary. They express a mystic awareness from which the idea of democracy is but one specific deduction: the vision of cosmic unity-in-diversity. That is the dominant impulse behind Transcendentalist catalogue rhetoric: the sense of the underlying identity of all things in the universe as manifestations of the divine plenitude. The catalogue, in short, is the most natural literary form for expressing the Transcendentalists' most characteristic sense of the universal order.

Of course they might not have favored the form as they did had they not also been passionately fond of strings of images for their own sake. Emerson believed that "bare lists of words are found suggestive to an imaginative and excited mind" (*W*, III, 17–18); Ellery Channing compiled a large dictionary of odd usages; [8] Theodore Parker had a passion for weaving bits and bushels of arcane information into his sermons and his conversations; Cyrus Bartol, in his essays, would sacrifice all clarity for a string of apothegms; Thoreau was a passionate collector of facts, sayings, and names. "The name of a thing may easily be more than the thing itself to me," he confesses, with reference to the delight he took, on his Canadian trip, in hearing that he was passing by "Point aux Trembles." But Thoreau's reaction has a deeper basis than the sheer sound of the phrase, as he goes on to explain: "Inexpressibly beautiful appears the recognition by man of the least natural fact, and the allying his life to it. All the world reiterating this slender truth, that aspens once grew there; and the swift inference is that men were there to see them" (*Wr*, V, 20). What really excites Thoreau, after the first momentary pleasure at hearing the name, is that the act of naming was a paradigm of man coming into relationship with nature, which he himself is now re-enacting, and in the process making contact with all those who met nature on this ground before. Raised to a slightly higher emotional pitch, this recognition of unity across different points of time, space, and perspective leads directly to the catalogue as a literary form,

8 "A Manual of Words and Phrases (chiefly English) in great part, Recent or Obsolete," bMS Am 800.6, Houghton Library, Harvard University.

as in this well-known and remarkable passage from Emerson's journal:

The metamorphosis of Nature shows itself in nothing more than this that there is no word in our language that cannot become typical to us of Nature by giving it emphasis. The world is a Dancer; it is a Rosary; it is a Torrent; it is a Boat; a mist; a Spider's Snare; it is what you will; and the metaphor will hold, & it will give the imagination keen pleasure. Swifter than light the world converts itself into that thing you name. [*JMN*, VIII, 23]

The only way Emerson can properly speak of "the metamorphosis of nature" seems to be in a torrent of emblems.

Exuberance, profusion, endlessness, surprise—these are the most obvious qualities of Transcendentalist enumerations, and the principle that underlies them. To some readers, this combination will seem aesthetically defective. Charles Feidelson, for example, after quoting the passage above, cautions that to see the universe as "a spontaneous dance of self-determining and autonomous symbols" leads to "literary anarchy." [9] But even if this charge were correct, which I shall question in a moment, it would be somewhat beside the point, for a feeling of total openness is crucial to the catalogue. Without the sense of unpredictability, without the sense that Emerson could have kept on adding items to his list forever, the excitement of his passage would be lost.

A good catalogue, however, is unified as well as diverse, though its form is not of a conventional sort. Its items must not have the rigid order of rational discourse, which would ring as false as Swedenborg's codifications of nature, but there must be a suggestion of order. This can be supplied in two ways: by modulating from item to item by process of association, and by giving to the whole a certain sense of shape. Let us take another look at the heart of the Emerson passage, for instance:

[9] *Symbolism and American Literature* (Chicago: University of Chicago Press, 1953), pp. 146, 149.

> The world is a Dancer
> it is a Rosary
> it is a Torrent
> it is a Boat
> a Mist
> a Spider's Snare
> it is what you will.

Clearly there is a shape to this "arbitrary" list: syntactical parallelism, and the device of shortening the clauses to "a Mist" and then lengthening them again, into an all-inclusive assertion. The procession of images also has a sort of logic: the dancer and the rosary suggest stylized movement, unleashed in the next line by the torrent on which the boat floats and which turns to the mist that congeals into the spider's web. To change the present order of the items would weaken the whole effect. This is not literary anarchy, though it looks so at first glance. It is a juxtaposition of images which, while arresting in themselves, are enhanced by the sense of relationship and totality, as well as by dissimilarity.

Not that Emerson's lists are always so coherent. For fairness' sake, we should not omit the rest of the journal passage.

There is nothing small or mean to the soul. It derives as grand a joy from symbolizing the Godhead or his Universe under the form of a moth or gnat as of a Lord of Hosts. Must I call the heaven & the earth a maypole & country fair with booths or an anthill or an old coat in order to give you the shock of pleasure which the imagination loves and the sense of spiritual greatness? Call it a blossom, a rod, a wreath of parsley, a tamarisk-crown, a cock, a sparrow, the ear instantly hears & the spirit leaps to the trope.

[*JMN*, VIII, 23]

There is still much to admire here: the fecundity of invention, the excited tone, the imaginative reach in connecting moth and gnat with Lord of Hosts; the modulations in the last sentence, with the blossom/rod flowering into the vegetable, then the shrub, and then the two birds—the link being the cock's comb, no doubt. But the passage as a whole is not as coordinated as the sequence before. Not that I would press this criticism too far, for I expect that most readers will appreciate (or dislike) this half of the passage about as much as the first. As long as the catalogue moves a certain amount in the direction of unity upon close reading, that is all one should expect. If the quest for unity seems useless, or if it is too easy, then the catalogue fails. "A too rapid unity or unification and a too exclusive devotion to parts are the Scylla and Charybdis" (*J*, VII, 118), Emerson sums it up. His philosophy tended toward Scylla, his rhetoric toward Charybdis, but surprisingly often he steers between.

Whitman's catalogue poetry, likewise, will reward a closer formal analysis than it has yet been given. A seemingly simple poem like "There Was a Child Went Forth" proves to be built around two quietly elaborated progressions in the imagery. The first (lines 4–11 of the 1855 edition) [10] suggests seasonal advance and a corresponding growth in the boy:

> The early lilacs became part of this child
>   .   .   .   .   .
> And the March-born lambs . . .
>
> And the field-sprouts of April and May . . .
> And the appletrees covered with blossoms, and the fruit afterward . . .

The second movement (lines 12–30) is an expansion outward in space, starting from a point, with the image of the child's conception, moving to pictures, to family influences,

[10] For aesthetic reasons, my quotations from "Song of Myself" and "There Was a Child Went Forth" are from the 1855 edition. Quotations from other poems are from *Leaves of Grass: Comprehensive Reader's Edition,* ed. Harold W. Blodgett and Sculley Bradley (New York: New York University Press, 1964), except when I call attention to changes in wording.

> The mother with mild words . . .
> The father, strong, selfsufficient, manly, mean, angered, un-
>   just

outward to city scenes,

> Men and women crowding fast in the streets

outward again to a distant view of

> The village on the highland seen from afar at sunset

to still more distant images of ships in the harbor, the waves,
the clouds, and finally

> The horizon's edge, the flying seacrow, the fragrance of salt-
>   marsh and shoremud;
> These became part of that child who went forth every day,
>   and who now goes and will always go forth every day,
> And these become of him or her that peruses them now.

Finally the reader himself is involved in the horizon of the
child-poet's vision—realizing at the same time he himself has
re-enacted the role of the child in the reading (and in life), the
role that will continue to be re-enacted forever. This conclusion makes the poem totally open-ended, just as the enumerative technique itself—which Whitman relies on almost exclusively here—is meant to convey the total receptivity of the
child; and yet this vision is structured in a deliberate and gradual way.[11]

To provide an adequate demonstration of this, comparable
to what was done with the Emerson quotation, would of course
take an essay in itself. The weakness of the short account I
have just given, a weakness common to most attempts to describe the structure of Whitman's poems and Transcendentalist
prose, is that for the sake of economy one must stress the second
unifying feature of the catalogue, its total shape, at the expense

[11] Cf. Howard J. Waskow, *Whitman: Explorations in Form* (Chicago:
University of Chicago Press, 1966), pp. 130–135.

of the image-by-image progressions, which are usually its primary source of formal beauty.

> I hear the bravuras of birds . . . . the bustle of growing
> wheat . . . . gossip of flames . . . . clack of sticks cooking my meals.
> I hear the sound of the human voice. . . . a sound I love
> ["Song of Myself," ll. 586–587, 1855 ed.]

In this instance, one does not particularly care to learn that "the auditory imagery is progressing from the natural to the human level," which is obvious enough. The real challenge and pleasure are to see exactly how the birds become transformed into wheat, into flames, into the cooking utensils, into voices. One needs to connect the fields of birds with the crop below, the conversion of it into the foodstuff which is now being cooked in a friendly atmosphere of clatter and talk, reflected in the "gossip" of the heartening fire. This is the real unity of the catalogue, of any catalogue, the main way in which it becomes a microcosm of a fluid but cohesive universe.

Even when one is not obliged to simplify the work for analytical purposes, even in one's own private reading of it, the kind of transformations just described are easy to overlook. Because the catalogue has the appearance of mere reiteration, and because it depends originally upon the power of its individual images or parts for its success, one tends to single out the best lines and read only them. But this is a misinterpretation of Transcendentalist aesthetics. Emerson would not have agreed with F. W. Schlegel (at least most of the time) that "an aphorism ought to be entirely isolated from the surrounding world like a little work of art and complete in itself like a hedgehog." [12] On the contrary, "Power," for Emerson, "resides in the moment of transition from a past to a new state, in the

---

[12] *Dialogue on Poetry and Literary Aphorisms,* trans. and ed. Ernst Behler and Roman Struc (University Park: Pennsylvania State University Press, 1968), p. 143.

shooting of the gulf, in the darting to an aim" (*W*, II, 69). "All thinking is analogizing, and it is the use of life to learn metonymy," or the inter-substitution of images for the same principle. Inevitably, Emerson grounds this judgment in the nature of the universe, "the endless passing of one element into new forms, the incessant metamorphosis" (*W*, VIII, 15). It is ironic that Emerson's critics have found so much to praise in his theory of the symbol, but so little in his idea about the dynamics of symbolism, the "metamorphosis" or the "flowing," which is what really excited him. Such a reaction is in effect a step backward in the direction of typological rigidity, a tightening up of the formal requirements. The motivation for it, no doubt, is essentially philosophical: In our time it is intellectually appealing to consider man a symbolic animal, but appalling to consider the universe (the literary universe, at any rate) as a catalogue. Not that the latter is any less contemporary a view. On the contrary, it is as true or truer to the nature of things than the symbolic theory itself, which may be precisely why one shrinks from it. So did the Transcendentalists, indeed, in their more downcast moments; more of that later on.

So far I have been using the term "catalogue" rather loosely, to cover any passage in which enumeration is the main organizing principle. Within this general category, however, at least three basic types of catalogue rhetoric might be distinguished, according to the degree to which they depart from sequential thought and syntax. These types might be called expository, illustrative, and symbolic. The first, which is the most common and the least radical, consists of the development of a proposition by the use of overlapping statements in parallel form. Here is a sample from Alcott, rearranged graphically for the sake of emphasis:

> Books are the silent teachers of the young.
> They are elements of outward condition.
> Every sentiment expressed in them,

and received into the imagination of a child, influences
his mind.
          Every picture images forth a virtue,
                                   a truth,
                                   a vice;—
                                   a moral which sinks deep into the
                              heart.[13]

Perhaps this should not even be called catalogue rhetoric, but
merely oratorical or incantatory prose. It stands on the border-
line between rational discourse and enthusiastic celebration,
like many of the sermon excerpts treated earlier. This sort of
rhetoric is typical of Alcott, and of that side of Transcendentalist writing in general which is closest to homily. W. H. Channing and the early Orestes Brownson also read quite like this.
About half of what is said is essential to the point; half is repetition for emphasis. The catalogue technique, if it can be called
that, is still used primarily for purposes of exhortation as an
adjunct to expository prose; but in any case it is prose that has
committed itself irretrievably to the method of restatement.

From here it is but one step to the illustrative catalogue,
which consists of successive expressions of a general principle
in the form of analogous exempla or images. The Emerson
journal passage is of the latter sort, as are most of his catalogues,
since most of his writing centers around abstract concepts. Some
essays, like "Circles," could almost be described as one long illustrative catalogue. Whitman's portraits of men and women in
section 15 of "Song of Myself" ("The pure contralto sings in
the organ loft") and the self-avatars in the next section ("I am
of old and young, of the foolish as much as the wise") are more
concrete than Emerson's usual style but nonetheless catalogues
of the same sort, a list of instances of "the grass that grows
wherever the land is and the water is."

[13] "On the Nature and Means of Early Intellectual Education as De-
duced from Experience," in Kenneth W. Cameron, ed., *The Transcendentalists and Minerva* (Hartford: Transcendental Books, 1958), II, 443.

The earlier canto on the meaning of the grass, however, is a symbolic enumeration, that is, a series of meditations or guesses as to the meaning of a particular image. The grass is interpreted, successively, as "the flag of my disposition"; "the handkerchief of the Lord"; "itself a child"; "a uniform hiero-glyphic," meaning equality among all people; "the beautiful uncut hair of graves"; and the second growth or "utterance" of those who are in the graves. (Has anyone pointed out the beauty and fitness of this progression: I, Lord [or microcosm, macro-cosm]; childhood, mankind, death, rebirth?) Less artful than Whitman, but still worth rescuing from oblivion, is Cyrus Bartol's reaction to a group of icebergs his ship passed in the Atlantic on his voyage to Europe. Half playfully he makes them the subject of a metaphysical rumination. They are "migratory birds," "bits of the pole . . . with the cold instinct of death at their heart that they must hurry on to waste away"; yet despite their forbiddingness, they are also "monuments of power and tokens of purity," "chains of icy hills" yet resembling human constructions, a "manifold architecture,—Egyptian, Grecian, and Roman, by turns." One particular iceberg strikes Bartol as "a temple of God upon the deep," and this gives him an op-portunity to end his thoughts gracefully on a pious note that unconsciously says a good deal about the art of the catalogue:

Full in front of the rising sun, it swept onward . . . and whatever use did its part to serve in the great economies of nature, it, at least, answered well for any thoughtful observer the purpose of worship in the ministry of the soul. Slowly southward it moved and faded by degrees away, bearing some holy thought in its shrine of material sanctity, and taking its place in memory for ever— though its temporary and fugitive being is long since dissolved— among Bethels of prayer.[14]

How right, as Bartol sees, that the iceberg should melt, that it have a "temporary and fugitive being," since its value for the

[14] *Pictures of Europe, Framed in Ideas* (Boston: Crosby, Nichols, 1855), pp. 138–140.

observer is not in this but in its ministry to the soul. The evanescence of the material iceberg is part of the lesson the soul learns from it. And in another sense evanescence is the method of the catalogue itself: a rapid picking up and laying aside of various alternative glosses on icebergs, to none of which Bartol attaches much specific importance (witness his uncertainty as to what use the iceberg serves "in the great economies of nature"), but all of which have a generalized spiritual reference.

Bartol's meditation also introduces a disturbing element into the catalogue, to the extent that we are reminded of the inability of human perception to comprehend the evanescence of matter and form. Even more central to Transcendentalism than the celebration of cosmic unity in diversity is of course the desire to encounter the informing spirit face to face, and this desire can be a source of extreme pain as well as joy. Romanticist aesthetics as a whole is often defined as an endless yearning after the infinite, for better and for worse, and the same can be said of Transcendentalism in particular. The quest for the spirit underlying its particular manifestations can lead to an "Ode to Dejection" as well as to a "Kubla Khan." "Poetry," as one of Emerson's definitions has it, "is the perpetual endeavor to express the spirit of the thing, to pass the brute body and search the life and reason which causes it to exist;—to see that the object is always flowing away, whilst the spirit or necessity which causes it subsists" (*W*, VIII, 17). Emerson here seems to envision the poet almost as a kind of Sisyphus, having to prove himself "perpetually," always in danger of being victimized by Maya, or illusion. As the Bartol passage shows, catalogue rhetoric also tends to suggest this possibility, the more it disengages itself from traditional expository prose or lyric prosody. Bartol is finally defeated—though he doesn't recognize the fact as such—when he must admit his ignorance of natural process and dissolve into "Bethels of prayer." Again, Whitman's meditation on the grass ends victoriously, but the catalogue technique itself is used mainly to suggest the speaker's initial bafflement when faced with the rich mysteriousness of his emblem.

Such undertones as these suggest that the tone of the catalogue can be as deceptive as its simple-seeming form. In Transcendentalist writing, its tone is usually joyous, but it can also express striving, confusion, frustration, disillusionment, and even despair. For some of Whitman's twentieth-century successors, the catalogue has even become a hysterical phantasmagoria:

> I saw the best minds of my generation destroyed by madness, starving hysterical naked,
> dragging themselves through the negro streets at dawn looking for an angry fix,
> angelheaded hipsters burning for the ancient heavenly connection to the starry dynamo in the machinery of night.[15]

This is indeed philosophical, if not literary anarchy. The catalogue mirrors a world which is falling apart, in which the only "connection" one can make is a perversion of the "ancient" one. Of course no Transcendentalist went so far as these lines from "Howl," but there are echoes. Perhaps the closest is Whitman's old-age postscript to a high-toned preacher's omissions in a sermon on "The Rounded Catalogue Divine Complete":

> The devilish and the dark, the dying and diseas'd,
> The countless (nineteen-twentieths) low and evil, crude and savage,
> The crazed, prisoners in jail, the horrible, rank, malignant,
> Venom and filth, serpents, the ravenous sharks, liars, the dissolute;
> (What is the part the wicked and the loathesome bear within earth's orbic scheme?)
> Newts, crawling things in slime and mud, poisons,
> The barren soil, the evil men, the slag and hideous rot.

---

[15] Allen Ginsberg, "Howl," ll. 1–3, in *Howl and Other Poems* (San Francisco: City Lights, 1959). For an interesting discussion of how this and other features of Whitman's style have been inverted by modern American poets, see Adrian Birney, "Cursing America: The Tradition of the 'Anti-Whitman,'" *Genre*, 2 (1969), 303–313.

No doubt this was intended mainly as a tour de force, but it serves as a reminder that there are certain risks involved in attempting to write the poem of the universe. What *is* the part of the wicked and the loathsome in the whole scheme? One must include them too. At one time or another, the Transcendentalists all puzzled over this problem. Thoreau was overwhelmed by the desolation of the wilderness when descending Mt. Katahdin.[16] Theodore Parker had to admit, "There are many things in nature which are utterly incomprehensible to me. . . . Alligators devour their young, till they are too large. . . . Squirrels castrate each other. . . . What does all this mean." [17] Even Emerson, in his old age, came to the conclusion that "the way of Providence is a little rude. The habit of snake and spider, the snap of the tiger and other leapers and bloody jumpers, the crackle of the bones of his prey in the coil of the anaconda,—these are in the system, and our habits are like theirs" (*W*, VI, 7).

In these last two passages we again see the potential of the catalogue to express chaos and terror. Stylistically speaking, as much coherence can be found in these passages as in the catalogues discussed earlier; it is simply the vision that differs, the vision of a potentially sinister or indifferent universe.

None of the Transcendentalist writers seriously entertains such an idea. Emerson is typical in his assurance that snakes and tigers are somehow "in the system." The primary threat to the vision of an integrated universe for the Transcendentalists is not the instability of nature but the limitations of man. This

[16] I would dissent from the common interpretation of this experience as traumatic for Thoreau, however, for two reasons. First, it is a literary recreation, not to be read as a totally factual account; second, in any case terror is traditionally a basic aspect of the emotion of the sublime. The only safe biographical conclusion one can draw from the episode is that Thoreau simply felt more at home in a semidomesticated nature than in the remote wilderness.

[17] "Journal 1838–40," p. 6, Andover-Harvard Theological Library, Harvard University.

awareness often injects a note of frustration into an ostensibly affirmative passage, like this expository catalogue from the second chapter of *Walden*:

Shams and delusions are esteemed for soundest truths, while reality is fabulous. If men would steadily observe realities only, and not allow themselves to be deluded, life, to compare it with such things as we know, would be like a fairy tale and the Arabian Nights' Entertainments. If we respected only what is inevitable and has a right to be, music and poetry would resound along the streets. When we are unhurried and wise, we perceive that only great and worthy things have any permanent and absolute existence,—that petty fears and petty pleasures are but the shadow of the reality. [*Wa,* pp. 95–96]

Is this the voice of one who is in possession of the secret, or of one who has merely glimpsed it and longs to possess it fully? "When we are unhurried and wise"—the phrase seems to imply "would that we were all the time." Certainly the passage itself is not unhurried, but urgent; and though its advice is wise enough, it never says what reality is, nor does the rest of the sequence of which it is a part. Reality, reality, reality—the word is used over and over but only in the abstract. We see that the speaker is right when he finally admits, "I cannot count one" (*Wa,* p. 98).

Of course it serves Thoreau's dramatic purpose here to seem mystified and prospective, since he has not yet really begun to describe his life at Walden. But at the end he is still looking forward: "There is more day to dawn" (*Wa,* p. 333). Prospectiveness—that quality explains both the dark and light sides of Transcendentalist catalogue rhetoric as well as any single term. It is alive with vision, and strains eagerly toward its realization, but it cannot capture that ideal except momentarily. Its very profusion is a sign of insecurity. As J. Hillis Miller remarks of the baroque style in British literature: "A great flood of metaphors and symbols, doubling one another to infinity, strives desperately to say what a simple phrase of the old poetry, in its calm possession of its spiritual meaning, could say in a moment." [18] The form must always remain inchoate, because no man can live continuously in harmony with the universe. "We have had many harbingers and forerunners; but of a purely spiritual life, history has afforded no example," as Emerson says (*W*, I, 338). And just as man is inconstant, nature herself is always changing: "As the bird alights on the bough, then plunges into the air again, so the thoughts of God pause but for a moment in any form" (*W*, VIII, 15). To live always according to the spirit would require a consciousness so supple and exquisitely sensitive that we can scarcely hope to do more than envision it in our best moments. Or so the aging Emerson believed.

Perhaps his most provocative expression of this Transcendentalist dilemma is his poem "The Sphinx," a work of special authority in the Emerson canon since he placed it at the head of his collected poems.[19] The sphinx was for him, as for Carlyle, a favorite symbol of the "open secret" of nature. The poem itself has been a riddle to many readers, since it is at first hard to see why the sphinx evades the poet after he has repeated "correct" Emersonian doctrine to her. The point is, I think, that nature tests man's affirmations by requiring him to find them in her. She is his "eyebeam" (*W*, IX, 20). Abstract statement is not enough; there is no such thing as naked truth, to quote Dr. Channing again. Furthermore, although the Sphinx promises that "Who telleth one of my meanings / Is master of all I am" (*W*, IX, 25), it is also true that to read even one fact requires a perfect perception of the whole. Every individual expression of truth "is the absolute Ens seen from one side," Emerson says in *Nature*. "But it has innumerable sides" (*W*, I, 44). When the power of universal perception fails— as it in-

[18] *The Disappearance of God* (New York: Schocken, 1965), p. 7.

[19] Emerson's son removed the poem from its ⟨lead⟩ lead position for fear that its obscurity would frighten readers away from the volume (*W*, IX, 403).

evitably does, given human limitations—nature seems to become a succession of fleeting surfaces and the observer disintegrates into a jumble of moods.

Emerson's poem itself can be said to fulfill the Sphinx's requirements by grasping and embodying the man-nature relation in the form of a parable, rather than by making a bare assertion as does the poet therein. This may account for the merriness of the ending. Testimony to the truth of Emerson's idea is given by Thoreau, who wrote out a sixteen-page interpretation of the poem, trying to reduce it to a logical argument in the same way that the poet tries to answer the Sphinx, before being forced to conclude that "all commentaries must be finite, but a text is infinite." [20] The poem itself achieves the infiniteness of nature, although not by solving the Sphinx's riddle but by stating it adequately. The victory over nature is still prospective, and the appearance of victory is gained only by a clever mimicry of the riddlesome face which godhead presents to the world.

So it is that in many Transcendentalist catalogues the dominant tone is either a reverential vagueness or a knowing detachment. What is the grass? "How could I answer the child?" Whitman asks. "I do not know what it is any more than he." He is sure that the dead are "alive and well somewhere," but he can't translate the hints that the grass gives of them; his interpretations are all guesses. This is like Bartol's final disclaimer. Emerson, on the other hand, as he came to realize that nature could mean "fate" as well as "possibility," [21] adopted the posture

[20] MS Am 1280.214.1(1), Houghton Library. Thoreau also has a lengthy interpretation of the poem in *JT*, I, 229–237. My reading of this elusive poem is partly indebted to Thomas R. Whitaker, "The Riddle of Emerson's 'Sphinx,'" *American Literature*, 27 (1955), 191–193, whose analysis is the best I have seen.

[21] For Emerson's changing idea of nature and man's relation to her, see Stephen Whicher, *Freedom and Fate* (New York: Barnes, 1961), pp. 141–153; and Jonathan Bishop, *Emerson on the Soul* (Cambridge: Harvard University Press, 1964), pp. 203–215. Both discuss Emerson's shift from a

of benign aloofness. In "New England Reformers" he assumes
this pose at the expense of some of his erstwhile admirers:

What a fertility of projects for the salvation of the world! One
apostle thought all men should go to farming, and another that
no man should buy or sell, that the use of money was the cardinal
evil; another that the mischief was in our diet, that we eat and
drink damnation. These made unleavened bread, and were foes to
the death to fermentation. . . . Stop, dear Nature, these incessant
advances of thine; let us scotch these ever-rolling wheels! Others
attacked the system of agriculture, the use of animal manures in
farming, and the tryanny of man over brute nature. . . . Even the
insect world was to be defended . . . [*W*, III, 252–253]

Here we see the comic potential of the catalogue, which
Thoreau exploits in a drier and more sarcastic way in his dis-
quisitions against philanthropy and new clothes. The chaos of
the contemporary reform scene is evoked but kept comfortably
at arm's length by Emerson's tone of mock-lament. (Note also
that he organizes his material even as he reduces it to absurd-
ity, by moving progressively in the direction of the more trivial,
from farming to insect protection.) Emerson is usually more
serious when dealing with illusions, however.

Few have overheard the gods or surprised their secret. Life is a
succession of lessons which must be lived to be understood. All is
riddle, and the key to a riddle is another riddle. There are as many
pillows of illusion as flakes in a snow-storm. We wake from one
dream into another dream. . . . Everybody is drugged with his
own frenzy, and the pageant marches at all hours, with music and
banner and badge. [*W*, VI, 313–314]

This passage also moves from the more significant to the more
trivial: as the idea is restated, its dimensions shrink from divine

---

view of man as the (potential) master of nature to a view of man as nature's final product, from a millenarian view of utopia as possible now a
conservative view of utopia as the future result of gradual progress.

mystery to moral lesson to intellectual puzzle to natural hallu-
cination to fantasy to a degrading collage of madhouse and
childish game-playing. Emerson is dealing with the same subject of metamorphosis that so excited him in the journal passage discussed earlier, and he uses a similar reiterative method;
but his conclusion is precisely opposite: the partiality of every
perception instead of its inevitable truth.

The irony of the later Emerson seems to be a self-protective
device, a way of preventing himself from being demoralized by
the uncontrollable mutability of nature. Emerson maintains an
air of confidence by adopting a pose of knowing detachment;
if this impression convinces, the reason is simply that the mysteries that he once sought earnestly to solve are now quietly
taken for granted. Whitman's and Bartol's capacity for wonder
is another sort of defense, perhaps. Several times in "Song of
Myself," for example, the speaker fears that his own diversity
will pull him into chaos. His sense of touch usurps him; his
power of empathy condemns him to death ("Agonies are one
of my changes of garments"). Each time he dies or is pulled
apart he reassembles himself, but the ecstasy is a stressful experience while it lasts. It is comfortable for him to be able
to linger awhile in his role as observer, or else to prolong one
stage of his vicarious travels by indulging a lighthearted feeling
of escape:

> I jump from the cross-beams, and seize the clover and timo-
> thy,
> And roll head over heels and tangle my hair full of wisps.
> ["Song of Myself," ll. 166–167, 1855 ed.]

This is the quality that leads Richard Chase to see the whole
poem in terms of frontier humor, as a cosmic joke.[22] It *is* that,

[22] *Walt Whitman Reconsidered* (New York: Sloane, 1955), pp. 58–98.
This penetrating and sensitive reading of "Song of Myself" has not been
taken as seriously as it deserves.

but equally important seems to be the sense of willed innocence in the face of trials, disaster and even death, which has preceded and is certain to follow.

Whitman's primary way of evading mishap in "Song of Myself," however, is not to dally but, like Hart Crane in *The Bridge,* to move so fast through the circuit of forms that no catastrophe can touch him. The spirit triumphs over chaos by sheer energy. In the long run, this, not irony or confusion or fright, is also the most typical strategy of the Transcendentalist catalogue in general. It seeks to inspire or uplift by overwhelming all possible objection. "Cultivate poverty like a garden herb, like sage. Do not trouble yourself much to get new things, whether clothes or friends. Turn the old; return to them. Things do not change; we change. Sell your clothes and keep your thoughts. God will see that you do not want society" (*Wa,* p. 328). So Thoreau exhorts the reader at the end of *Walden.* If one should criticize this and similar Transcendentalist utterances as whistlings in the dark, Thoreau might reply that they are not merely a rhetorical ploy but a faithful expression of the way nature works, namely in ceaseless metamorphosis onward toward the light. As Emerson puts it in his proto-evolutionist way, the worm mounts through all the spires of form (*W,* I, 1);

> the eternal Pan,
> Who layeth the world's incessant plan,
> Halteth never in one shape,
> But forever doth escape,
> Like wave or flame, into new forms
> Of gem, and air, of plants, and worms.
> I, that to-day am a pine,
> Yesterday was a bundle of grass. [*W,* IX, 58]

The Thoreau passage looks forward to this same transformation, both in the sense that it leads up to several explicit images of metamorphosis which are given a moment later (e.g., the seventeen-year locust and the beautiful bug that emerged from the sixty-year-old table), but in the sense that it acts out on its own nature's process of continually uttering and reuttering itself. The catalogue is prized chiefly by the Transcendentalists as the closest verbal approximation they were able to achieve to the boundless vitality of nature.

That this vitality is not expressed haphazardly, at least in the best Transcendentalist literature, but has the analogical continuity and the sense of shape that nature itself had in the vision of the writers, I have tried to demonstrate. While the catalogue is not the sole or even the most important ordering principle in many of the works discussed, it is perhaps the most characteristic structural device. Once the reader has recognized its potential subtlety, the range of tones and nuances of which it is capable, he will have arrived at a deep understanding of the Transcendentalist sensibility and will be in a better position to appreciate its handling of form in more elaborate literary structures.

7 Thoreau and the Literary Excursion

Most of Thoreau's works might be described as catalogues extended through time and space. His favorite form, as noted earlier, is the romantic excursion: a ramble ("Walking")or trip (*Cape Cod*) or sojourn (*Walden*) which takes on overtones of a spiritual quest as the speaker proceeds. Thoreau's later journals have the same rhythm. Like the conversation, the sermon, and the essay, the excursion is also a potentially encyclopedic form. Though somewhat more controlled by the obligation to describe a particular setting, it tends to become, in effect, an account of the whole universe as it appears to the speaker, particularly in the two books Thoreau published during his lifetime. This comprehensiveness is due in large part to the extraordinary gift for microcosm which Emerson was the first to notice in him, the ability to infer the "universal law from the single fact" (*W*, X, 474). This very transcendental mode of perception gives rise to what John Broderick rightly calls the fundamental movement of Thoreau's prose—from observation to speculation and back again—and to his breadth of allusion. Thoreau did not travel far in his lifetime; but, as John Christie has shown, his imagination ranged throughout the world.[1]

---

[1] Broderick, "The Movement of Thoreau's Prose," *American Literature*, 33 (1961), 133–142, rpt. in *The Recognition of Henry David Thoreau*, ed. *Wendell Glick* (Ann Arbor: University of Michigan Press, 1969), 324–334. Christie, *Thoreau as World Traveler* (New York: Columbia University Press, 1965).

Whereas Emerson built his essays around concepts of universal order, Thoreau began with his environment and tried to invest it with meaning. Temporal continuity in his writing is usually more important than the continuity of abstract ideas which unifies Emerson's prose and characterizes most of the rest of Transcendentalist literature. Thoreau's excursions, consequently, cannot be considered as typical of the movement to the same degree as the forms and techniques discussed earlier. Still, the excursions can be called representative in the Emersonian sense, in that they attempt to carry out to practical fulfilment the spirit of the Transcendentalists' largely theoretical fascination with nature. Nearly all of Thoreau's adult life was devoted to proving the validity of correspondence in his own experience. Few of the Transcendentalists except for the Concord group took Thoreau's example very seriously, at least during his lifetime, but most endorsed both the general principle of living close to nature and the romantic excursion as a literary form.

Thoreau's choice of form reflected the prevailing taste of his age. Travel writing of various kinds had always been very popular in America: scientific expeditions (e.g. Darwin's *Voyage of a Naturalist Round the World*), records of exploration (Brackenridge's *Journal of a Voyage up the River Missouri*), shipwreck and captivity narratives (Melville's *Typee*), grand tours of foreign and domestic parts by literary gentlefolk (Goethe's *Italienische Reise*), and so forth. Indeed on both sides of the Atlantic, in the early years of the 19th century, it seemed to one reviewer that almost everybody who "happens once in his life to wander from the precincts of his own native village, thinks it his duty to enlighten the publick with a narrative of his adventures." [2] The *North American Review* regularly devoted two or three major articles each year to travel books; Thoreau is known to have

[2] Jared Sparks, "Riley's Narrative," *North American Review*, 5 (1817), 390.

read at least 146 of them, including all the works just listed.[3]

There were several reasons for the vogue of travel writing, especially in America: the rise of romanticism; [4] the largely unexplored condition of America; the self-consciousness and provincialism of the new nation, which stimulated intense interest among Americans in European travelers' reports about them and in compatriots' reports of Europe; [5] and the didactic orientation of the American aesthetic. Like lyceum lectures, travel literature could be delightful without ceasing to be ostensibly instructive. Fascinating glimpses of exotic spots could be purveyed as "scientific information." Such works were also relatively easy to produce. "He must be dull indeed," one critic declared, "who cannot give a tolerably interesting account of very interesting places." [6]

For all these reasons, many of the prominent serious and popular writers in America during the nineteenth century tried their hand at travel writing, including the Transcendentalists.

[3] Christie, p. 42. Actually, his bibliography of those works (pp. 313-333) excludes a few works which might also be put into the travel literature category, such as William Gilpin's *Remarks on Forest Scenery, and Other Woodland Views,* a book which is as close or closer to Thoreau's own sort of travel book than almost any of the 146 listed works.

[4] For a discussion of the idea of travel as a romanticist phenomenon, see George B. Parks, "The Turn to the Romantic in the Travel Literature of the Eighteenth Century," *Modern Language Quarterly,* 25 (1964), 22-33. For a particular example example of romanticism in travel literature, see Herbert Barrows, "Convention and Novelty in the Romantic Generation's Experience of Italy," in *Literature as a Mode of Travel,* ed. Warner G. Rice (New York: New York Public Library, 1963), pp. 69-84.

[5] For an analysis of Americans abroad during this period, see Neil Harris, *The Artist in American Society* (New York: Braziller, 1966), pp. 124-168; for Europeans in America, see Max Berger, *The British Traveler in America 1836-60* (New York: Columbia University Press, 1943). For American interest in domestic travel, see Robert C. Bredeson, "Landscape Description in Nineteenth-Century American Travel Literature," *American Quarterly,* 20 (1968), 86-94.

[6] W. P. Mason, "Delano's Voyages and Travels," *North American Review,* 5 (1817), 245.

Poe wrote two fictional narratives; Melville began as a travel romancer; Cooper's fiction has a strong travel interest, as does Hawthorne's *Marble Faun;* Washington Irving, Bayard Taylor, and George William Curtis each wrote several literary travelogues. Among the Transcendentalists, the roster of travel books includes not only Thoreau's work but also Emerson's *English Traits,* Margaret Fuller's *Summer on the Lakes* and *At Home and Abroad,* Bartol's *Pictures of Europe,* James F. Clarke's *Eleven Weeks in Europe,* and (in a sense) Ellery Channing's *Conversations in Rome.* These books varied widely in style and scope and quality, from the hurried reportage of Clarke and Fuller's European book to the analytical overview of *English Traits* to Bartol's serious attempt at prose poetry. But all share a basically literary, rather than factual, approach. To the extent that they make any claims on the reader's attention, then or now, it is as imaginative reinterpretations of their subject rather than as guidebooks or as compendia of information, although they do supply generous amounts of data and moral directive. All the Transcendentalist authors, especially those who traveled in Europe, were well aware that they were going over ground already covered many times before, and that their own contribution, such as it was, would consist in supplying new points of view—in deploying the resources of their wit, descriptive ability, capacity for original reflection, and eye for the out-of-the-way detail.

Literary criticism of travel writing is still in its infancy, and virtually nothing has been written about the formal conventions of such works,[7] partly because the genre is so miscellaneous.

[7] Most of the extant criticism deals with content rather than style. Christie is representative: on Thoreau's interest in travel, travel reading, and allusions to travel books, he is definitive; on problems of form he is sketchy. But see his last two chapters (pp. 245–271) for some discussion of the travel book as a formal model for Thoreau. I know of no satisfactory study of the stylistic conventions of American travel writing during the early nineteenth century, though of course much has been done on the interest of writers in Europe and the frontier.

The travels of Marco Polo, Harriet Martineau, Thor Heyerdal, and D. H. Lawrence apparently have little in common; even the Transcendentalist works listed above vary greatly in style and structure. Nevertheless, some generalizations can be made about the state of travel writing in the early nineteenth century which will help clarify Thoreau's literary purposes and those of the Transcendentalists as a whole.

To start with, we must realize that the *literary* travel book was then in a transitional state, just beginning (in America at least) to be distinguished from a factual account or analysis, but not yet recognized as different in kind. For Howells and James, living in the era after the Civil War, travel writing was unambiguously an art, to be judged by the same high standards of stylistic refinement and formal coherence as would be applied to prose fiction. James, for example, considered the traditional epistolary or journalistic methods of organizing travel books unsatisfactory even for a talented writer: "His work will doubtless furnish a considerable amout of entertaining; but there will yet be something essentially common in its character. The book will be diffuse, overgrown, shapeless; it will not belong to literature." [8] Earlier critics, however, were less stringent in their literary standards than James, though they too complained of the slipshod ease with which many such works were written. Jared Sparks, for example, was inclined to think that "the eye of criticism should pass gently over the pages of the traveller,— it should be contented with gazing on what is new and interesting from its intrinsick value, although it may not be dressed out in so good a taste, and under so attracting a form as could be desired." [9] This remark suggests that the reviewer looks to travel literature primarily for new information, rather than for high art. Sure enough, he continues: "There is one indispens-

[8] "Howell's Italian Journeys," *North American Review,* 106 (1868), 336–337. For additional strictures by James, see his reviews in *The Nation,* especially 16 (1873), 152; 20 (1875), 279–280; and 21 (1875), 29–30, 264–265.

[9] "Riley's Narrative," *North American Review,* 5 (1817), 391.

able requisite however, in books of travels, without which they can have neither interest nor value;—we mean veracity." [10] Inaccuracy is to Sparks what "want of method" is to James, and the same applies to most other early *North American* reviewers. The primary demand they made of the travel writer was that he be "a just and clear observer"—especially if he happened to be a European traveling in the United States.[11]

Traveler's who mixed fact and fancy were suspect, even if their writing showed talent. Francis Bowen objected to George Borrow's account of the Gypsies on the ground that imaginative liberties "seriously impair[ed] the credibility of the book." [12] Another critic scoffed at what he called "imaginative" travelers who went to the Holy Land "in order to write poetry," since "their journals are not trustworthy records of what they saw and heard." [13] *Two Years before the Mast* was highly regarded not because it was well-written, although Boston reviewers agreed that it was, but because it gave an "accurate" and above all moralistic description of the life of sailors. Its fictive virtues were, in the opinion of the *Christian Examiner,* a positive disadvantage, inasmuch as they tended to lure the reader into seafaring.[14]

When the reviewers of the 1820s and 1830s took it upon themselves to outline a model for prospective travel writers to follow, what they usually recommended, therefore, was not that the genre should become more amusing or more elegant or more imaginative but that it should be more rigorously analytical. "The only sort of travels that will, we think, hereafter be much

10 *Ibid.*

11 W. B. O. Peabody, "Travels of Reed and Matheson," *North American Review,* 41 (1835), 493.

12 "The Gypsies," *ibid.,* 55 (1842), 73.

13 C. Emerson, "Robinson's *Travels in Palestine and Arabia,*" *ibid.,* 53 (1841), 176.

14 William Ware, *"Two Years before the Mast,"* Christian Examiner, 29 (1840), 270. See also Edward Tyrell Channing's review in the *North American Review,* 52 (1841), 56–75.

sought for," opined Edward Everett, will concentrate rather "on topics of statistical and political information, on the condition, pursuits, and manners of the people, than on pictures, statues, and ruins." [15] An entertaining popularizer with a careful eye for detail was welcome, another reviewer conceded, but what the field really needed was more "rigidly honest" scholarly investigators.[16]

The concession is significant, however. Apart from their role as arbiters of taste, the reviewers did appreciate travel literature for its entertainment value; and they were also aware of, and to some extent sympathetic to, a growing popular interest in imaginative travels, coinciding with the rise of the romantic movement. One critic traced travelers' preoccupations with "fanciful speculations" to the influence of Mme de Staël's *Germany;* [17] other sources were Wordsworth's poetry and Byron's *Childe Harold;* eighteenth-century topographical poetry and prose picturesque; and the sentimental journeys of Sterne and Goethe. The collective impact of these influences was such as to encourage a more subjective and loosely "poetic" approach to travel description. Though Boston reviewers could not, as a matter of principle, prefer it to the factual approach, they were capable of appreciating it when they met with it in a favorite author like Washington Irving.[18] The *North American Review* even printed an occasional excerpt or manuscript by subjective-poetical travelers. One such example is the record of a short "Pedestrian Tour" of New England by one "H. Tudor" in 1817. Here is an excerpt:

June 1st. To Keene, 43 miles.—Overslept ourselves at Pepperell, set off after breakfast, and walked six miles, then being tired of moving so slow from home, took the stage, and arrived here at

[15] "Italy," *North American Review,* 12 (1821), 200.
[16] C. Emerson, "Robinson's *Travels,*" p. 177. Cf. John G. Palfrey, "Von Raumer's *England,*" *North American Review,* 43 (1836), 446.
[17] J. C. Gray, "Foreign Travel," *North American Review,* 9 (1819), 260.
[18] Review of Irving's *A Tour on the Prairies, ibid.,* 41 (1835), 1–28.

8, P.M. We have passed to day through a number of "clever towns," but have seen nothing worth remarking, except the Monadnock mountain, at a distance, and seven beautiful girls *en passant,* which I have observed this day; it is remarkable, and I mention it for the benefit of artists, what a fine, warm, and mellow tone, objects like these, in the front ground, give to a landscape; one of these maidens, with a sparkling, open countenance, rose-tinted, transparent complexion, falling shoulders, and rounded arms, light elastic step, small foot, and tapering ancle, [*sic*] (it must be observed that,

> Brachia et vultum, teretesque suras
> Integer laude)

formed one of the most picturesque *studies* I ever saw, and I sighed that I was not an artist. The latter part of this road is a gentle descent for two miles, shaded by tall trees, and with a fine stream running by the road side.[19]

Tudor's log resembles Thoreau's usual travel style, despite obvious differences, in its day-by-day structure, its attempt to intermix facts and entertainment, its academic wit, and its tendency to overrefine ideas. There is no reason to believe that Thoreau ever saw Tudor's account but he would have found some of the same qualities in authors he did read, such as Gilpin, Goethe, Purchas, and Sterne.

As the century progressed, the imaginative approach to travelwriting continued to gain ground, not only because the romantic movement encouraged an expressivist approach to writing

[19] *North American Review,* 4 (1817), 176–177. This style should be contrasted with that of another New England traveler, whose work Thoreau knew well, Timothy Dwight, *Travels in New England and New York* (1822; rpt., ed. Barbara Solomon [Cambridge: Harvard University Press, 1969]). Dwight's book is a compendium of information on the region, based on many years and some 18,000 miles of traveling. It was books like Dwight's, which in themselves had enough of the quaintness of amateurism to appeal to the imagination of a Thoreau, that led to more scholarly accounts of their subject on the one hand, and supplied the factual groundwork for more creative travelers like Thoreau on the other.

and an idealized view of exotic locations and the life of adventure, but also in part because the sheer volume of previous travel books had made it impossible to say anything distinctive about the usual watering places unless one was extremely creative, or else intimidatingly thorough. Gone were the days when "the mere circumstance of traveling" was thought sufficient to allow a gentleman"the right of forcing on the public an account of his breakfasts and nights' lodgings." [20] The gentleman amateur and his wilderness counterpart, the untutored explorer, were being replaced by two different kinds of reporters: the professional writer on the one hand and the professional historian, sociologist, geographer, naturalist, or archaeologist on the other. Even today it is still of course possible for anyone who circumnavigates the globe in a small sailboat or travels to mainland China to publish his impressions, just as in the early nineteenth century any literate person who had seen Japan or Tahiti or Africa was assured of an American audience and a review in the *North American*. But the opportunities for amateurs are much more limited now, and during the nineteenth century they shrank progressively. George William Curtis summed up the situation for the literary travelogue in 1855 when he declared that if the work is not "poetic" it will be "soon forgotten." [21]

The center of literary interest in such writing, Curtis goes on to say, is not what the traveler sees or the adventures he experiences, but the self-portrayal of the traveller himself.[22] In this, as in several other respects, Curtis was the child of Transcendentalism. The Transcendentalists, in general, departed from the Unitarian line of travel-writing in the same way they did on other issues: by stressing the importance of the individual mind over that of empirical fact. Caleb Stetson, for example, reviewing Fuller's *Summer on the Lakes,* was pleased to find that she "is much more occupied with what is passing in her own soul,

[20] Edward Everett, "Italy," *North American Review,* 12 (1821), 198.
[21] "American Travelers," *Putnam's Monthly Magazine,* 5 (1855), 564.
[22] *Ibid.,* p. 568.

than with the objective realities which present themselves to the senses." His only complaint was that "she does not let her thought or emotion write itself out" sufficiently.[23] Frederic Hedge, in the same vein, declared that what "we care to read about" in travel books is not paintings and churches and rivers and mountains, "but the reflection of these in genial and original minds. The most interesting travels are those that have the least to say about the very things which we go abroad to see, —such books as Eothen, and the Sentimental Journey. . . . For the same reason, we like travels at home better than travels abroad." [24] Hedge's last sentence touches upon the essential idea of travel as expressed in "Self-Reliance" and the "Conclusion" to *Walden*. True travel is spiritual travel, an exploration of one's own higher latitudes. Travel is interpreted, in other words, in the same idealized way as the religious terminology discussed in Chapter 4, above. Actual travel is useless, in the Transcendentalist view of things; the chances are that it may even be a stumbling block to spiritual advancement, like the doctrine of miracles. For example, Emerson's principal notion about travel, based on personal experience, was that in most cases it signifies a futile attempt at self-escape (*W*, II, 80–82; VI, 145–146). He and other Transcendentalist travelers, therefore, hedged their reports with admonishment that home is best, that travel is merely a preparative to better living at home. "The traveller learns many precious lessons," effused Bartol, "but perhaps the most precious of them all, for which alone it is well worth one's while to take a long journey, as perhaps else it cannot be learned, is that the crown of life is in no change of place, but is to be in one's home." [25]

Not that Bartol and other Transcendentalist travelers sought to deny the peripatetic impulse, however—far from it. They simply desired to make it spiritually valid, or, in Thoreau's

[23] "Summer on the Lakes in 1843," *Christian Examiner*, 37 (1844), 274, 275.

[24] "European Travel," *ibid.*, 53 (1852), 240.

[25] *Pictures of Europe* (Boston: Crosby, Nichols, 1855), p. 15.

case, to make the best of their inability to gratify it fully. Such motives reinforced their natural literary predilection for the abstract and subjective dimension. Emerson talked about his experience in England in terms of an analysis of the essence of the English character; Bartol used the scenes he saw on the continent as illustrations for moral meditations; Fuller (in *Summer on the Lakes*) and Thoreau interspersed descriptive sketches with verse fragments, prose poetry, and quaint bits of historical lore. In all these cases one becomes conscious of an interplay between the sequence of actual observations and the interests of a subjectively imposed mood or design. Neither dominates to the exclusion of the other; rather, the works oscillate between the two structural principles.

This sort of oscillation, which is to be found in many literary travelogues of the romantic period as well as among the Transcendentalists, was one of the features of the genre which most perplexed conservative critics. Edward Everett, for instance, enjoyed Irving's *A Tour of the Prairies,* but did not know quite what to make of it:

To what class of compositions the present work belongs, we are hardly able to say. It can scarcely be called a book of travels, for there is too much painting of manners, and scenery, and too little statistics;—it is not a novel, for there is no story; and it is not a romance, for it is all true. It is a sort of sentimental journey, a romantic excursion, in which nearly all the elements of several different kinds of writing are beautifully and gaily blended into a production almost *sui generis.*[26]

Thoreau had but a limited interest in the purely picturesque; but his mode of writing does resemble Irving's in most of the ways listed here—in its descriptive, peripatetic, and miscellaneous or hybrid character: part sketch, part information, part narrative, part wit, part philosophy. This resemblance is well worth insisting upon, as a reminder that the Thoreauvian ex-

[26] *North American Review,* 41 (1835), 5–6.

cursion is not a great deal more sui generis than Irving's actually was. Thoreau criticism of the last few decades has tended to convey this impression by its intense concentration upon the intricacies of his literary strategies.[27] Much of this scholarship has been first-rate, and it has succeeded admirably in showing Thoreau's dedication to his vocation as a writer. But in the process it has created a somewhat unbalanced picture of his work, and by extension that of other romantic travelers also.

In the first place, the prevailing critical approach to Thoreau carries with it the somewhat misleading implication that literary architectonics was (or should have been) of immense concern to him. In fact, none of his books, not even *Walden,* is very tightly unified, nor probably designed to be, for the romantic excursion is as much a record of events and impressions as it is a poem. Even in the course of so analytical a work as *Walden,* there are all sorts of meanderings and digressions: the song the speaker sings when chopping timber, the length of the diatribe against philanthropy, the inclusion of the "complemental verses," and

[27] The most important analyses are F. O. Matthiessen, *American Renaissance* (London: Oxford University Press, 1941), pp. 166–175; Sherman Paul, *The Shores of America* (Urbana: University of Illinois Press, 1958), pp. 293–353; Lauriat Lane, Jr., "On the Organic Structure of *Walden,*" *College English* 21 (1960), 195–202; J. Lyndon Shanley, *The Making of Walden* (Chicago: University of Chicago Press, 1957), pp. 74–91; and Charles R. Anderson, *The Magic Circle of Walden* (New York: Holt, Rinehart & Winston, 1968). My own critical preferences are closer to those who continue to approach Thoreau as a stylist but who regard that style as governed not by the demands of literary structure but by the demands of his vision: e.g., Jonathan Bishop, "The Experience of the Sacred in Thoreau's *Week,*" ELH, 33 (1966), 66–91; Joseph Moldenhauer, "Paradox in *Walden,*" *Graduate Journal,* 6 (1964), 132–146, rev. rpt. in *The Recognition of Henry David Thoreau,* pp. 351–365; Reginald Cook, "Ancient Rites at *Walden,*" *Emerson Society Quarterly,* No. 39 (1965), 52–56, rpt. in *Twentieth Century Interpretations of "Walden,"* ed. Richard Ruland (Englewood Cliffs, N.J.: Prentice-Hall, 1968), pp. 93–100; and Ethel Seybold, *Thoreau: The Quest and the Classics* (New Haven: Yale University Press, 1951).

so forth. It is not that these passages bear no relation to the over-all drift of the book,[28] but that their charm lies more in their heterogeneity and unpredictableness than in their contribution to an overarching whole. Like a Whitman catalogue, Thoreau's writing is to be more appreciated as process than as product, more for its irregular flow than for any patterns which can be abstracted from it, although the awareness of such patterns naturally enhances one's pleasure in the work.

A related problem with Thoreau criticism is that it has over-emphasized the symbolic implications of Thoreau's writing, to the point that one recent analyst of *Walden* has felt obliged to *argue* that the book really does have a factual level.[29] Yes, that was a real loon, a real woodchuck—they are not just metaphors. Like all literary travel narratives, *Walden* is an aesthetic mongrel, a mixture of the actual and the fictive, a report of real occurrences which have been reshaped, in different degrees, by the processes of selection, reflection, ordering, heightening, and mythologizing.

These points are obvious enough, to be sure. The problem is not so much with our responses to Thoreau as with our literary tools. It has become second nature for criticism to approach a work as a literary construct unified by a certain theme or themes to which the separate parts are subordinate, whereas what Thoreau actually wrote is a somewhat different article. It may not change our critical preferences, but it should help to clarify the expectations we bring to Thoreau, if we see his work as one outgrowth or variant of a larger development in excursion-writing during the romantic period.

By way of summarizing the conventions of the romantic ex-

[28] Cf. Raymond Gozzi, "The Meaning of the 'Complemental Verses' in *Walden,*" *Emerson Society Quarterly,* No. 35 (1964), 79–82.

[29] William Reger, "Beyond Metaphor," *Criticism,* 12 (1970), 333–344. Reger proves his point conclusively by quoting Thoreau's directives to would-be bean farmers: "Plant the common small white bush bean about the first of June," etc.

cursion vis-à-vis literary Transcendentalism, the following can
be said. As to method of organization, most travelogues used
one of two models: the sequential, sometimes day-by-day (Tudor's "A Tour," Irving's *Tour,* Brackenridge's *Journal*), or the
topical (Mme de Staël's *Germany,* Tocqueville's *Democracy in
America,* Emerson's *English Traits*). Thoreau preferred the
former model in general, though he used the latter in *Walden.*
A literary travel book was not expected to have a very coherent
structure; one of its pleasures, indeed, as James Russell Lowell
said in his review of Thoreau's *A Week,* was in its "happy
fortuity." [30] A talent for observation and description was a sine
qua non, but romantic travelers were expected to go beyond
this and tell not simply "what has happened to them," but "how
they have happened to the universe," in Thoreau's words (*Wr,*
I, 348). This was not to be interpreted as a blank check to the
imagination, however: "To write a true work of fiction even,
is only to take leisure and liberty to describe some things more
exactly as they are. A true account of the actual is the rarest
poetry" (*Wr,* I, 347). As these remarks suggest, there were no
special ground rules for the order in which a travel writer
should proceed—that would depend on the order of observation
or reflection, but there was an unspoken commitment to totality. Edward Everett, as we have seen, wanted more compen-
dious tomes than the usual fare; one of James F. Clarke's purposes in writing about his trip was to demonstrate "how much
may be seen now in Europe, in a comparatively short time"; [31]
Thoreau demanded that the observer enter into a total relation
with the thing observed. Emerson, even more transcendentally,

---

[30] "A Week on the Concord and Merrimack Rivers," in *Pertaining to
Thoreau,* ed. Samuel A. Jones (1901); book rpt. in *Emerson Society Quarterly,* No. 62, Suppl. (1971), 15. Jones's collection and *The Recognition of
Henry David Thoreau,* ed. Wendell Glick, contain most of the significant
early criticism of Thoreau.

[31] *Eleven Weeks in Europe and What May Be Seen in That Time* (Boston: Ticknor, Reed, and Fields, 1852), p. viii.

declared that true travel consists "in sounding all the stops of
our instrument.

> If I have had a good indignation and a good complacency with my
> brother, if I have had reverence & compassion, had fine weather
> & good luck in my fishing excursion & profound thought in my
> studies at home, seen a disaster well through; and wrought well in
> my garden, nor failed my part at a banquet, then I have travelled,
> though all was within the limits of a mile from my house. [*JMN,*
> VIII, 18]

This gets at the heart of what the excursion meant for Thoreau,
both in life and as a literary endeavor. It was a succession of
confrontations with nature, from each of which the observer is
expected to extract as much as he can, the mark of success being
not so much in the planning of one's itinerary or imaginative
rearrangement of events as in the way in which he runs the
gamut of events as they occur.

In light of all this, the question of Walden's structural and
poetic integrity seems less important than it is often represented
as being; and *Walden* as a whole seems less important relative
to Thoreau's other works, which have been somewhat unjustly
neglected. Even when considered as a travelogue, *Walden*
emerges as Thoreau's masterpiece, of course, for not only does
it carry the principle of significant travel as interior travel farther than any other Transcendentalist work, it is also more
thorough and sophisticated on the level of observation than the
rest of Thoreau's writing. *Cape Cod, The Maine Woods,* and
A Yankee in Canada, indeed, differ from the general run of
tourist accounts only in being a bit more perceptive and fluent.
At the same time the generic approach reminds us that these
works *can* bear comparison to *Walden;* that *Walden* is not in a
class by itself, but a variant or extension of a form which all
share loosely in common; and that *Walden's* present critical reputation relative to Thoreau's other books is partly a modern

accident, insofar as it derives from *Walden*'s being (1) more conducive to metaphorical interpretation and (2) more cohesive than the other travelogues with their arrangement of narrative plus digressions. The nineteenth century cared less about either virtue. Though *Walden* was even then generally conceded to be Thoreau's best work, it was not elevated to such unapproachable stature as it enjoys today. John Weiss, for example, preferred *Cape Cod* (because it was less preachy and more genial), and Edwin Morton even considered *A Week* to be a more "artistic and beautiful performance" in respect to form! Of course Morton was only a Harvard undergraduate.[32]

Of all Thoreau's books, *A Week on the Concord and Merrimack Rivers* is probably most illuminated by an understanding of the travel-writing tradition, because it presents on the surface the most perplexing mixture of subject matters and levels of style. The usual explanation for the book's apparent vagaries is Thoreau's immaturity as a writer: he had not yet found his own medium; besides, he wanted to memorialize his juvenilia and thus turned his book into something "perilously like a library of the shorter works of Henry Thoreau," as Canby wittily remarks.[33] A good deal of the apparent vagary of *A Week*, however, might better be explained as an attempt to master the tendency toward the poetic which we have remarked in the romantic excursion. Thoreau's affinities with this popular tendency should not be overstated, in view of the notorious commercial failure of the book (although the one popular magazine which reviewed it gave it a very favorable notice) [34] and the fact that several romanticist critics showed as much impatience as twentieth- cen-

[32] Weiss, "Thoreau," in Jones rpt., p. 46. Morton, "Thoreau and His Books," *ibid.*, p. 23.

[33] *Thoreau* (Boston: Houghton Mifflin, 1939), p. 272.

[34] [Sarah Josepha Hale], review in *Godey's Lady's Book*, Glick, p. 4. Mrs. Hale mistook the author for Whittier, however, and may perhaps not have read as far as the free-thinking parts of "Sunday."

tury readers with its digressiveness (though much of their objection was based on dislike of Thoreau's ideas).[35] Nevertheless,
Thoreau should not be pictured simply as an artist with a
unique combination of interests trying, as yet unsuccessfully, to
create in solitude a harmonious fusion of philosophy and local
chronicle. He was writing in a day when pedestrian tours which
juxtaposed statistics, alluring wenches, and Latin quotations
were publishable in the best journals; when self-confessed pot-
pourris of prairie anecdotes and descriptive sketches received
good reviews; and the ex-editor of *The Dial* could attempt to
finance her summer on the lakes by dashing off a concoction of
gossip, preachment, platonic dialogue, and Indian lore, and
receive favorable notice in the *Christian Examiner*.[36] The problem was rather that Thoreau, being a more serious writer than
Fuller and Irving and H. Tudor, carried the experiment too far
in the transcendental direction, for too long, and too impiously
(in "Sunday") for his first book to make any headway against the
natural indifference of a reading public which had never heard
of him.

Lowell's impatient thrust gets at the heart of the matter: "We
were bid to a river-party, not to be preached at." [37] In the popular romantic excursions of the era there is, so to speak, a
convention of levity, a tacit assumption that the prevailing atmosphere is going to be bucolic reverie or musing, which will

[35] Lowell, Jones rpt., pp. 15–16; George Ripley, "H. D. Thoreau's
Book," *ibid.*, pp. 9–12; review of *A Week* in *London Athenaeum*, Glick,
pp. 4–5. John Weiss evidently considered the idea of reflective digressions
a virtue but disliked Thoreau's carping tone ("Thoreau," Jones rpt., p. 46).
Moncure Conway ("Thoreau," *Fraser's Magazine*, 73 [1866], 448–452) and
H. S. Salt (*The Life of Henry David Thoreau* [London: Richard Bentley,
1890], p. 141) found the digressiveness charming.

[36] Perry Miller contends that Thoreau received from *Summer on the
Lakes* "much of the impetus" for *A Week* (*Margaret Fuller: American
Romantic,* ed. Miller [New York: Doubleday, 1963], p. 116). This is pure
conjecture, however.

[37] Jones rpt., p. 16.

furnish both author and reader an escape from business and the city into a pastoral dream-world. George William Curtis, for instance, begins his book of sketches, *Lotus-Eating:*

Not four days away from the city, I have not yet done roaming, bewildered with the summer's breath, through the garden, smelling of all the flowers, and returning to lie upon the lawn, and bask, dreaming, in the July sun." [38]

The passage is startlingly like the first canto of Whitman's "Song of Myself"—and justly so, because that poem also takes its impulse from the same theme as the poetic excursion, the idyllic escape. (Another parallel is that Curtis' topographical musings range freely in space and time over much of America and Europe.) Much of Whitman's poetry could in fact be categorized also in terms of the other conventions of the romantic excursion described above.[39] The difference between Whitman and Thoreau and the popular excursion, in addition to the fact that their writing is simply more difficult, is that they refuse to do no more than daydream; they must also prophesy, whereas Margaret Fuller is largely content to remain on the level of description and anecdote.[40] This made Whitman and Thoreau less popular but truer to Transcendentalist ideals of art.

Now that we have looked at the Thoreauvian excursion in its nineteenth-century context, it may be worthwhile to examine

[38] *Lotus-Eating: A Summer Book* (New York: Harper, 1854), pp. 11–12. This was really the sort of book Mrs. Hale thought she was recommending (see note 34, above).

[39] The motif of travel in Whitman's poetry has often been pointed out, e.g., Gay Wilson Allen, "The 'Long Journey' Motif," *Walt Whitman as Man, Poet, and Legend* (Carbondale, Ill.: Southern Illinois University Press, 1961), pp. 62–83. Allen and other commentators emphasize the symbolic aspects of this motif, but it is quite likely that on one level Whitman would have responded to a writer like Curtis, for his sensuous evocation of sights and scenes.

[40] At the opposite extreme, Cyrus Bartol, in *Pictures of Europe,* is far more preachy than Thoreau and Whitman, but he carries it off by presenting his work quite frankly as a series of sermons on exotic texts.

A Week in detail. Relatively few readings have been attempted, and almost none which scrutinize it in its entirety—probably because it is a very hard book to hold in one's mind.[41] The criticism which exists, furthermore, is divided rather sharply between those who see *A Week* primarily as a narrative with philosophical interpolations which mar its unity,[42] and those who see it as a thematic progression with certain unassimilable elements.[43] From the foregoing, it would seem that both these lines of thought are based on inaccurate assumptions about the genre.

[41] The most detailed general interpretation is Sherman Paul, *The Shores of America*, pp. 191–233, especially pp. 210 ff, though Paul has relatively little to say about events after Tuesday. He sees *A Week* essentially as the record of the "ecstasy" Thoreau felt during his Walden years. William B. Stein interprets the book as a movement toward spiritual enlightenment along Oriental lines, ("Thoreau's First Book: A Spoor of Yoga," *Emerson Society Quarterly*, No. 41 [1965], 3–25; "Thoreau's *A Week* and *Om* Cosmography," *American Transcendental Quarterly*, No. 11 [1971], 15–37). Jonathan Bishop, in "The Experience of the Sacred in Thoreau's *A Week*," reads the excursion into nature as an encounter with a more westernized God and draws a provocative analogy between Thoreau's ambivalent feelings about wilderness and about the deity. V. K. Chari briefly discusses the relationship between narrative and philosophical levels in "The Question of Form in Thoreau's *A Week*," in *Indian Essays in American Literature: Papers in Honor of Robert E. Spiller*, ed. Sujit Mukherjee and D. V. K. Raghavacharyulu (Bombay: Popular Prakashan, 1969), pp. 99–112. Carl Hovde gives a detailed account of Thoreau's use of literary sources and manuscript revisions in his Ph.D. dissertation, "The Writing of Henry D. Thoreau's *A Week on the Concord and Merrimack Rivers*: A Study in Textual Materials and Technique" (Princeton University, 1956), (a part of which has been revised and published in "Literary Materials in Thoreau's *A Week*," *PMLA*, 80 [1965], 76–83).

[42] This was the opinion of Lowell, whose review is the best nineteenth-century essay on *A Week*. Among those modern commentators in general agreement are Canby, *Thoreau*, pp. 270–275; Chari, p. 111; and especially Walter Harding, *The Days of Henry Thoreau* (New York: Knopf, 1965), pp. 247–248, and Harding, ed., *A Week on the Concord and Merrimack Rivers* (New York: Holt, Rinehart & Winston, 1963), pp. xi–xviii.

[43] Among those who take this view are Paul, Stein, and Bishop.

A Week has other claims on our attention here. It is Thoreau's most "transcendental" work; it is also, in an important way, the most ambitious book which the movement produced, with the exception of Theodore Parker's *A Discourse of Matters Pertaining to Religion,* which attempts a comprehensive theology. In respect to scope, even *Walden* is parochial by comparison, being confined to a more limited geographical area and frame of reference, and in this sense suggesting the narrowing of Thoreau's intellectual range which reaches its conclusion in the later journal and the posthumous travelogues. Undoubtedly *A Week* is a less finished performance. But if one applies Thoreau's own touchstones of "extravagance" and "obscurity" set forth in *Walden's* "Conclusion" (understanding these terms as Thoreau did, as terms of praise), then *A Week* compares very favorably. For it attempts nothing less than to encompass the whole of Thoreau's intellectual and spiritual development, indeed to take in the whole cultural history of mankind. This is clearly a quixotic task, but by the same token it puts *A Week* in the same category with those other great American failures, from Melville to Dreiser to Williams, which together make up so much of what is interesting in our literary history.

Finally, *A Week* seems also to suggest a certain awareness of failure, notwithstanding the general verdict that it is a "joyous" book, "a soul's voyage gaily taken on the tides of youthful hope." [44] Despite its frequent exuberance, *A Week* has a marked elegiac quality, which increases as the days wear on. Unlike *Walden,* which ends with the renewal of spring, *A Week* begins in summer and ends in fall. Whatever somberness it may contain no doubt derives originally from its nominal "muse" or inspiration, Thoreau's dead brother; but beyond this, it displays some of the same anxieties about the natural order as a whole that we have seen in Transcendentalist catalogue rhetoric and will see again, more dramatically, in the poetry of Channing.

[44] Paul, pp. 195, 194.

8 *Thoreau's* A Week

Written largely during his years at Walden Pond, *A Week on the Concord and Merrimack Rivers* comes closer than any of Thoreau's later writing to an unguarded expression of his relationship to nature.[1] In *Walden* the speaker is obviously much more familiar with his surroundings, but he is also more detached in his presentation of them: he begins and ends in polemic and the account of his experiences is subsumed within an analytical framework throughout. Much of *A Week,* one feels, *might* have been taken straight from a journal, but very little of *Walden.* This helps to make *Walden* a better book, critically speaking, but it makes *A Week* a more interesting record of the Transcendentalist sensibility. Although *A Week* was of course actually written some years after the original excursion, it gives the impression of chronicling the succession of a sensitive mind's meditations in nature. From this point of view, the book's loose consecutiveness, and even the lack of close coordination between its reflective and descriptive parts, enhance its interest, to the extent that they allow the speaker's perceptions freer play. Like catalogue rhetoric, *A Week* is best understood and appreciated when read as a series of epiphanies leading from one to another by process of association, fitting here and there into larger patterns, threading back and forth precariously between the infinite and the concrete. Since these qualities are common to much Transcendentalist literature, in

---

[1] For previous works on *A Week,* see Chapter 7, note 41, above.

different degrees, the following chapter may serve in some measure not simply as an explication of *A Week* but also as an illustration of how the Transcendentalist sensibility unfolds over the course of a lengthy work.

"Concord River" fulfills Thoreau's apparent literary objective in the book as a whole: to immortalize the excursion by raising it, in all its detail, to the level of mythology. The chapter begins with fact and ends in myth. The Concord is a particular river with a particular ecology, but it also turns out to be the familiar river of time, which can mean "progress," "fate," or even death—it can be benign, neutral, or somber (*Wr*, I, 11), like nature herself. As emblem and as natural force, the river is also timeless. The name of the Concord has changed, and so has the civilization around it, but it "winds mindful still of sannup and of squaw" (3), as old as the Nile or Euphrates, ultimately at one with all the famous rivers of history and legend: Xanthus, Scamander, Mississippi, Ganges, Nile.

The movement of the chapter acts out this paradox of timelessness versus time. The motto, from Emerson, foreshadows it: the river is still an "Indian rivulet," but along its banks dwell the farmers, "supplanters of the tribe." Through the imagery of the first few pages, Thoreau insists on time's flow: contrasting then with now, moving from a description of the raw March wind to the white summer honeysuckle and clover (now seen no more) to a reference to haying in the marsh in winter, and ending with a provocative image of scythes cutting tufts above the ice (5). Again, a voyage upstream, if only to nearby Sudbury, is seen hyperbolically as a journey back to the primitive, to Labrador and the Northwest and heroic times of old (5–6).

But now, having implied that time can be reversed, Thoreau changes his approach at mid-chapter, by remarking that although "yesterday and the historical ages are past, as the work of to-day is present, nevertheless some flitting perspectives, and

demi-experiences of the life that is in nature are in time veri-
tably future, or rather outside to time, perennial, young, divine,
in the wind and rain which never die" (7). This transition introduces the poem "The respectable folks," the first of
Thoreau's doggerel interpolations. It celebrates a model life-
style, a life according to nature which is respectable in a true
and not a conventional sense. Like all the poetry in the book,
as well as the prose "digressions," the passage causes an abrupt
change of pace: it interrupts the prose sequence, and as poetry,
it must be read more slowly, thereby creating the sense of
double time, or rather of an escape from time altogether into
the timeless world of meditation.

The transition was awkward; the poem is weak; but now the
line of thought finds a more worthy expression. As Thoreau
shifts back to prose he continues to stress the perennial qualities of the river. History, change, and motion subside as we get
an overview of the Concord. Its current is gentle, almost nonexistent; its course through the town seems less like a forward
movement than a circling, nine times around a field verdant.
Three essentially static pictures follow: a description of the surrounding landscape, the excerpts from Johnson's *Wonder-
Working Providence* (which do not so much contrast history
with the present as reassert the marshiness of the region
throughout time), and the indentification of the Concord with
various famous rivers. The general effect is to set up several
thematic possibilities, which will not so much direct the flow of
events and thoughts as bind them loosely together ex post facto.
Like the river, like the trip itself, the speaker's imagination in
A Week moves both upstream and down, forward toward self-
realization but simultaneously back into time: the biographical
past, the regional past, even the cultural past, as far back as the
beginnings of civilization. When Thoreau insists on these metaphors, we shall start to see the voyage not as a line but as a
circle, from Concord to new Concord (almost) and back again,
during the archetypal circuit of a week, which stands for all

time, and potentially for regeneration and perfection as well.[2] However, the narrative will keep us from experiencing this circle as much more than a periodic reminder; primarily we will be subjected to a flux of events, each one tumbling into the next, and our problem will be to follow Thoreau's course through all its reaches and bends. In the later stages of the book, perhaps unintentionally, this impression of flux will conspire with the mood of autumn and the awareness of the circularity of the voyage to convey the same sense of fatality that one gets at the end of "Concord River," or at least the sense of drifting toward an unknown and vaguely ominous future.

"Saturday" is another sort of introduction, and as such it complements "Concord River." (As in *Walden,* the other chapters, we shall see, also occur in pairs.) In "Saturday" the movement from the mundane world to the mythical is re-enacted on the narrative level. First, the two brothers formally take leave of the town: they perform their "shore rites" (14), salute their friends with a volley of gunfire (14), and pay their respects to "the St. Ann's of Concord," Ball's Hill (19). These details initiate a movement backward in time toward an ideal, Arcadian world. The rest of the chapter, accordingly, is largely taken up with an account of the natural environment: the vegetation on the banks of the river and especially the fish that swim in it. Here Thoreau's "scientific" side comes to the fore more than anywhere else in the book, but in a casual way he also uses ichthyology for metaphorical purposes.[3] The sunfish is a "jewel of the river" (26); the shiner is an infant; the pickerel is a wolf

[2] See J. J. Boies, "Circular Imagery in Thoreau's *Week,*" *College English,* 26 (1965), 350–355; and Joyce Holland, "Pattern and Meaning in Thoreau's *A Week,*" *Emerson Society Quarterly,* No. 50, Suppl. 1 (1968), 48–55. They point to such other symbolic circles as the cycle of ebb and flow, the water cycle, the circular pile of stones on the bottom of the river and around campfires, and the potholes in the Merrimack.

[3] The next two paragraphs are partly indebted to Sherman Paul, *The Shores of America* (Urbana: University of Illinois Press, 1958), pp. 213–215.

(29); the horned pout squeaks like a minister (29). The classifications get more playful and anecdotal as they go along, culminating in the mock-tragic lament for the shad and some well-honed invective against the Billerica dam (35–37).

On a deeper level of meditation, the figure of the fisherman serves as a focal point for much of the metaphorical activity in the chapter. The narrator presents himself as a symbolic fisherman. Just as fishing is a contemplative man's recreation, so "science," he says (meaning the sort of nature lore he purveys) is "only a more contemplative man's recreation" (23). Also, travelers are fishermen: half dreamers, half adventurers in nature; and like the kind of journey these travelers have undertaken, fishermen suggest both the beginning and the end of time. Fishing was, for Thoreau, one of "the pleasures of my earliest youth" (21), as well as a livelihood and favorite pastime for Concordians of old. By the same token, fishing is also associated with age, in Thoreau's memory of the old man who practiced it as "a sort of solemn sacrament and withdrawal from the world, just as the aged read their Bibles" (23). The ritualistic withdrawal, again, suggests the brothers' leavetaking, and sure enough, the "last of our townsmen whom we saw" was a fisherman (21).

The end of the chapter, with the description of pitching camp for the night, gives the impression that the departure from civilization has been completed. Though Thoreau spoke earlier about sailing into the future, it is as if they have arrived back at the beginning of time. The boat seems like "the first encroachment of commerce on this land" (39); the surrounding countryside seems "a place for fauns and satyrs" (38); and the brothers drink from the stream in primitivistic fashion "to propitiate the river gods" (38). To be sure, they also hear fire alarms in nearby Lowell and the continual barking of house dogs, but these sounds are transformed by their remoteness and by the experience of camping into things of the wilderness, just as the train in *Walden* sounds like the scream of a hawk.

The feeling of natural antiquity carries over to "Sunday" morning. The color of the dawn seems to date "from earlier than the fall of man" and still preserve "a heathenish integrity" (42). But, Thoreau adds, this aura vanishes with the dew, "and not even the most 'persevering mortal' can preserve the memory of its freshness to midday" (42).[4] This graceful albeit hackneyed contrast of natural piety and Christian jargon points the way for the rest of the chapter. Sunday is a holy day, but the religiosity of present-day New England is played off against the sacredness of nature and the wisdom of the ancients. Both "Sunday" and "Monday" are indeed laregly given over to meditations first on spiritual then on ethical life from the viewpoint of one who has withdrawn at least temporarily from the mundane into the realm of its symbolic opposites: nature, timelessness, the orient, the primitive, the sacred.

Thoreau begins by describing the "natural Sabbath" (45). The scene has an "ideal remoteness and perfection," which invites comparison with the things of man: "Why should not our whole life and its scenery be actually thus fair and distinct?" Thoreau asks (45).

The sense of disparity between the things of man and the things of nature intensifies as the boat passes the town of Billerica, which seems old not with the antiquity of nature but with decrepitude. Thoreau becomes droll and then indignant at the thought of the town fathers imposing their puritanism on the "howling wilderness" (49), as they called it, and displacing the

[4] This supports Jonathan Bishop's argument that twilight in the book is "sacred," while noon is "profane." On "Monday," however, noon is sacred. Bishop's other examples of sacred-profane polarities are very suggestive and hold more generally: distance, depth, wildness, solitude, leisure are sacred; nearness, surface, cultivation, society, and labor are profane ("The Experience of the Sacred in Thoreau's *Week*," *ELH*, 33 [1966], 72–73). But Thoreau abides by no formulae; he would rather invert a conventional expectation than be consistent with his symbols. Note, for instance, the difference between his treatment of labor in "Sunday" and "Monday."

Indians even to the point of plowing up their bones. Thoreau
sees and respects the settlers' achievement but, as always, remains sentimentally attracted by "all wildness" (54). Although
the era of the gardener and the era of the hunter both have
their places, he sides with the hunter, as personified especially
by the Indian.

This era was the age of fable, and this coincidence provides
Thoreau the opportunity for a long passage in praise of fable,
which he (like Emerson) sees as a model for poetry today. This
is the first of a series of discussions of the nature and history of
literature, which progresses more or less chronologically from
the primitive to the Greek to the Roman to the "modern";
taken together, they give a sense of Thoreau's aesthetic. For the
moment, however, his interest is not in the literary but the
mythological side of fable, in its diverse and universal appeal
for men. The concept of myth gives him a club with which to
attack institutionalized religion, as he soon proceeds to do.

What follows is an entertainingly flippant discussion of
Christianity and other ancient religious traditions as comparative mythology, in both the complimentary and disparaging
sense of the term. God is God, no matter what avatar you worship; the spirit must not be confined to the letter. When it
comes to choosing gods, "I swear by the rood, / I'll be slave to
no God" (70)—although Pan and Buddha, Thoreau emphasizes,
are more appealing to him than Christ; though again: "I like
him too" (68). Thoreau's strategy here, of course, is to shock
his reader out of conventionalism, into a truer way of looking
at things. Not that his purpose is purely didactic. Thoreau's
natural mode of argument, like Emerson's, is triumph by aphorism: being insistent but antidogmatic, he prefers to affirm rather
than prove or even communicate. His meditation on religion
is therefore a literary tour de force as well as a sermon, just as
religion itself is to him not doctrine but fable in the best sense.
Nature is again used as the standard against which to judge
"Christian" behavior. Christianity is too otherworldly for a

woodchopper; fishing is more fun than the New Testament. (Though the apostles were fishers too, they were "of the solemn race of sea-fishers, and never trolled for pickerel on inland streams.") Conscience itself is unnatural, only "instinct bred in the house" (75).

Thoreau ends his critique with a longish quotation from Saadi, which praises the transcendent god who towers "above the flights of conjecture, opinion, and comprehension." Fortified by this vision, he returns to the narrative and establishes a truer relation with the next person they see, the lock-keeper who lets them into the Merrimack. "With him we had a just and equal encounter of the eyes, as between two honest men" (80).

Thoreau is presently reminded that they are passing through "an old battle and hunting ground" (84); and the excitement which this inspires adds to the strongly epic quality of the long geographical description of the Merrimack which follows, paralleling the earlier, quieter account of the Concord. The Merrimack is a river of greater stature, "the only key which could unlock" the "maze" of New Hampshire's hills and valleys. Its tributaries flow past mountains which slumber "like tumuli of Titans," "by many a pastured Pelion and Ossa, where unnamed muses haunt," etc. (86). Unfortunately civilization has not enhanced the region. From end to end the Merrimack is now exploited commercially, and the only signs of the Indian are place names and the ruins of fishing weirs. The whistle of the steam engine has replaced the fishhawk's scream and the fish are "comparatively few" (90). Still, the fact that the shad and alewives keep coming back "cannot but effect our philosophy favorably"; the scenery is pastoral; the day is still "glorious" at noon (92); so without any feeling of inconsistency the travelers can rest or row with pleasant thoughts.

As they consult their "Navigator," the gazetteer, Thoreau is abruptly reminded of the subject of books in general and especially of poetry, since from the "bald natural facts" of the gazet-

teer they "extracted the pleasure of poetry" (92). The transition
is lame but what he has to say is appropriate. This is his afternoon meditation, which supplements and overlaps his morning
thoughts. His emphasis here is on the literary expression rather
than the spiritual inspiration and its source, on secular writing
rather than sacred. But in his eyes the ingredients for both
are similar. The loftiest wisdom is poetic; true poetry is religious. A touchstone for both is nature. "As the oak bears an
acorn, and the vine a gourd, man bears a poem" (94); the poet
must be "as vigorous as a sugar-maple" (101); in Homer,
Thoreau's model for the poet as Pan is the model for his deity,
"it is as if nature spoke" (94). As with the meditation on religion, Thoreau's approach is to bring a brief assessment of
ancient tradition and general principles to bear on today; and
the effect of this, as before, is to negate time. The *Iliad* still
embodies "all the sunlight that fell on Asia Minor," and still
"lies in the east of literature, as it were the earliest and latest
production of the mind" (97). Some modern classics, conversely,
"already seem ancient, and in some measure have lost the traces
of their modern birth" (102).

Thoreau ties his discussion to the context of the journey by
speaking of writing as an art of navigation, a voyage of discovery (100). The voyage should be of the same sort as the
one he is undertaking at the moment: not an easy flowing or
impetuous rush downstream, but a measured and deliberate
effort. Sentences should be "truly *labored*," he says, in a related
metaphor (109). Presumably we are to remember that Thoreau
is "writing" his book as "we thus worked our way up this
river" (113). His defense of labor as the basis of writing is also
perhaps an indirect justification for their Sabbath-breaking.

In contrast to the Thoreaus are the two befuddled travelers
(one of several mirror images in the book for the brothers) who
call to them from the bank. They too are bound upstream, but
have been "waylaid by the Sabbath," because they prefer to
travel the "smooth way" (rather than the labored way) by com-

mercial transportation. For them nature is "a rough and uncivil place" (115–116). Thoreau's short sketch of the history of the island on which they (unwittingly) stand implies that the brothers have the hardihood of the first permanent settler, Jonathan Tyng, while the strangers are like his hired men who ran away for fear of Indian attack. Not that the brothers themselves are immune: they nearly experience "a pilgrim's fate" in their pursuit of what seems to be a sturgeon (the emblem of the Merrimack) but is really a buoy (117); later, their sleep is interrupted, and one of them has nightmares (119).

Monday is a day of activity after a day of rest, and the opening of Thoreau's next chapter reflects this change: "When the first light dawned on the earth . . . all men, having reinforced their bodies and their souls with sleep, were invited to unattempted adventures" (121). The epic tone recurs throughout the chapter. Military language abounds. The two epigraphs from the Robin Hood ballads give the sense of adventure. The historical sections dwell upon the Indian wars. When the brothers camp for the evening, they are inspired by the sound of a drum, and they sleep to the sound of a violent wind roaring outside. All this is a fitting extension of the Monday mood they now observe at the local ferry, which seems "busy as a beaver dam" (122)

The brothers' quest, however, is at cross-purposes with such quotidian activity. The ferry ride "is only a *transjectus,* a transitory voyage, like life itself, none but the long-lived gods bound up or down the stream" (122–123). Thoreau gives notice here that he will continue the critique begun on "Sunday." His main concern in this chapter, though, is not with his countrymen's beliefs so much as with their practical morality, as befits the nature of the day. While the narrative sections play with images of activity and derring-do, the reflective passages examine the value of action as opposed to contemplation, often in terms of the contrast between Western and Eastern ethos. (The two levels are further linked by Thoreau's sly pun, Indian-Indian [153]).

Thoreau's first topic, characteristically, is the local history of the region, which gives him the opportunity to take a few additional pot-shots at the ways of "our brave forefathers" as well as those of "their degenerate children" (124). He delights in the bathos and inaccuracy of the "Ballad of Lovewell's Fight" and so turns the affair into mock-epic, mourning more for "the crippled Indians" than for the settlers (126). At the same time, he does accept the epic approach to New England history to the extent of conceding that "we have need to be as sturdy pioneers still as Miles Standish, or Church, or Lovewell" (124).

A feeling of meditative languor now begins to qualify the speaker's mood of moral restlessness, leading him into his main theme, the contrast between the Oriental mentality as intellectual and contemplative and the western or Christian way as moralistic and activivist. "There is a struggle between the Oriental and Occidental in every nation; some who would be forever contemplating the sun, and some who are hastening toward the sunset" (147). Thoreau's attitudes toward this issue are as mixed as they are about the "sturdy pioneers." He himself is at the least an armchair reformer, who has practiced civil disobedience and admires the mood of defiance in *Antigone* (139–140); and he is well aware of the narcissistic side of a life of pure contemplation. His first thought as he warms to his subject is the perennial need of man and society to be reformed (128). But the thought quickly tires him, and he adds that "all laborers must have their nooning, and at this season of the day, we are all, more or less, Asiatics, and give over all work and reform" (130). This sets the tone for what follows. Thoreau makes it stay noon for the next twenty-five pages while he discusses Indian scripture, which "belongs to the noontide of the day" (156). He stands as an advocate for the Orientals, as being unjustly neglected by his contemporaries and attractive to him personally. Their antiquity appeals to his sense of romance, their proverbs appeal to the poet in him, and their austerity appeals to his puritanism. Perhaps most of all he is excited, just as on Sunday, at having discovered new truth in something exceedingly remote.

After the long nooning, it is hard to resume the trip. The voyagers are repeatedly sidetracked, by such diversions as a garrulous old man's "fisherman's tales of floating isles in bottomless ponds" (167); or a side trip to the Dunstable graveyard (176–178). In a way, the hodgepodge of geography and anecdote in this section has the effect of offsetting the meditation; in another way it is a continuation, for it stresses both the antiquity of the region and its newness to the voyagers. The charm of local history, like Hinduism and the rest of the remote past, is its exotic quality: old John Lovell lived till he was a hundred and twenty; the Indians Wars "sound incredible to us" after almost two hundred years (176); Dunstable's "wild and antiquated graveyard" has a "heathenish" look (176).

Perhaps by sheer happenstance, this feeling of progressively greater remoteness coincides with the first appearance of what turns out to be a fairly important motif in the book, the recollection of another past excursion—in this case to the western part of the Nashua River, whose estuary they have just passed. On the simplest level, this sort of reminiscing adds an informal coloring to the narrative ("That reminds me of . . . "); but in addition, the device reinforces the effect of double consciousness, suggesting possible analogues—or contrasts—with the voyage. The speaker remembers the Nashua excursion, for example, as something the brothers long dreamed of, like Rasselas, but hesitated to carry out, for fear that if they left their Happy Valley "thereafter no visible fairy-land would exist for us" (173). How did the trip turn out? Thoreau does not say, nor does he make any comment as to whether it is better to dream about distant lands than to try to reach them. One wonders if the brothers will be in for the same disappointment that he foresees for the two boatsmen who passed them earlier in the day.

The chapter ends triumphantly, however. Having begun with a picture of everyday bustle, it ultimately succeeds in transcending time altogether. The eschatological imagery of the graveyard and the sunset and the drum are followed by a sudden experience of unity with the universe:

> idle time ran gadding by
> And left me with Eternity alone.   [181]

The drum music seems to have catalyzed this transformation, and Thoreau gives the usual cosmic explanation: "Music is the sound of the universal laws promulgated" (184). The amateur drumming becomes the music of the spheres, just as the speaker recalls the telegraph wire seeming like an aeolian harp, "its message sent not by men, but by gods" (185). As in his early essay "The Service," Thoreau uses this idea of music as inspiration to reconcile the vocation of the hero or man of action with the vocation of the artist: music is the quintessence both of art and heroism, the "flower of language" and the inspiration which "brings out what of heroic lurks anywhere" (182–183).[5] Appropriately Thoreau follows this insight with two passages of poetry expressing heroic aspiration.

Tuesday opens with a predawn meditation which recalls a hike up Mt. Greylock. As the book's most sustained reminiscence of a previous excursion, it brings to a focus the anecdote of the previous afternoon, and several more which follow. In addition, it both revives and concludes the spiritual exhilaration of Monday night. Thematically, the episode is like an extra day to the week: it takes exactly one day (from one morning to

[5] Stein connects Thoreau's meditation on music with yoga, in "Thoreau's First Book: A Spoor of Yoga," *Emerson Society Quarterly*, No. 41 (1965), 15.

the next) and serves in some ways as an epitome of the present voyage. Because of its self-contained and archetypal nature, it has probably been discussed more thoroughly than any other part of the book, but more remains to be said.[6]

Climbing a mountain was always a sacred act for Thoreau, and this excursion, appropriately, was a pilgrimage which led to a transcendent experience. At the summit, he was alone above the clouds, witnessing day break as if on a "new world," "such a country as we might see in dreams, with all the delights of paradise" (197–198). Unfortunately, the experience does not last. Thoreau has visions for a moment of even further bliss: "As I had climbed above storm and cloud, so by successive days' journeys I might reach the region of eternal day" (198). Instead the clouds rise ("owing, as I think, to some unworthiness in myself" [156]), and he is left in a drizzle. But undaunted, he now sets his course "for a fair lake in the southwest," and is off on another excursion (200).

The narrative proper reduplicates this pattern, of course. The previous night he has had another mystical experience; now he is encased in fog, but he is hopeful that it will rise, as it eventually does. For the future we shall find more such alternations of illumination and dulness. The "fair lake in the southwest" also appears elsewhere, as a symbol of ideality (157); as in "Walking," this direction has a magical appeal for Thoreau. Nevertheless, it is saddening to think that the Greylock experience is not a "real" event in *A Week,* but an analogue from the "past" (for although it actually took place some years later than the boat trip, it is presented as a completed action.) [7] Be-

---

[6] See especially Paul, pp. 220–225, and Bishop, pp. 73–76. Both these accounts rightly see the excursion as the spiritual high point of the book, a model of Thoreau's quest for the sacred, but they need to take into account all the implications of the fact that the passage is only an anecdote.

[7] For a short account of the original excursion in 1844, see Walter Harding, *The Days of Henry Thoreau* (New York: Knopf, 1965), pp. 171–172.

ing past, it is no longer accessible except to the imagination. It is ironic that the moment of intensest ecstasy does not take place during the week itself. This fact, plus the attitude toward the past maintained by Thoreau and Transcendentalism generally, keeps the experience from assuming the same authority in *A Week* as, say, the ascent of Mount Snowdon has in *The Prelude*. The theme of the growth of man's mind is alien to Transcendentalism; Transcendentalism recognizes, so to speak, no continuity between past and present; and once the experience of ecstasy is past there is no knowing whether it can be recovered.

References to the past, in any case, continue as the boat proceeds upstream. "Tuesday" is indeed that chapter of *A Week* most steeped in the past, both because of the amount of personal reminiscence, and because the landscape continues to be described in terms of remoteness and antiquity. The brothers pass springs along the river banks, "fountains of innocence and youth" "along life's stream" (203). The country is "wild and solitary" (247); the farms have a medieval look, as if "the few inhabitants were retainers to a lord, and a feudal state of things prevailed" (205). Thoreau sees traces of Indians and, as always, is reminded of numerous anecdotes about the early settlement of the area.

But his most beautifully provocative passage on the relationship between past, present, and future is inspired by the subject of commerce, of all things. "Being now fairly in the stream of this week's commerce, of all things. "Being now fairly in the stream of this week's commerce" (220), Thoreau reflects on the life of the boatman, which he finds pleasant, carefree, healthful, even romantic. He recalls his excitement as a boy at seeing the "fabulous river-men" come into Concord (222–224) from far-away places, or so he thought. "Such is Commerce," he concludes, expansively: "Who can help being affected at the thought of the very fine and slight, but positive relation, in which the savage inhabitants of some remote isle stand to the

mysterious white mariner, the child of the sun?" (224). Here
Thoreau is simultaneously the savage welcoming the boatsmen
and the mariner, himself a boatsman bound up the exotic
Merrimack. As such, he is acting out his boyish dreams. He may
not see girls in grass skirts, but he does espy "some shagbark
trees, which, as they do not grow in Concord, were as strange
a sight to us as the palms would be, whose fruit only we have
seen" (227). Thoreau's praise of commerce is thus as much a
way of romanticizing his adventure as is his comparison of life
at Walden to an "enterprise." Unfortunately, in the present
case he is also aware of the sequel: "Since our voyage . . .
there is now but little boating on the Merrimack. . . . Now
nothing is carried up the stream" (225). This will be the last
voyage. Thoreau has only the stock Transcendentalist consolation, that there is "no need to travel . . . so similar are the
lives of men in all countries" (227).

In addition to the idea of questing, commerce suggests relationships between people; and that is a no less important concern in "Tuesday" and *A Week*. It is relevant that Thoreau's
hike up Greylock is a solitary climb, and the anecdote conveys
a strong sense of isolation from (and superiority to) other
people. The local inhabitants try to persuade Thoreau to climb
by the conventional trail, but he takes "the shorter and more
adventurous way" (191). At the top, "my only companions were
the mice" (196) and he has his morning vision all to himself.
Though it is anticlimactic to descend, he can take some satisfaction in proceeding "by my own route" and finding that for the
rest of the world "it had been a cloudy and drizzling day
wholly" (200).

The chapter's next reminiscence of a past excursion is more
directly concerned with relationships. Passing a native who seems
humane under an "uncivil" surface, Thoreau is prompted
to thoughts on the distinction between "civil and uncivil,"
which in turn lead to the recollection of a hike along a tribu-
tary of the Connecticut, where in an area just as remote as this

he spent the night with a farmer who was "rude as a fabled satyr" (217), but eventually betrayed "a gleam of true hospitality and ancient civility" (218). (Though only after Thoreau offered to pay him in advance—a detail which is glossed over.)

This anecdote about hospitality suggests the general direction in which Thoreau's mind is moving. Up until this chapter he has established an almost unbroken impression of the brothers' willed isolation from other people. Now, without exactly reversing himself, he seems more interested in defining further his relationship with mankind. In the warmth of his feeling about boatmen, he finds it "pleasant to hail these sailors of the Merrimack from time to time, and learn the news which circulated with them" (226). He speaks almost approvingly of the "quiet agricultural and pastoral people" that live in these parts (226). One gets the feeling, altogether, that the countryside has become wild enough to make civility something of a relief. Disembarking at a lonely spot, they are pleased to find wild apple trees. "These gentler trees," says Thoreau, "imparted a half-civilized and twilight aspect to the otherwise barbarian land" (246). As in "Ktaadn," Thoreau did not like his nature *too* unharnessed. Some of the less successful touches in this chapter might also be put in this context: for example, his meditation on the "tragedy" of the deaths of animals (236–237), partly inspired by the brothers' having killed squirrels and then been unable to eat them, is an attempt to humanize nature; and his anecdote of the friendly seventeenth-century Indian petitioning the governor to protect him against bad Indians suggests Thoreau's own inability to fit comfortably into the role of noble savage.[8]

If we visualize "Tuesday" as recurringly preoccupied with the subject of human relationships, we may begin to see some point to the prominent and seemingly intrusive noon-time

[8] Cf. Bishop's argument that Thoreau's inhibitions about savagery in nature are related to his mixed feelings about God and the savagery of Indians, in that both seem simultaneously to be desired and vaguely feared as threatening (pp. 84–88).

passage on Anacreon. This would seem to be a prime example
of a passage which was stuck in simply because Thoreau happened to have written an essay on the subject, and very possibly
this was the case. Nevertheless, the essay is quite pertinent to
Thoreau's interests in this chapter and the next. Just as *A Week*
itself is an oblique commemoration of John Thoreau, so the
poems here translated are love poems, frequently couched in
natural imagery: swallows, vines, doves, snakes, horses, bees,
even fishes. No matter that the love in Anacreon is amorous
rather than fraternal; the tantalizing balance between nearness
and distance, longing and content, binds them both. (Perhaps
this is why Thoreau insists that the lyrics "are not gross, as has
been presumed, but always elevated above the sensual" [240]).
Also significant, maybe, is that Thoreau invokes Anacreon in
person, as a "minstrel." This is to be a convivial occasion, a
sociable rather than mystical nooning. Thoreau begins by com-
plimenting the ancients in general as the most "refined society"
imaginable—though he attributes the pleasure of their company to the fact that "we can converse with these bodiless
fames without reserve *or personality*" (238). It comes as no
surprise, then, to find that the brothers wish to pitch their camp
in complete seclusion, "on a large rock in the middle of the
stream" (248).

This proves impractical, and the next morning, ironically,
they find that they have made their camp in a pathway. "This
was the only time that we were observed on our campground"
(249). This remark plus the chapter's epigraph ("Man is man's
foe and destiny") point to the main concern of "Wednesday,"
friendship. This chapter, and particularly the thoughts on
friendship, I take to be the thematic climax of the book, the
ultimate object of Thoreau's literary quest.[9] It takes him quite

[9] The essay on "Friendship" was evidently one of the last parts of *A
Week* to be written. This might suggest that it was no more than an
afterthought. But it is also possible that the essay was designed as a
capstone.

awhile here to build up momentum, for not only must he report what he has seen, he continues to be preoccupied with the
subjects of questing-in-nature and the significance of the past.
These subjects, however, eventually turn out to be ways of
leading up to his main theme; for the kind of friendship which
matters to him (as well as the particular friendship which he
seeks to memorialize) is adequately described only in terms of
remoteness of time and place, and the nature of that friendship
is the same as the nature of nature.

Thoreau begins, accordingly, by meandering through a series
of observations which revive the impression of him as search-
ing rather restlessly for some indefinite goal. They pass the
smaller bittern, "the genius of the shore" who seems to be trying to wrest "the whole of her secret from Nature," or to be
looking "forward to some second advent of which *he* has no
assurance" (250). Somewhat reluctantly, Thoreau identifies with
the bird: "We, too, were but dwellers on the shore"; their
quest, too, amounts to no more than the pursuit of "the wrecks
of snails and cockles" (255) in a minor stream. But he resigns
himself to making the most of this small-time quest—a typical
Thoreau gesture. "The smallest stream is a *mediterranean* sea"
(253); the ocean can be "deeper known" by standing on the
beach and seeing what it casts up than by sailing on its surface
(255); the locksmen's houses are more interesting than "palaces
or castles"; life here has the serenity of Arcadia and the Orient
(256–257). Not that he intends to settle down and participate
in the life of the local community. Generally, the brothers resist the temptation to land on the "low, inviting shore" (252).
The image of a New England Arcadia gives way before a tribute
to islands as little self-contained continents, as if to shrink from
the tie to society.

Having withdrawn in space, Thoreau now withdraws in time.
Turning to his gazetteer, he is inspired to another passage of
historical geography (consisting mainly of a disquisition on
potholes in the river), and this leads him to the book's most de-

finitive statement on the antiquity of the region. No matter if America lacks the ruins of the old world, says Thoreau, with seriocomic grandeur, "Our own country furnishes antiquities as ancient and durable, and as useful, as any: rocks at least as well covered with lichens, and a soil which, if it is virgin, is but virgin mould, the very dust of nature" (265). In keeping with his goal of art as nature, Thoreau tentatively includes his book in the list of natural antiquities. Also included are a series of local worthies, white and Indian both. All are dead, but Thoreau asks, "Who is most dead,—a hero by whose monument you stand, or his descendants of whom you have never heard?"

Thus Thoreau travels a devious but characteristic intellectual circuit during the first twenty or so pages of the chapter. He begins by drawing archetypal images out of his surroundings, which at first attract him to them but then become standards against which his environment is judged; he secedes from it to bask in thoughts of the eternal, the primitive, the antique, but finding these qualities in the local environment he returns to it with a somewhat more abstract, selective affection.[10] The same ambivalences underlie what he soon has to say about friendship.

The main points of Thoreau's idea of friendship are quite simple and explicit. True friendship is a relation between souls, in which material considerations and petty prejudices have no place. Friends should make the highest demands upon each other and themselves, conceiving their relationship as a means of attaining a spiritual level above their normal state. "Let our intercourse be wholly above ourselves, and draw us up to it" (289). This extreme high-mindedness resembles Emer-

---

[10] This pattern may be seen in a great many other places in the book, of course. Essentially it is the familiar Thoreau movement from concrete to abstract back to concrete, but with a couple of specific features: the paradoxes of society versus solitude, withdrawal from the present in time and space versus acceptance of the present, and satirical versus affirmative tone.

son's, except that Thoreau goes even further in his emphasis on
a certain tension or rivalry at the heart of friendship.

> Let such pure hate still underprop
> Our love, that we may be
> Each other's conscience,
> And have our sympathy
> Mainly from thence.   [305]

One's best critic (either by rebuke or example) is one's best
friend. Whereas Emerson is self-deprecating in his essay on
"Friendship," speaking as one conscious of his inadequacies,
Thoreau is pugnacious. So few friendships are worthy of the
name; are *you* worthy? Such is the tone throughout. It is not
just that Thoreau is wary of mixing with strangers. Even true
friendship "is a miracle which requires constant proof" (289).
His disdain, however, seems to mask a greater longing for
friendship than that of Emerson, who treats friendship as a lux-
ury which he has resigned himself that he will never possess.
Thoreau is not yet so blasé. He has known the pain of loss, and
the pain of misunderstanding ("It is impossible to say all that
we think, even to our truest Friend" [300]), but still he clings
to the vision of an ideal human relationship.

To the extent that Thoreau's essay is built around this aspiration, it partakes of the same questing atmosphere as the rest
of the book. "The Friend is some fair floating isle of palms
eluding the mariner in Pacific seas," or like "The Atlantides,"
to which many voyage but none have seen (278). Again, the
search for the friend is like standing on a promontory waiting
for the ship to come in, with the ocean all the while roaring
"Of wrecks upon a distant shore, / And the ventures of past
years" (279). On a more personal level, as this couplet implies,
these thoughts are a voyage back in time to a particular friendship. The ideal friend "is not of some other race or family of
men, but flesh of my flesh, bone of my bone. He is my real
brother" (302).

The quest for friendship, like the book as a whole, has both an elegiac and a hopeful quality. Thoreau regrets the loss of the "gentle boy" who might have been his friend, but trusts that "If I but love that virtue which he is," they shall still be "truest acquaintances" (276, 277). Though in one sense there is no such thing as an ideal friend, the experience of friendship abides forever, even beyond the grave, "as surely as . . . the manifold influences of nature survive during the term of our natural life" (303). Nature is Thoreau's main analogue for friendship, as for all other subjects. Friends are "cis-Alpine"; acquaintances are "beyond the mountains." The theory of friendship is to the real thing as "botany to flowers" (303). And Thoreau's conclusions about both are the same: man's relation to the Friend is as constant, and as fleeting, as his relationship to nature.

The rest of the chapter bears out this paradox, as well as the friendship/nature analogy. At the close of the meditation, ominously, the first thing the brothers do is separate, one going ashore and the other remaining aboard (307). The canal-boaters whom they outraced catch up and act hostile; they meet a gentle boy who wants to join them, but his father refuses to let him (308). At the chapter's end, however, Thoreau has a dream in which the memory of an old quarrel with a friend is somehow eased, so that the day ends affirmatively. More important, his evening thoughts are full of assurance and peace, like Monday night's. Thoreau seeks to affirm the sublimity and transforming power of "the inward morning" despite full awareness of the fleetingness of such moments. Our "summer life" is as transient as mist, but by the same token we may at times float "high above the fields with it" (314).

The marked self-consciousness of Thoreau's exuberance here makes his evening meditation a proper culmination to his thoughts on friendship. Like the latter, the passage is mainly theoretical: on the nature of sublime visions, a surrogate for the real thing rather than the thing itself (in which respect it is a marked comedown from Monday night and even Tuesday morning.) The sense of ecstasy as a transcendence of insuperable obstacles is also a carryover from the discussion of friendship. Finally, it is right for Thoreau to move from the issue of friendship to the issue of the sublime experience, for that is the chief benefit of friendship in his view. The promise of friendship is: we shall be as gods.

Wednesday evening is beautiful; Thursday morning it rains. One feels a general sense of decline, not only in the week and the weather but also in the quest. "This was the limit of our voyage" (318); they go farther on foot, but in a way that doesn't count, since the boat trip is over. They do not climb the hill which "affords the best view of the river," evidently because the bad weather would obscure the view (321). Finally they reach the end of their walking trip, Mt. Agiocochook, where the Merrimack has its source, only to be reminded of the stanza from Herbert's "Vertue," which ends:

> The dew shall weep thy fall to-night,
>   For thou must die.   [335]

Allen Hovey points out that the Indians considered Agiocochook as the abode of the Great Spirit and regarded it with superstitious dread.[11] Perhaps this is the reason why, in retrospect, Thoreau chose to emphasize not the triumph of having climbed it but the fate in store for those who had.

It also seems relevant that the writers Thoreau discusses in "Thursday," Persius and Goethe, are inferior by his standards to the ones he has praised earlier, just as Anacreon was inferior to Homer. "There is a sad descent" from the Greeks to Persius (327); Thoreau values only "some twenty lines" (330) and has harsh things to say about his genre. Goethe is a "city boy," a consummate artist who "lacks the unconsciousness of the poet" (349, 348). Like all the Transcendentalists, Thoreau was both drawn to and repelled by Goethe's cosmopolitanism.

[11] *The Hidden Thoreau* (Beirut, 1966), pp. 76–78.

"Go where he will, the wise man is at home. . . ."—the chapter's epigraph (317)—suggests feelings toward the quest both of consummation and resignation. The relation to nature is the sum of wisdom, but the wise man is not a purposeful quester so much as a spiritual vagrant. Indeed a later passage which echoes the epigraph seems a positive renunciation of questing: "Go where we will on the *surface* of things," says Thoreau, "men have been there before us" (323). He goes on to point toward the next stage of existence (in which he himself happens now to be living).

> The frontiers are not east or west, north or south, but wherever a man *fronts* a fact, though that fact be his neighbor, there is an unsettled wilderness between him and Canada, between him and the setting sun, or, farther still, between him and *it*. Let him build a log-house with the bark on where he is, *fronting* IT, and wage there an Old French war for seven or seventy years, with Indians and Rangers, or whatever else may come between him and the reality, and save his scalp if he can.   [323–324]

For those who know *Walden,* these words are a declaration that Thoreau is now ready to "front the essential facts of life" in a more genuine manner than *this* book will show. *A Week* has been his grand tour; now he has found that "continued travelling is far from productive" (326) and he is ready for a profounder excursion on a more limited geographical scale. He has seasoned into the mature albeit unglamorous woodsman described in the epigraph, which comes, of course, from Emerson's "Woodnotes," for which Thoreau was rumored to be the model. It is pleasant to suppose that one reason this turning point takes place on Thursday is that Thursday is the day of Thor, with whom Thoreau liked to link his own name etymologically.

In any case, the hiking trip is described very hastily, often in generalized terms: "Sometimes we lodged at an inn. . . . There we sometimes read." (326); "Suns rose and set" (333), etc. The only detail on which Thoreau dwells is the upland encounter

with the young soldier, whose greenness is perhaps an image of
Thoreau's own past. In general, he seems in a hurry to get back
to the boat—partly for structural rather than thematic reasons,
of course. But in addition, he seems to intend a certain personal
parallel to the horrific tale of Hannah Dunstan's escape from
the Indians. The brothers too decamp on Thursday morning
from "the very spot" which a tribe of Indians occupied awhile
ago (318); they now ply the same downstream route at the same
time of day ("probably") as Hannah (341), not terrified as she
but also heading home away from wilderness. The connection
is obliquely reinforced by another passage which moves from a
sense of the remoteness to a sense of the presentness of the Indian wars and the ancient past (345–347), and by a comparison
of the art of composition to the act of scalping—Hannah's act
(351).

Throughout the book Thoreau has scattered foreshadowings
of fall. Thursday night is "the turning-point in the season"
(356). The brothers go to bed in summer and awake in autumn,
and the autumnal mood dominates "Friday," the last, downstream chapter of *A Week*. The water looks grayer; the wind
has picked up; the cottages on shore look "more snug and comfortable"; the leaves have begun to turn; Thoreau begins to
ruminate about Concord's annual cattle show. The crowd of
farmers there sounds like the rustling of autumn leaves. Thoreau gives his image of the autumn festival a timeless dimension
by comparing it to "the ancient festivals, games, and processions
of the Greeks and Etruscans" (359–360). The overall effect of
the reference, however, is to accelerate the flow of time, for the
cattle show is not due to take place until later in the fall. Some
of Thoreau's other descriptions also look forward to October
and November, making the change of seasons seem more abrupt
than it really is. The principal historical allusion is to the great
flood of October, 1785 (380). This deepens the elegiac note in
the chapter. Summer, the trip upstream, seems like a previous

existence: "The places where we had stopped or spent the night in our way up the river, had already acquired a slight historical interest for us" (376). As they pass the tributaries of the Merrimack they wonder if they will ever see them again. Things seem to be hastening to their end, though with some promise of another incarnation, as in Channing's poem to autumn quoted by Thoreau:

> So fast we hasten to decay,
> Yet through our nights glows many a star,
> That still shall claim its sunny day.   [378]

The fast pace of the downstream journey quickens the tempo, too; at one point the boat almost seems to be flying (385).

The tempo briefly shifts when they reach the Concord and once more have to row upstream; the day is warmer now and it seems as if summer has returned (391). But Thoreau continues to float "in imagination farther down the stream of time" (391). The mild weather and slow progress set up a dreamy mood, which he now identifies with autumn and senescence, in contrast to the morning briskness, which now seems to recall an earlier and more vigorous era. The towns they pass, compared to those upriver, have an antiquated look, and Thoreau is reminded of "poets of a milder period than had engaged us in the morning" (391). In the morning he had meditated on "the stern and desolate poetry of Ossian"; now his thoughts turn to Chaucer, who is something of a comedown: indoorsy, unheroic, witty rather than inspired.[12] In contrast to primitive poetry, Thoreau says, "our summer of English poetry . . . seems well advanced toward its fall" (391). He goes on, however, to exempt Chaucer

---

[12] Ossian, in his own way, also suggests the declension of the season, being a more "wintry" poet than Homer (*Wr*, I, 366). This detail, however, is less important than the functions of the Ossian passage (plus the remarks on inspiration which precede it) as a contrast to the state of the arts today and as a warm-up for the statements of aspiration for the ideal life which occur later in the chapter.

from a good deal of this censure. Chaucer may be decadent compared to Ossian, but he is youthful in contrast to us. His "innocence," "serenity," "love of Nature," and "reverence" are all "childlike," just as historically he is "the child of the English muse" (398). "In many respects," then, Chaucer is "the Homer of the English poets," "so natural and cheerful, compared with later poets, that we might almost regard him as a personification of spring" (393). But this praise, in turn, gives way to a passage of more complex tone, which describes the characteristics of a work of genius by disparaging the comparatively superficial poetry and criticism of the present day (400–403).

As his journey nears its end, Thoreau begins to have intimations of immortality. "In the hues of October sunsets, we see the portals to other mansions than those which we occupy" (403). These are not conventional heavens, however; they are "not far off geographically" (403). The kind of immortality he envisions, "the true harvest of the year," is rather an immortality within nature, gained when one's life has become totally *"naturalized"* (405). "Here or nowhere is our heaven" (405). It consists of "a *purely* sensuous life"—meaning not a life purely according to the five senses, but a life according to the "pure senses"; for "our present senses are but the rudiments of what they are destined to become." Our ears, for instance, must be able to hear "celestial sounds" (408). Thoreau looks to "the immaterial starry system, of which the [material universe] is but the outward and visible type" (412). The way to this discovery is not through disembodied meditation but "to educate and develop these divine germs called the senses" (408).

This new world remains to be discovered. The voyage about to be completed is merely a symbol and preparative. Underlying Thoreau's affirmations here is a certain sense of frustration, evidenced in his repeated calls to discover the brave new world, and two interpolated poems in which the speaker identifies with the fading autumnal sun (404) and a transitory bouquet of flowers (410–411), respectively. In function, these poems suggest the little lyric in "The Ponds" chapter of *Walden,* where the speaker also identifies his soul with nature. In each case, the poetic identification supplies a kind of climax for Thoreau's thoughts on the man-nature relation. But in *A Week* the identification brings as much pain as pleasure, ending in an anticipation of death. The sun says:

> The winter is lurking within my moods,
> And the rustling of the withered leaf
> Is the constant music of my grief.   [404]

The bouquet in "Sic Vita" is consoled somewhat, however, by the thought that the flower bed will thrive from having been thinned (just as Thoreau is careful to follow the first poem with a more optimistic prose passage).

By the time Thoreau has finished his meditation on immortality, the sun is setting and the boat is almost back in Concord. The book ends, or almost ends, with a succession of redundantly emblematic sunset images (416–418), and then the famous passage on silence. It is both a triumph and a defeat.[13] Silence is celebrated, as a soothing and welcome refuge, and as "Truth's speaking-trumpet, the sole oracle" (419). But it is also an enigma which one cannot interpret. It is a vast unfathomable sea (the end of every life-river-journey). It is a challenge which men perpetually fail to meet; even after six thousand years it "is little better than a sealed book" (420). The sense of the whole passage boils down to something like this: praised be silence, the rest is silence.

Although in one chapter it is impossible to fathom the intricacies of a 400-page book, the foregoing analysis has at least tried to give a sense of the rich and often beautiful play of

---

[13] For a quite different interpretation of this passage, see W. B. Stein, "Thoreau's *A Week* and *Om* Cosmography," *American Transcendental Quarterly,* No 11 (1971), 36. In my view, Stein ultimately imposes the analogy of yoga too heavily on Thoreau, but his two articles on *A Week* are significant as the most ambitious attempts ever made to view Thoreau in terms of Oriental thought.

sensibility manifested in *A Week*. Thoreau's excursion does
not have the kind of formal cohesiveness which modern readers
have been trained to expect, but it does have a sinuous continuity, reminiscent of those lengthy Chinese scroll paintings en-
titled "Mountains and Rivers without End." The images are
isolated and often abrupt, eccentrically spaced apart by sky and
clouds. The artist seems to have been inconsistently selective:
here we see a person sketched in a few strokes and a few trees
made to represent a whole wooded hillside, while the contours
of a particular hill or gnarled tree are outlined with an almost
surrealist attention to detail. Still, the work does have a defin-
able movement, and the parts relate. In the case of *A Week*, the
main movements are: first, the withdrawal into nature, which
has its emotional culmination on Monday night and Tuesday
morning and continues until Thursday; second, the counter-
point theme of the relation of self and others, which emerges on
Tuesday and especially Wednesday; and third, the theme of declension (both historical and seasonal), which begins as early as
Sunday and takes over the book on Thursday. If this reading of
the book's flow is accepted, all the chapters can be seen as loosely
knit units, and most of the major meditations are functional.

In addition to the structure just described, we have found
certain recurring motifs, some of which scholarship has already
identified, some not. Minor configurations include circular
imagery, confrontation with pairs of people, recollections of
other past excursions, and special nuances surrounding the time
of day: the morning and/or afternoon meditation, the languor
of noon, the serenity of evening. Of greater importance are the
various ways in which Thoreau manipulates the sense of time.
He experiments with pace, making time stand still in one spot
(Monday), speeding it up in another (Thursday, Friday). He
interweaves several different types of history: the personal, the
regional, the cultural, the mythic, and handles them in a number of characteristic ways. He may emphasize the presentness or
the remoteness of the past, the transitoriness or the eternality of

the present, the superiority or the inferiority of tradition to
today—all of which strategies are used, however, with a view
to praising and preserving what is infinite in the particular fact,
whether it be Homer, the Indian wars, or the smaller bittern.
On the other hand, this sense of the infinite is not allowed to
dominate the book, except at intervals. Thoreau presents rather
a succession of guesses or graspings at the transcendent. For each
excursion or sortie into meditation and nature there is an inevitable return, which amounts to a defeat as well as the completion of a cycle. Although time is continually being suspended
or slowed down during the course of *A Week,* the narrator
makes no lasting headway against time, for it is the course of
time and events which ultimately determines the continuity of
both the voyage and the book.

This fact, in turn, reminds us that the way the shaping imagination works in *A Week* is not primarily to pursue and inter-
weave a set of motifs but to seize upon each image or idea as
it comes along and develop it for what it will yield, then let it
go by. Although *A Week* is indeed rich in patterns, it is still
basically a book about Ball's Hill, the Merrimack dam, the sunfish, the Dunstable graveyard, Homer, Hinduism, mountain-
climbing, Hannah Dunstan, phony bardic poetry, thoughts on
music and silence, and a thousand other things which Thoreau
spins together with spider-like filaments. The unity of Thoreau's literary universe consists not in the smoothness with
which these lead into one another but in the analogical relations
which he is able to draw out of them.

Still farther on we scrambled up the rocky channel of a brook,
which had long served nature for a sluice there, leaping like it
from rock to rock through tangled woods, at the bottom of a ra-
vine, which grew darker and darker, and more and more hoarse
the murmurs of the stream, until we reached the ruins of a mill,
where now the ivy grew, and the trout glanced through the crum-
bling flume; and there we imagined what had been the dreams and
speculations of some early settler. But the waning day compelled

us to embark once more, and redeem this wasted time with long
and vigorous sweeps over the rippling stream. [246–247]

This comes near the end of "Tuesday" as the last part of a passage describing a brief foray on land. By any normal standard of
literary economy, it should be excised; it has no (direct) bearing
on the book's "main action"; but who would want to see it cut?
It is a beautiful piece of description and justifies itself as such.
That is one's first response, probably also the basic cause of its
inclusion. But then the analogizing perception sets in. The side-
excursion has a microscopic quality: the trip up a mini-river
towards what is more remote, wild, ancient; the attempt to
empathize with the original pioneer; and of course the re-em-
barkation—one does not stay permanently in these parts. The
old-fashioned religious rhetoric, "redeem this wasted time,"
gives a provocative coloring to the whole quest: it is done
partly out of a sense of duty, it seems; these puritans have to put
in their time before they can get to the saints' everlasting rest.

Such resonances as these, possible extensions of the particular,
are the heart of the book. Like the Silence, they are complex
beyond telling, and they seem to vanish in a cloud when one
stands at a remove from the books and looks for skeletal form.
But if one enjoys nuance and tone and is willing to read *A
Week* part by part, he may do so in the assurance that the parts
do add up to something, even if it does happen to be the Indefin-
able. In any case, the quality of endless suggestiveness is a much
better literary embodiment of the "purely sensuous life" to
which the speaker of the book aspires than the qualities of precision or cohesiveness. Despite its recurring immaturities both
in style and philosophy, *A Week* is indeed the most manysidedly
sensitive public account of the soul's encounter with the Not-me
which the Transcendentalist movement produced.

9 Ellery Channing: The
Major Phase of a Minor Poet

To most students of American literature, William Ellery Channing II is known only as the protégé of Emerson, the friend and biographer of Thoreau, and the joke of criticism from Poe to the present.[1] He has been cited regularly, even by

[1] The critical history of Channing's work is quickly told. Emerson reviewed his poetry in *The Dial* (Emerson, *Uncollected Writings* [New York, Lamb, 1912], pp. 137–152), and in the *United States Magazine and Democratic Review*, 13 (1843), 306–314. Years later, he also wrote a preface to Channing's *The Wanderer* (Boston: Osgood, 1871). Margaret Fuller mentioned Channing in her essay "American Literature," *Literature and Art*, ed. Horace Greeley (New York: Fowler and Wells, 1852), II, 132–133, as did Channing's cousin William, in "Poems of William Ellery Channing," *The Present*, 1 (1843), 30–32. All these notices are mixed but generally sympathetic. Poe, however, partly in reaction against critical backslapping among the Transcendentalists, devastated Channing in an 1843 review (*The Complete Works of Edgar Allan Poe*, ed. James A. Harrison [New York: Crowell, 1902], XI, 174–190), since which time no one has ever quite been able to take Channing seriously as a poet. It is almost as if Lowell's strictures on Thoreau had remained unquestioned. F. B. Sanborn, in his preface to Channing's *Poems of Sixty-Five Years* (Philadelphia: James Bentley, 1902), simply confirmed this impression by praising Channing's "poetical temperament" (p. xlix) but noting, rightly, that he wrote far too much. Thoreau was of the same opinion, and recommended in his Journal that a good antidote to Channing's "sublimo-slipshod style" would be "to write Latin, for then he would be compelled to say something always, and frequently have recourse to his grammar and dictionary" (*JT*, III, 118). The only significant modern critical study of Channing, Robert N. Huds-

fellow Transcendentalists, as a case history of the dangers of taking Transcendentalism too literally. "Whim, thy name is Channing," said Bronson Alcott (*JA*, p. 420), and he seems to have been right. Channing neglected his wife and children; he lived by sponging off his father, Emerson, and others; he was capricious with his friends. In his poetry, too, he distressed Emerson by seeming to take the doctrine of inspiration at face value, refusing even to correct grammatical mistakes in the poems he submitted to *The Dial*. As Walter Harding remarks in the introduction to Channing's *Collected Poems,* "It is significant that his best-known poem, 'A Poet's Hope,' was written on the spur of the moment," and that it became well-known not for its "unity, structure, or significance . . . as a whole, but for one brief line—'If my bark sinks, 'tis to another sea,'" which was quoted by Emerson and Thoreau in better known works.[2] Channing's biographer, Frederick McGill, Jr., implicitly goes along with this view by making only passing reference to his poetry and taking toward the man a tone of good-humored indulgence.[3] Channing himself seems to have welcomed his own oblivion in later life. One report, possibly apocryphal, has it that he would "haunt the Boston secondhand shops, buy up his own 'works,' and burn them." [4]

I believe that Channing's verse merits a fresh look.[5] The best

---

peth's "Ellery Channing's Paradoxical Muse," *Emerson Society Quarterly*, No. 57 (1969), 34–40, is sympathetic but concludes that Channing's poetry was good as a psychological outlet but mediocre as art.

[2] *The Collected Poems of William Ellery Channing the Younger,* ed. Walter Harding (Gainesville: Scholars' Facsimiles and Reprints, 1967), p. xviii. All page references are to this edition.

[3] *Channing of Concord: A Life of William Ellery Channing II* (New Brunswick, N.J.: Rutgers University Press, 1967). Robert Hudspeth, however, takes Channing more seriously, in "A Perennial Springtime: Channing's Friendship with Emerson and Thoreau," *Emerson Society Quarterly*, No. 54 (1969), 30–36.

[4] "Last of the Concord Seers," Detroit *Journal*, 24 Dec. 1901.

[5] In what follows I have little to say about Channing's prose, although some of it is quite interesting (see Chapter 1, note 43, above), because

of it still makes good reading; and his work as a whole is a provocative complement to that of Emerson and Thoreau, in that it too tends to be informed by the rhythms of nature, but in a different way. The rhythms most likely to inspire Channing's poetry are not those of ascension, as in Emerson, or cycle and renewal, as in Thoreau (with the partial exception of *A Week*), but those of decline: sunset and the decay of the year into fall and winter. These often supply the occasions for his short lyrics and the structures of his longer poems. When surveyed as a whole, this body of work furnishes the best example in Transcendentalist literature of the frustrations inherent in a life and aesthetics according to nature.

In approaching so obscure a figure as Channing, it is perhaps first necessary to show that his work is worth the trouble to read. To see that he was indeed capable of writing well, it is best to begin with small things. Often Channing shows a talent for finding the word which gives a deeper tone to a straightforward image or proposition, as when he speaks of the "impression" of shadows on the grass as a metaphor for the transience of fame (103); of philosophical maxims as "fungi / Of the Understanding" (442); of time as "the cenotaph of things" (341); or of the relationship of nature to spirit:

> The issues of the general Soul
> Are mirrored in its round abode. [298]

"Issues" suggests both spiritual laws and natural progeny. Elsewhere in Channing too, the issues of Transcendentalism are stated as well as in the best of Emerson or Thoreau, as when he describes the separation from nature one feels when walking in a barren spot, under a bare sky:

> Between, I stand, a creature taught
> To stand between two silent floors. [314]

---

most of his prose is unpublished and (more important) because most of his creative effort went into verse. He was the only significant Transcendentalist except for Jones Very of whom this is true.

"Creature taught / To stand" captures the split image of man as a natural being educated into an artificial posture, which isolates him from his environment.

Related to this sort of tension are the mixed feelings Channing has in the following passage on New England religion. Gazing from Mt. Wachusett on the surrounding countryside, he sees

> From every village point at least three spires,
> To satiate the good villagers' desires,
> Baptist, and Methodist, and Orthodox,
> And even Unitarian, creed that shocks
> Established church-folk; they are one to me,
> Who in the different creeds the same things see,
> But I love dearly to look down at them,
> In rocky landscapes like Jerusalem.   [242–243]

This is a nice balance of disengagement and empathy. The hill-top vantage point is appropriately transcendental: the four spires are literally one to him who sees the panorama, and he is literally "looking down" on them as on a state of being from which he has evolved. But though he is skeptical, he is also fond. The "rocky landscapes" are barren, but he also reveres them as proof of the analogy his ancestors drew between New England and Canaan.

Emerson credited Channing with a painter's eye, and perhaps he is most consistently successful at putting tonalities into images of color and shape. The sense of the four steeples composed into one is an example. Later on, looking from the same hill at sunset, the poet sees that "on some faint-drawn hillside fires are burning, / The far blue smoke their outlines soft in-urning" (257), prefiguring the "death" of the day which soon follows. Other provocative shape images are the "forked orchard's writhing mood" (411); the "pine harp-shaped" (479); a picture of Niagara Falls "dwell[ing] alone in the pride of its form" (35); and most characteristically, his sense of the texture of light. The "Earth Spirit" says:

> I have woven shrouds of air
> In a loom of hurrying light.   [26]

In several other instances the metaphor is reused to good purpose, as in the beautiful apostrophe to "Una":

> We are centered deeper far
> Than the eye of any star,
> Nor can rays of long sunlight
> Thread a pace of our delight.   [110]

Here star and sunlight are complementary, as night and day;
the star suggests the soul, sunlight the form of love. Elsewhere,
Channing uses sunlight in woods as "spidery interlacings," as
the setting sun "drew bright webs out of the twigs" (481).

Such touches as these show that Channing had at least the
sensibility of a true poet. Sometimes, though rarely, his inspiration will sustain itself for the length of a poem, and the whole
will be as memorable as the part. Such a case is "Boat Song,"
which can also serve us as an introduction to the themes which
most distinguish his work.

> The River calmly flows
> Through shining banks, through lonely glen,
> Where the owl shrieks, though ne'er the cheer of men
> Has stirred its mute repose;
> Still if you should walk there, you would go there again.
>
> The stream is well alive;
> Another passive world you see,
> Where downward grows the form of every tree,
> Like soft light clouds they thrive;
> Like them let us in our pure loves reflected be.
>
> A yellow gleam is thrown
> Into the secrets of that maze
> Of tangled tree, that late shut out our gaze,
> Refusing to be known;
> It must its privacy unclose,—its glories blaze.

Sweet falls the summer air
Over her form who sails with me,
Her way like it is beautifully free,
Her nature far more rare,
And is her constant heart of virgin purity.

A quivering star is seen
Keeping its watch above the hill;
Though from the sun's retreat small light is still
Poured on earth's saddening mien:
We are all tranquilly obeying Evening's will.

Thus ever love the Power;
To simplest thoughts dispose the mind;
In each obscure event a worship find
Like that of this dim hour,—
In lights, and airs, and trees, and in all human kind.

We smoothly glide below
The faintly glimmering worlds of light:
Day has a charm, and this deceptive night
Brings a mysterious show;
He shadows our dear earth, but his cool stars are white.

[51–53]

The stanzas, with their varying line lengths, seem designed to
meander like the Concord River, which surely was the original
for the poem. The initial effect is calmness, passiveness, at times
even stagnation. First and last this is a lazy idyll, such as one
would expect from an afternoon of boating, especially if the
boatsman were that comic-strip Transcendentalist, shiftless
Ellery Channing. But the poem is not idyllic without a struggle. First, the river is not entirely inviting: the glen is "lonely";
it lacks the "cheer of men"; it is tenanted by the conventionally
ominous owl. "If you should walk there, you would go there
again"—but not without misgivings, not with the same "mute
repose" as the river. The mute repose is more an aspiration

than a fact, then, for the poet. The next stanzas suggest the source of the problem. Let "our pure loves" reflect ourselves as faithfully as the water reflects the trees, it asks—implying that at present this is not the case. The idea seems to be that the self —whether hers, his, or both at once—still harbors something secret within it.

Stanza three contains a hopeful emblem: the sunbeam penetrates "the secrets of that maze/Of tangled trees, that late shut out our gaze,/Refusing to be known." This new light is faint, only a "gleam," but it promises a total revelation of the forest's "privacy." Sure enough, the next stanza (which comes at the exact center of the poem) seems to bring fullfillment—at least on the surface. For the first time, the poet turns from the river and its environs to look directly at the lady, who is "beautifully free," as free as the air. But the consummation is only partial. They do not make contact; the lady is described in the third person, whereas elsewhere she is addressed directly; she is abstractly described—her "form," "her way," "her nature"; she is an object of reverence, not a companion. In a way, the poet's idealization of the lady is consummation enough; certainly one expects nothing deeper than this face-value equation from sickening clichés like "her constant heart of virgin purity." In the next stanza, furthermore, when he returns to speak of their surroundings, they seem to be in harmony with nature: "We all are tranquilly obeying Evening's will." The injunction in the next-to-last stanza ("Thus ever love the Power"), which parallels that of the second, suggests a desire for *continuation*, not fulfilment. Underlying this, though, is a sense of loss. The blaze of glories promised in the third stanza is annihilated by "sun's retreat"; as it darkens, earth has a "saddening mien." The transition between stanzas four and five suggests that the "virgin purity" of the lady has metamorphosed her into the "quivering star"; she lights the poet's world but coldly, as a constellated goddess. Whether or not this specific implication was intended by Channing, it tallies with the gen-

eral atmosphere of the poem: love is suffused into spirituality,
passion is diffused into languor. The last line expresses per-
fectly this mixture of loss and gain: in the light/dark imagery
which Channing often uses: "He shadows our dear earth, but
his cool stars are white."

"Boat Song," then, is both subtle in tone and sophisticated
in structure, the last stanza echoing the first, the sixth the second, and the fifth the third, with the fourth highlighted as a
result. As far as the quality of the imagery goes, this stanza is
pure sentimental cliché—like most love scenes in American
romanticism—but altogether the poem has so much going for
it that it is hard to forgive Channing for not always writing as
well as this. Certainly "Boat-Song" is better than almost any
poem of Thoreau's and as good as most of Emerson's.

But perhaps this would have been perceived long ago, were
it not for the fact that Channing was a (professed) follower of
those two men. In the long run, his reputation, like Jones
Very's, is going to depend not upon evidence that he *could*
write respectably, so much as proof that he was in some ways
different from his mentors, more than a reflection of their
genius. At first glance, he seems simply to be competing with
Emerson and Thoreau on their own ground. "Boat-Song" is
like a piece of *A Week,* only without Thoreau's concreteness;
"Una" and "The Earth Spirit" seem to imitate Emerson's
gnomic style but without his intellectual rapidity and invention. The charge of imitation is false; Channing developed his
gnomics independently of Emerson, as he was quick to tell
those who thought his "Spider" (1835) an imitation of "The
Humble-Bee" (1837); and "Boat-Song," along with many other
Channing idylls, was written before Thoreau had published
anything. But the fact remains that Channing did less than his
friends with the modes they shared in common, and that his
independence was arrested—as he himself confessed—when he
came within their orbit.

Yet Channing's poetry does have an originality of a sort, in

the sense that it emphasizes certain notes which Emerson and
Thoreau sound but do not stress. One is the idyllic. Emerson
and Thoreau often speak of the need to "acquiesce" and live
"deliberately as nature" but surprisingly seldom do their styles
themselves create the feeling of unbroken tranquillity. Emerson's is generally restless; Thoreau's is tense and aggressive, or
else compulsively informational, when he is marshalling his
facts. Channing had different inclinations. He was still something of a Puritan, but a decadent one; his muse was moralistic,
but with a large dose of hedonism. Whereas Thoreau and Emerson, in their theory of poetry, dwell more on bardic rage than
Wordsworthian wise passiveness, Channing rarely pictures the
poet as a Merlin or an Ossian, even though he was much more
tempted than his friends to cast himself in the role of *the* New
England bard, after the publicity Emerson gave his early verses.
Herrick, significantly, was his favorite poet. He likes best to
think of the poet as the "master of the calm" (96), sitting content come what may. He is Emerson's "Saadi" carried to an
extreme degree. The Emersonian invitation to acquiescence
becomes in Channing almost a narcissistic impulse to oblivion:

> . . . I would my simple being warm
> In the calm pouring sun; and in that pure
> And motionless silence, ever would employ
> My best true powers, without a thought's annoy. [151]

As in this passage, and in "Boat-Song," Channing loves to entertain the sensation of drifting and dreaming. "Calm," "tranquillity," "passiveness," "content," "willingness," and other such
terms appear again and again in Channing's poetry. Sometimes,
unfortunately, the dream-impulse takes the form of sentimental
romantic medievalism—papier-mâché Keats and Spenser—a
strain which links him with the soft side of Hawthorne and accounts, I think, for Channing's admiration of Hawthorne's tales.
But usually the idyll takes place in nature, specifically in Concord. The favorite images of tranquillity, to which Channing

continually recurs, are the low hills and fields of Concord and
especially the slow-moving river:

> Thou lazy river flowing neither way
> Me figurest . . . [86]

For Thoreau, the Concord's sluggishness was a joke; for Hawthorne it ruined the swimming; for Channing it was a personal
emblem. Thoreau was right in calling him the poet of Concord.

But that is not all he was. As the undercurrents in "Boat-
Song" suggest, Channing was, for all the delight he took in
easeful lolling, a very melancholy poet at times. The melancholy is the other side of the idyll. His favorite context for his
nature poetry is a context of loss: sunset is his favorite time of
day, autumn his favorite time of year for poetry, and always
these settings are redolent with death. Indian summer, for instance, is like "a new mood in a decaying man" (74), or

> like the hectic cheek
> Of a consumptive girl who ere her time,
> In some gay anguish half renews her prime. [256]

Neither Emerson nor Thoreau is so apt to dwell on these associations, nor upon the parallel Channing likes to draw between the Indian's near extinction and the time of year which
is named for him.

Channing's love of pastoral calm and simultaneous preoccupation with declines in nature are reminiscent of Robert Frost;
and in each man's work the intermixture has a lot to do with
a fear of mutability. "There's no stay to life" (434), Channing
complains, in a Frostian echo. Both were insecure and unhappy
men who turned to nature for relief but could not quite bring
themselves to trust her. As Channing, in a typical instance, seeks
to celebrate and identify with her, the remembrance of the
passing of the seasons draws him back to this thought:

> . . . where shall man, feigning his ignorance
> To be in league with her, at last arrive,—

Or is he but a leaf tossed on the wave
Creative, one more joint to pass along
Tomorrow, to a meaner thing, a throw
Of her wise finger, then displaced. [432]

He stifles this heresy immediately, but it keeps coming up, and intensifies as he grows older. The series of notebooks which he kept during the 1850s and 1860s—in imitation of Thoreau, Emerson said—show a painfully self-divided effort to experience a meaning in nature. Emerson and Thoreau, in their worst moments, felt frustrated; Channing felt desperate.

At such times he would break out in mocking satires of his friends or complain that he had been hoodwinked into a life-style unsuited to him. "Nature & myself are utterly and entirely apart," he writes in 1867. "I neither shall, I neither do know or imagine or suppose the faintest connection between myself & these objects, or between myself & these thoughts, than if I had never heard of them either. And so it will be to the end." He goes on to bewail his unfitness for the writer's vocation. Recalling the early encouragement given him by Emerson and others, he declares, "Had I known then, what I know now, I would never have written a line, or the smallest part of a line, at least to be printed." "The process of writing with me," he insists, "is something artificial and unnecessary," a matter of habit.[6]

In the long run, Channing did not blame the Transcendentalists or nature for his problems, but himself. He admired Emerson, even though he snipes at him cattily in "The Sage" ("The answer that I needed bad /Ne'er reached my ear, nor gay nor sad; /'That might be so,' the sage would say, / Exactly flat as mere 'Good day.' " [1010]). He described Thoreau condescendingly as a crank, but at bottom he worshipped Thoreau's memory, Emma Lazarus declared.[7] This admiration, as well as

[6] Manuscript diary, 'Out-of-door Life," pp. 5, 11, 42, bMS Am 800.6, Houghton Library, Harvard University.

[7] McGill, p. 169. The vicissitudes of Channing's feelings toward Thoreau need systematic research. Channing was just as complicated a character as

Channing's own sense of inferiority comes out dramatically in the prefatory dedication to Thoreau in his long pastoral, *Near Home*. Here Channing pictures himself as an insignificant "reed," passing "a weak life consumed in trivial thought" (417), and he calls upon Thoreau to be his "muse," so that

> Thy abiding faith in God's great justice
> Might arise, and so might I be just,
> And trust in him!   [419]

Channing's image of himself as the weak reed sustained by Henry suggests still another reason why he was unable to find abiding consolation in nature. He was too dependent upon people. The problem of loneliness, felt by both Emerson and Thoreau, was especially acute for him; and it grew more so as he aged, outlived them, and developed a reticence even greater than theirs had been. It is typical of Channing to center his "Boat-Song" around a human figure, and then to make that figure tantalizingly remote. The sense of solitude always filled him with a longing for society. He was torn between a theoretical preference for nature as superior to man and the desolation of a world populated only by muskrats, pouts, and perch. As he climbs Mt. Wachusett, he professes to "love old solitude and hate new show" (241), but once he is at the summit he is glad to see "Plenty of farmers' clearings, and some woods, / But no remote Sierra solitudes" (242). The same thing happens in another hilltop meditation. After a bit of gazing around, the speaker wishes for "some chat with roguish lad"; indeed he feels so lonely that he would welcome "idle gossip fresh from parlors full / Of sewing"; or even "the dry call of herd-boy to his cows / His endless *goaf*" (528). In writing elsewhere of New England traits, Channing seems quick to rebut the charges of

---

Boswell, even if he was less of a literary talent. For an example of his satires of Thoreau, see Francis B. Dedmond, "William Ellery Channing on Thoreau: An Unpublished Satire," *Modern Language Notes,* 67 (1952), 50–52.

dreariness, inhospitality, and unfriendliness—partly because he senses them to be true.

Equipped with the sensibilities just described, Channing handled the usual Transcendentalist topics in ways rather different from Emerson and Thoreau. Only Channing, for instance, could have concocted this mixture of abasement, gloom, and natural piety:

> I love thee, Autumn, ruthless harvester!
> Thou dost permit my stagnant veins to flow. [299]

As a Concord poet, Channing could no more get away from nature as his primary poetic subject than he could evade the stereotype of young ladies as creatures of "virgin purity." His imagination fed on the very thing from which, at moments, it felt most alien. His sense of dualism was thus more severe than that of his friends, although disguised by his ways of coping with the problem—passiveness and self-effacement in his poetry, for the most part; humor and wit in his conservation and his prose. Channing really did doubt the efficacy of a life according to nature, for himself if not for his betters. The very "superficiality" and "caprice" for which his friends reproached him gave him a perspective on their existence which they lacked. He could see its ludicrous side. On the whole, one feels that Channing would have been far happier in literary New York than he was in Concord. He was a sparkling conversationalist; he had a gift for social satire; he entertained the ambition of writing a comic novel in the tradition of Cervantes and Rabelais; and the autobiographical tale he published in *The Dial*, "The Youth of the Poet and the Painter," shows a sprightly insouciance which might have been converted into successful popular fiction had Channing travelled in the right circles. But in Concord serious literature was de rigueur. As an Emersonian poet, Channing largely suppressed his comic sprightliness and sublimated it into a wistful melancholy. The result was something like what might have happened to Nathaniel Parker Willis if he had remained in Boston.

Channing chose, then, to remain in Emerson's orbit, take daily walks with Thoreau, and meditate on the mysteries of nature. Despite many misgivings, he was in the long run prepared to be damned, if it should come to that, for the glory of nature. As he told himself in one poem, he had no more right to complain than any other creature at the way she creates life and then destroys it. It would be going much too far to raise Channing to the level of a tragic figure, since it is often doubtful whether he is writing from his heart or from convention, and since a good deal of the time he evinces no deep self-knowledge but only a nameless disaffection ("I am possest / With strange Unrest" [203]). But his most ambitious work gives provocative and at times even memorable expression to the issues which plagued him. "October has hardly tinged our poetry," Thoreau remarks in "Autumnal Tints" (*W*, V, 249). As we shall see in a moment, Channing came closest among the Transcendentalists to filling this gap, to poetizing the elements of autumn which are present in *A Week* only as a somber undertone.

During his lifetime, Channing published seven volumes of poetry, as well as miscellaneous verses: three collections of short poems (1843, 1847, 1849); then four long works in blank verse: *Near Home* (1858) and *The Wanderer* (1871), two local descriptive poems; *Eliot* (1885), a dramatic monologue; and *John Brown, and the Heroes of Harper's Ferry* (1886), a closet drama. His poems which have been anthologized are all from the 1840s, but taken alone they present an incomplete picture of his work. Usually Channing is thought of as a lyricist, but if the later poetry is taken into account, he emerges as primarily a descriptive and dramatic poet. Many of the poems in the first three volumes also are in these veins. Like Thoreau, he is most consistently good in poems which establish an interplay between a natural setting, real or imaginary, and the thoughts of a first-person observer. Such works might be called romantic excursions in verse. In the early poetry, "Boat-Song" is such a poem, as are "Inscription for a Garden," "The River," "Still-water," "The Lonely Road," "Wachusett," and "Baker Farm," to name the most successful. Most of these poems, significantly, are in pentameter couplet or blank verse. Although Channing was capable of getting good effects with stricter forms, in general he did not have the talent, or the discipline, to master them, and in any case he needed a more open form for the free play of his thought.

Channing's achievement in the descriptive-reflective vein, such as it is, can be represented by "Wachusett," *Near Home, The Wanderer,* and *Eliot.* The first is a hilltop meditation in the topographical tradition dating back to Denham's "Cooper Hill" and including Emerson's "Monadnoc," as well as Thoreau's prose descriptions of climbing Wachusett, Saddle-back (in *A Week*), and Katahdin (in *The Maine Woods*). The next two poems are also topographical, set for the most part in the vicinity of Concord. *Eliot* has a wilderness setting, some-where on the midwestern frontier.

"Wachusett" is the most ambitious and in many ways the best of the early poems. Neatly organized, it begins with the climb and a brief look from the summit, ends with a corre-spondingly panoramic view of the sunset, and centers around an inner debate between a hypothetical "student" and the speaker. The student sees three evils in the surrounding coun-tryside: a devotion to utility rather than beauty, a crass mate-rialism, and a tradition-bound religion. The speaker answers each of these charges in turn, with Emersonian arguments: (1) to make a good engine is not a mechanical act but "one of the purest ministries of Art" (244); (2) the law of competition will ensure that everybody seeks his own level, in contrast to the feudalism in the so-called age of romance; and (3) if the forms of religion have a validity to the worshipper we should not censure them. Neither these arguments, nor the objections they are designed to counter, make the poem interesting so

much as the happy expression which is sometimes given to
them and the unusual (for Channing) thoroughness with which
they are made to dovetail. Each leads nicely into the next, and
upon finishing the poem and going back to the beginning, one
has the pleasure of finding that the introductory descriptions
have been fashioned, unobtrusively, so as to lay the groundwork
for each of them.

The really provocative part of the poem, though, is its final
section. The poet has hinted that it might be summer, but now
we see that it is fall, from the oak tops "Which light October
frosts color like wine." It is still warm, but the rising wind
brings a sense of urgency: "the Indian summer's voice, / Bids
me in the this last tropic day rejoice" (254). But he cannot;
instead the immediately sees "How brown the country is, what
want of rain" (254), associating this with the Puritans' devasta-
tion of the Indian tribes. "Where are they?" he asks.

> Ah, like this summer, they did fade away
> Into the white snows of that winter race,
> Who came with iron hands and pallid face.   [255]

In just a few lines the speaker has, in effect, conceded all the
student's objections to the civilization he has previously defended. Once he has put dialíectics aside and opened himself
to the influences of nature, his sense of its relentless cycle refutes his dogged optimism.

Now he notices the approach of night. Sunset comes like the
end of the world, "As if at last old earth had caught on fire, /
And slowly mouldering, sank into the pyre" (256). He himself
feels like the "last man" alive. But curiously enough, his sad-
ness disappears, though the imagery of death continues for fifty
lines more, until the end of the poem. "Who can be sad and
live upon this earth?" he cries (257). In an access of the same
mutability which has just led him into gloom, his painter's eye
is overcome by the beauty of the sunset. "Each instant changes
everywhere the scene, / Rapid and perfect turns the Indian

screen"—the local Indian becomes the Asian Indian, the sad transience of Indian summer now seems like an exotic piece of Oriental art (258). "New England drear" seems positively Mediterranean to him now; and his enthusiasm bursts out in patriotic fervor: "He is not right, who our New England says / Is a dread, cold inhospitable realm" (259).

In short, his sunset meditation has come full cycle, re-enacting the rhythm of the debate: melancholy, rescued by affirmation. His personal fear of nature's mutability gives way to his delight in her mastery of the art of change. In the nine remaining lines, the serenity is maintained (or is it?) as the sinking sun turns the sky to "purest roseate," which modulates to "gentle red,"

> Then dies within that stormy mountain cloud,
> That masks him proudly in a leaden shroud.   [260]

Why "proudly"? Does it add the last touch of dignity to the sunset, or does it mark the cloud's final triumph over the sun? The speaker's heart is content, no doubt about that, but only because he has made himself the passive receiver of contra-dictory impressions.

Near Home is a much more diffuse and uneven work than "Wachusett," partly because it is twice as long—almost a thou-sand lines. In its scope it is a more ambitious treatment of the theme of the going-down of the seasons. The poem opens with a sunrise in spring and ends with the coming of autumn. The movement is guided by two structural principles: shifting scenes according to the season and the topic the poet wants to broach; and the conflict between hope and gloom, à la "Wachusett."

The conflict here, however, is less regulated and more oblique: the device of the second persona is dropped, and the speaker's way of coping with doubt is usually to evade it, by changing the subject.

The spring sunrise, for instance, calls to mind the origin of the world, which leads to thoughts about the diminution of man since his Arcadian beginnings, raising the possibility of the future extinction of the race, from which, however, the speaker abruptly draws back: "Of this / We phrase not here" (422). His subject is local, not epic. He is then visited by an ominous image of the regional past, the Indians, but this is quickly superseded by his pleasure in nature and the awareness that "I do not walk alone; / For still I feel thy arm is round me, / . . . Thou, who art all in all" (422–423). But at once, in another metamorphosis of sensibility, this presence is transformed into a sense of human companionship:

> I do not walk alone, for still the Spring
> Calls up my old companions. [423]

This in turn leads into a eulogy of Home, the pleasures of friendship and family, thoughts which give him inexpressible comfort and security. "Safe in my heart is home with all its joys"—the idea, and the language too, suggest to him the way

> the dimpling river laves,
> Safe in its pure seclusion, the green base
> Of yonder hill, bleached to its core with shells,
> Things of the Indian. [424]

But, alas, the poet finds himself betrayed again by reminiscence, betrayed even by nature, for the mention of Indians now calls to mind the whole tragedy of their race, gone like leaves, like grass.

> Thus drop the races,
> Annihilated and spoiled, not to return.
> Yet at their base the dimpling river laves,
> Base of those low, lone hills. [425]

Luckily the poet is able to return to the river and seize on it as an image of constancy. This cheers him up again; he makes ready to cast himself on the bosom of nature, and "Leagued with the universal law pursue / Like it, a sympathetic journey"

(426). Never complain about loneliness in nature, he tells himself; look at all the natural life around you, and the testimony it affords to "the revelation of abiding grace / Continuous" (428).

But try as he will the poet cannot sustain this mood. He cannot help thinking of the fate of the Indians, the mutability of the seasons, his loneliness in nature, and the possibility that nature may be planning to annihilate him without a trace. He changes the subject, he changes the scene from river to meadow, from inland to seashore, but somber intimations still pursue him. It is not necessary to trace all the twistings and turnings of his thought; its subjects vary but the range of tones is about the same as in the sample I have just discussed, which comprises the first 170 lines or so. That sample should suffice to illustrate the main virtue of the poem, its subtle emotional texture. In its better portions, there is a continual modulation of tone, reminiscent of the changes in the autumn sunset in "Wachusett." Since the language and imagery of *Near Home* are less interesting, this quality of modulation may not strike the reader at first, and even if it does he might argue that it testifies rather to Channing's dreamy capriciousness than to conscious art. That may be true in part, though I hope I have made a case for Channing as a conscious artist in the other poems I have discussed. Certainly, despite anything Emerson said, one must have some respect for the conscientiousness of a writer whose surviving manuscript poetry shows fairly extensive revision; who withheld a great number of poems from publication, feeling they were not good enough to print; who after the age of thirty had serious doubts about his artistic abilities.[8] Even if one assumes that Channing did meander a good deal in *Near Home,* the effect is often happy: a procession of tonal shifts within an emerging design.

At the end of *Near Home,* as in "Wachusett," Channing "re-

8 Sanborn's preface and Channing's manuscripts substantiate these claims.

solves" the cosmic question raised by the coming of autumn through a triumphant lapse into resignation:

> Learn from the joy of Nature, so to be
> Not only quite resigned to thy worst fears,
> But like herself superior to them all.   [465]

Though we may be destined for a wintry fate, we may warm ourselves with the fires of our own serenity, thus "annihilating change" (466). This solipsistic affirmation is clinched by appeal to the example of "Vernon" (elsewhere identified as Thoreau), the same muse invoked in the preface.

But this consolation was soon lost. Thoreau died four years later, leaving Channing without his closest friend. That may partly explain why his next poem, *The Wanderer,* begins on a more somber note than we have ever heard him strike before. Standing on a hill, the speaker surveys first his village, then the sky, and then he turns once more to the perennial subject, the meaning of nature. The season is winter; the silence and loneliness are intense; the frost is "like a nettle robe" (482). How can a person withstand, much less fathom, such relentless force? "Well, I could pray," he thinks, for an intermission of winter; but what good would that do?

> And then fancy the dull man wandering round
> As I, vexing the sly world with questions,
> Heard his queries solved and plainly answered:
> Came, by some taste of learning, to the sense
> Of all the senseless facts.   [482]

What then? Even with such theoretical knowledge, "might I so front the wood? / Should it not flout and leer?" Why should man have the effrontery to probe "the end of Nature's bashfulness" (483)? Compared to nature, the oldest man's life is scarcely less ephemeral than the youngest's.

At this point, about a hundred lines into the poem, the speaker begins to move about. He shifts the scene from hill to field to riverside, and he turns away from personal meditation to portray first a struggling farmer, then—at length—an ideal student of nature. The inquest into nature is not dropped entirely, but it is pursued in a much different manner for the rest of *The Wanderer*'s considerable length (about 2500 lines). The poem falls into seven sections, grouped according to setting into three main units, "Wood," "Mountain," and "Sea"; and the progression from one to the next is, broadly speaking, a progression from solitude to society, from private to public. "Wood" counterpoints the impressions of the speaker with the portraits of the ideal student of nature and a crotchety hermit, the two of whom, taken together, make up the split image of Thoreau in Channing's mind. "Mountain" describes two social scenes. First, the poet takes an excursion with the hermit to the side of a hillside summerhouse, frequented also by a group of their friends, whose good times are recalled. Next, he camps out with the hermit near the wigwam of an interesting old Indian, and recalls how several acquaintances visited them there. In "Sea," finally, Channing moves beyond personal reminiscence to take in the whole course of history. The prospect of ships at sea calls to mind the spread of western civilization from its beginnings in America, and the colonization of America in particular. A beautiful mansion overlooking the bay, and its well-bred inhabitants, stands as an image in his mind of the attainments of American culture, though the poet cannot quite forget the great social problems which exist outside the charmed circle of the estate. Such intimations call to mind the social responsibility of the artist: he caps his panorama and ends his poem with a vision of the kind of poetry the new age requires: not bardic tales, not classical myth, but "the myth to-day," "the scholar's song" (134,133), based on close observation of nature and contemporary life.

In its design, *The Wanderer* is Channing's most ambitious work. In its execution, though, it is inferior to "Wachusett" and *Near Home,* except for the first section, which seems to me to contain the best poetry Channing ever wrote. Once he moves away from his initial posture of soul- and nature-searching, the poem rapidly loses force; the emotional pressure of the inner dialectic is diffused into set-pieces of description, which get more and more insipid as they get more public and range farther away from Concord.

Eliot is the last major poem in which Channing shows a persona in confrontation with himself and nature. Here the speaker's isolation and withdrawal are extreme: he has been a hermit for almost twenty years, and still he does not feel at home in nature:

> And yet the everlasting voice I hear,
> And never find the silence.   [613]

But there is a special secret to his sorrow. He has killed his rival in love, and banished himself to the wilderness; and as a result of both acts his wife has died of grief. Now he is continually tortured by guilt about the two deaths and by fantasies of the lover and especially the wife, whom he loved dearly despite his neglect of her. The fact that he must kill animals to stay alive is a reminder of his crimes; the stream speaks in the voice of his abandoned children. Even crucifixion, he thinks, would be "Far happier than this slowly dropping rust/Curdling about my unprotected thoughts" (640).[9]

At the end of the poem, he feels himself to be dying. Still as far away as ever from peace of mind, he manages nonetheless to gain a certain satisfaction from looking over the mementos he has with him, including some of the poetry he used to write, and pronouncing a "testament" or epitaph on his life. The following lines are of special interest as an indicator of their author's poetic development.

> In those my early days, amid the trees,
> I thought to raise an altar to the Muse,

[9] This poetic situation can of course be autobiographically interpreted, as both expressing and legitimatizing (as tragic rather than tawdry) Channing's personal loneliness and guilt at mistreating his children and his wife, whose death was hastened by his neglect of her.

And with these lines to consecrate its front,—
The Muse that haunts these bowers and bends their lives.
Time rubs away the outward, leaves within,
Merely the cerements that once owned life.
And, when my numbers failed me, I essayed
To dwell as might some anchorite austere;
O'er the cold stones to drag the nights with prayer,
And mortifying arts the convent knew.   [700–701]

This is the confession of a failed nature poet. Like a good deal of the material in *Eliot* having autobiographical reference, this passage is not particularly relevant to the career of the fictive persona, but it says a lot about the career of his author, and explains some of the differences between *Eliot* and the long pastoral poems discussed before. *Eliot* is not much concerned with guessing at the riddle of nature, with the interplay between the mind of the observer and the thing seen. The restless mind is turned inward; the question of nature's meaning now seems ephemeral compared to the speaker's own spiritual crisis. The thought of nature's calm, constant persistence amid all temporary mutations and suffering occurs to him, but is not enough to draw him away from himself to her, as it was for the speaker of the earlier poems. The tone here is thus much more intense: nervous, self-pitying, distracted, even hysterical at times. This makes for greater force, but not, unhappily, for better poetry. Just as a too heavy dose of descriptiveness in *The Wanderer* leads Channing *away* from sharp imagery and into trite abstractions, so an excess of psychodrama lures him into another sort of conventionalism, the histrionics of Byronism. *Eliot* is Manfred redivivus. To perform at his best, Channing needed to strike a balance between the inner and the outer lives.

The syndrome described in Eliot's speech infected Emerson and Thoreau as well as Channing. All three believed that the success of poetry was dependent upon the poet's insight into nature, and that if this failed his only recourse was a life of austere self-discipline. Indeed, this should be his regular practice, since, as Emerson said, "the sublime vision comes to the pure and simple soul in a clean and chaste body" (*W*, III, 28). But it was terribly frustrating if the visions would not come, as Emerson and Thoreau realized as they aged. Here is the point at which Channing's work supplements theirs most importantly: his frustrations was the keenest; and he owned up to it most candidly, and portrayed it best in his work. Since his writing, like his personality, is less self-restrained than theirs, it is in some ways a more faithful record of their spiritual lives. In particular, its vacillations of mood read more like their journals than their own essays do. Their rambling, aphoristic style gives their essays the appearance of spontaneity, but their tone is almost maddeningly self-assured. The reader knows that this contrast between turbid syntax and confident tone hides something; and it takes Channing—or their journals—to show what it is.

Emerson was right, therefore, when in his review of Channing's early poems he categorized them as "verses of the portfolio," more revealing though less polished than good poetry is.[10] If we may go one step further than this and say that a number of passages in Channing's poetry are also well-written, perhaps some may even be persuaded to follow Emerson's advice and read it.

[10] *Uncollected Writings*, p. 139.

PART IV

THE FIRST PERSON

In the last two sections we have approached Transcendentalist literature as inspired utterance and as a form of nature. The Transcendentalist was no more deeply interested in spirit and nature, however, than he was in the human consciousness which experiences their power and the relationship between them. "Persons alone interest us," affirms Emerson (*JMN*, VIII, 13). "Nothing, not God, is greater to one than one's self is," says the poet in "Song of Myself" (l. 1271). William B. Greene rightly observed that "Transcendentalism sinks God and nature in man," [1] in the sense that the Transcendentalists were ever-conscious of the centrality of the self as receiver of divine and natural influences, and as the initiator of all heroic action—social, literary, or otherwise.

[1] William B. Greene, *Transcendentalism* (West Brookfield, Mass.: Cooke, 1849), p. 5.

It is fitting, therefore, that the last of the three major parts of this study deal with the vision of the self as a subject and as an aspect of technique in Transcendentalist writing. Although the personality of the Transcendentalist writer does not in most cases obtrude in his work, much of the literature of the movement is a literature of self-examination and relies heavily upon the effective use of personae to convey its characteristic views of the self. The following chapters will attempt first to relate those views and ways of speaking about the self to the autobiographical traditions which the Transcendentalist inherited, and then to concentrate on the literary use of the first person in the four most interesting cases: Emerson, Thoreau, Very, and Whitman.

10 Transcendentalist Self-Examination and Autobiographical Tradition

Unlovely, nay, frightful is the solitude of the soul which is without God in the world.

—Emerson

A recent critic of Melville has rightly remarked that "the American writer continually sings a 'Song of Myself.' "[1] A number of American literary classics are autobiographies, from Benjamin Franklin to Richard Wright. In Afro-American literature, autobiography is the dominant genre; the tradition of the slave narratives of the nineteenth century has its contemporary analogues in Eldridge Cleaver and Malcolm X. Much of the best American fiction is also first-person narrative, in which the persona often seems strongly autobiographical: *Moby-Dick, The Great Gatsby, The Sun Also Rises,* and *Invisible Man* are representative examples. American poetry is overwhelmingly lyric; American drama—the genre least compatible with the autobiographical impulse—virtually nonexistent before the First World War.

It is not hard to conceive of reasons for the American preoccupation with the self. First, the ideology of individualism encourages interest in the careers of single persons, especially those which re-enact such culture myths as the American dream of success or the pioneer's conquest of nature. Another stimulus has been the tradition of religious self-examination imported

[1] Edgar A. Dryden, *Melville's Thematics of Form: The Great Art of Telling the Truth* (Baltimore: Johns Hopkins University Press, 1968), p. 19.

from Europe in the colonial period, which produced the *Personal Narrative* of Jonathan Edwards, the *Journal* of John Woolman and countless other pious diaries and conversion narratives running well into the nineteenth century. During that century, in the third place, the interest in self was quickened by the influence of the romantic movement, under whose auspices was first produced in America a literature worthy of the name, and which still remains our dominant tradition. It was during the romantic era that the diary and the autobiography became significant as literary forms, on both sides of the Atlantic.

More puzzling than the presence of a strong autobiographic tendency in American writing is the lack of critical attention to it. Though individualism as a subject and as a life-style for American authors has long been a topic of analysis, seldom has it been discussed in relation to rhetoric and genre except to support the very general thesis that American writing is oriented against tradition and towards experience and experiment. Only in the last few years has there arisen a significant body of scholarship on the characteristic techniques, motifs, and conventions in American autobiographical writing.[2] The most logical explanation for prior neglect is simply the relative underdevelopment of theoretical criticism of autobiography. Modern formalist criticism was naturally first attracted to poetry, then to drama and prose fiction; only now that it has ceased to make significant new advances in those areas has it turned its attention to less purely aesthetic genres.[3]

[2] I am thinking especially of Robert Sayre, *The Examined Self: Benjamin Franklin, Henry Adams, Henry James* (Princeton: Princeton University Press, 1964); Daniel B. Shea Jr., *Spiritual Autobiography in Early America* (Princeton: Princeton University Press, 1968); and David L. Minter, *The Interpreted Design as a Structural Principle in American Prose* (New Haven: Yale University Press, 1969), which deals broadly with first-person narrative.

[3] For the theory of criticism of autobiography, the works which have helped me most have been Roy Pascal, *Design and Truth in Autobiography* (Cambridge: Harvard University Press, 1960); John Morris, *Versions*

So far the new scholarship in American autobiographical writing has dealt mainly with individual examples; a complete survey is called for. When it is written, the American romantic period, and particularly the Transcendentalist movement, is sure to come in for extended treatment. To begin with, it was in Transcendentalist writing that the three traditions just mentioned—spiritual self-examination, romantic self-consciousness, and democratic individualism—converged for the first time in American history, with the result that the self became a more important entity for the Transcendentalists than for any of their forbears. They were acutely conscious of living in "the age of the first person singular," when, as Emerson put it,

the poet is not content to see how "Fair hangs the apple from the rock," "What music a sunbeam awoke in the groves," nor of Hardiknute, how

"Stately stept he east the wa,
And stately stept he west,"

but he now revolves, What is the apple to me? and what the birds to me? and what is Hardiknute to me? and what am I? [*W*, XII, 312]

This appraisal, shared by all the Transcendentalists, led them to take great interest in literary representations of the self, in accordance with Schiller's maxim that whereas the "simple" or primitive poet merely imitates Nature, the "sentimental" or modern poet *"reflects* on the impression produced on him by objects; and it is only on this reflection that his poetic force is based." [4] The Transcendentalists tended to disdain the novel, somewhat moralistically, as frivolous and artificial, but they

of the Self: Studies in English Autobiography from John Bunyan to John Stuart Mill (New York: Basic Books, 1966); Wayne Shumaker, *English Autobiography: Its Emergence, Materials, and Form* (Berkeley: University of California Press, 1954); and Francis Hart, "Notes for an Anatomy of Modern Autobiography," *New Literary History*, 1 (1970), 485–511.

[4] "Simple and Sentimental Poetry," *Essays Aesthetical and Philosophical* (London: George Bell, 1884), p. 289.

appreciated fiction as a revelation of character. "True" histories they prized. Emerson and Alcott agreed in 1838 that auto-biography was the best kind of book (*JMN*, V, 99). "Is not the poet bound to write his own biography?" Thoreau asked. "Is there any other work for him but a good journal?" (*JT*, X, 115). "Writing is worthless except as the record of a life," declared Margaret Fuller. One's "book should be only an indication of himself." [5] Small wonder, then, that the editorial preface to *The Dial* concluded with the resolution "not to multiply books, but to report life":

Our resources are therefore not so much the pens of practised writers, as the discourse of the living, and the portfolios which friendship has opened to us. From the beautiful recesses of private thought; from the experience and hopes of spirits which are withdrawing from all old forms; and seeking in all that is new somewhat to meet their inappeasable longings; from the secret confession of genius afraid to trust itself to aught but sympathy; from the conversations of fervid and mystical pietists; from tear-stained diaries of sorrow and passion; from the manuscripts of young poets; and from the records of youthful taste commenting on old works of art, we hope to draw thoughts and feelings, which being alive can impart life. [*Tr*, p. 250]

Such a statement of intent, however, conveys a misleading impression of the kind of writing the Transcendentalists actually did. This is a second, more idiosyncratic aspect of their handling of the first person which invites analysis. Although they attached great theoretical importance to the self, most of what they themselves wrote seems quite impersonal, including their own private journals. Their poetry is highly intellectual; their prose metaphysical rather than familiar. The most egoistic movement in American literary history produced no first-rate autobiography, unless one counts *Walden* as such. The same is even more embarrassingly true of Transcendentalist attempts at

[5] *Life Without and Life Within,* ed. Arthur B. Fuller (Boston: Brown, Taggard and Chase, 1860), p. 26.

autobiographical fiction: Brownson's *Charles Elwood,* William Channing's *Ernest the Seeker,* Ellery Channing's *The Youth of the Poet and the Painter,* and Margaret Fuller's short stories. The great journals of Emerson and Thoreau are superior specimens of their kind, but because of their brilliance of thought and description, not for their intimate disclosures. The caveat with which Richard Henry Dana, Jr., prefaces his journal might apply to the Transcendentalists also: "I shall set down nothing here which is untrue," he says, but some things he will keep to himself, for "our Maker knows & each man's own soul knows that there are thoughts & intents of the heart, sometimes put forth in act, which no man would be willing or need or ought to open to all observers." [6]

Though one certainly finds differences among Transcendentalists, such as Emerson and Thoreau, in respect to personal tone, all shared a basic inhibition about revealing themselves. It was not so much a Victorian sense of propriety which restrained them, although that did enter in, as it was a matter of principle. If the first axiom of Transcendentalist thought was that the individual is potentially divine, the second was that the individual is valuable only sub specie aeternatis, in his universal aspects. At the meetings of the Transcendental Club, Alcott recalled, "It was the fashion to speak against personality . . . and the favorite phrase was 'Impersonality.'" [7] Emerson maintained simultaneously that "the soul's emphasis is always right" (*W,* II, 145) and that "the individual is always mistaken" (*W,* III, 69). This led to a rather strict self-censorship policy. "That which is individual & remains individual in my experi-

[6] *The Journal of Richard Henry Dana, Jr.,* ed. Robert F. Lucid (Cambridge: Harvard University Press), I, 3.

[7] "Alcott's 'Conversation' on the Transcendental Club and *The Dial,*" ed. Clarence Gohdes, *American Literature,* 3 (1931), 17. Alcott's biographers point out that he disagreed with Emerson on the subject of personality, believing—especially in his later years—in a more personal relation between individual and God than Emerson would admit.

ence is of no value," he writes in his journal. "What is fit to engage me & so engage others permanently, is what has put off its weeds of time & place & personal relation" (*JMN*, VII, 65). Emerson was somewhat distressed by the "mountainous ME" which Margaret Fuller projected (*Ossoli*, I, 236). But Fuller herself also favored a certain amount of literary restraint. "You may tell the world at large what you please," she advised a young essayist, "if you make it of universal importance by transporting it into the field of general human interest. But your private griefs, merely *as* yours, belong to yourself, your nearest friends, to Heaven and to nature." [8]

The criterion of representativeness, however, did not prevent the Transcendentalists from the appreciation and continual practice of first-person writing. Emerson made the definitive comment on this score in his distinction between true and false subjectivity. A writer's use of the "I," he says in "Thoughts on Modern Literature," is to be welcomed or censured according to whether his work "leads us to Nature, or to the person of the writer. The great always introduce us to facts: small men introduce us always to themselves. The great man, even whilst he relates a private fact personal to him, is really leading us away from him to an universal experience" (*W*, XII, 314–315). Though here as always Emerson deprecates subjective experience as such in favor of the universal truth it contains, he gives his general approval to the "subjectiveness" of modern literature as a hopeful sign, marking "the uprise of the soul" (313). Thus the leading Transcendentalists, despite their distrust of egoism, relied heavily on first-person approaches and thereby helped to prepare the way for the culmination of romantic egoism in America, *Leaves of Grass*. This is the third and most far-reaching reason why Transcendentalist writing is of interest to the historian of American self-consciousness. Though its definition of the self was too pietistic to produce a full-blooded tradition of autobiography, the notion of the link (and the discrepancy) between the personal "I" and the cosmic "I" did

[8] *Life Without and Life Within*, p. 69.

lead to some interesting and significant first-person strategies, which as we shall see later on, became an integral part of the American literary heritage through *Walden* and *Leaves of Grass*.

The Transcendentalist paradox of self-preoccupation versus self-transcendence has its origins in the three traditions of democratic, romantic, and (especially) Protestant thought. As students of romanticism have pointed out, "Subjectivity was not the program but the inescapable condition of romanticism," the central problem which it had to confront and overcome as a result of the legacy of eighteenth century mechanism, which seemed to alienate the human spirit from the universe.[9] In romanticist literature, therefore, subjectivity "becomes the subject of poems which *qua* poetry seek to transmute it," as Geoffrey Hartman says.[10] The poet's basic faith is that if only he looks far enough inward, or merges himself with the world-soul through nature, he will reach the unconscious or universal. Thus for Wordsworth and Coleridge, just as for Emerson and Thoreau, the sense of being spiritually isolated is tragic, and Byron is the most somber of all the English romantics in those works which are most obsessively self-conscious. English and American romantics, in general, seem to have been more aware of the risks of self-consciousness than their European counterparts, which is perhaps why they did not accept the epithet "romantic."[11]

[9] Robert Langbaum, *The Poetry of Experience* (New York: Norton, 1963), p. 28.

[10] "Romanticism and 'Anti-Self-Consciousness,'" in Harold Bloom, ed., *Romanticism and Consciousness* (New York: Norton, 1970), p. 53. Several other essays in this excellent collection, notably Bloom's "The Internalization of Quest-Romance," also shed light on the subject. For comparisons between English, French, and German romanticism vis-à-vis individualism and self-consciousness, see Lillian Furst, *Romanticism in Perspective* (New York: St. Martin's Press, 1969), p. 55–115.

[11] Those Transcendentalists who use the term, Emerson and Fuller, following Goethe, declare a preference for the "Classic" over the "Ro-

The tradition of religious confessional valued the personal self even less than the romantic, inasmuch as the writer was chiefly preoccupied with seeing his life in relation to a paradigm of grace. He attached no intrinsic importance, for example, to originality, individualism, literary innovation; if anything, these betokened vanity or perverseness. The religious autobiographer, as Daniel Shea says of the Puritans, tended to make "Providence the chief character of his narrative, his own life merely the setting for its actions." [12] That is why so many conversion narratives read like imitations of each other, even those of some writers with demonstrable literary talent, like Edward Taylor. The spiritual journal was less likely to become stereotyped, being more taken up with day-to-day events, but it too was interested in these events not for their own sake but as providential tokens.

"Democratic individualism," finally, is also something of an oxymoron. It means mass rule as much as it does individual freedom. Tocqueville even went so far as to claim that "freedom of opinion does not exist in America"—which he thought was the reason why America had not produced any great writers.[13] The broadening of the base of political power that took place during the Jacksonian era was an acknowledgment of the dignity of the individual, but it also ensured that the particular citizen would have less influence in the political process than formerly. Most of the Transcendentalists found this trend somewhat confusing (to the extent that they thought about it

---

mantic," associating the first with universality and the second with idiosyncratic caprice on the writer's part (*W*, XII, 303–305; *Life Without and Life Within*, pp. 129–131).

[12] *Spiritual Autobiography in Early America*, p. 119. An earlier discussion which deals with the individual versus typical qualities of the diary and the autobigraphy in early America is Kenneth Murdock, *Literature and Theology in Colonial New England* (New York: Harper, 1963), pp. 99–135.

[13] *Democracy in America*, ed. Phillips Bradley (New York: Knopf, 1945), I, 275.

at all), because their notion of the dignity of the individual was conditioned by an elitist upbringing (either moral elitism or social elitism or both), which also made them feel threatened by "the people" or "the great mass" as an actual force. At heart, most of them were for natural aristocracy rather than egalitarianism. At the same time, individualism for them had to be validated by its representativeness: genius is a larger imbiding of the common heart; civil disobedience must be grounded on divine law, and so forth. This awareness is what differentiates, say, Emerson's *Representative Men* from Carlyle's *Heroes and Hero-Worship*. The same doubleness characterizes a number of the classic American autobiographies, which explicitly or implicitly view the life of the writer in the context of his times. Franklin, Henry Adams, and Richard Wright are cases in point. The hero (or anti-hero) is such essentially by virtue of his re-enactment of the national experience.

To relate Transcendentalism's paradoxical attitude toward self-consciousness to the three traditions which informed it does not, however, explain the peculiarities of Transcendentalist style. One may still ask, for example, why the closest thing to *The Prelude* which the movement produced was Alcott's vapid *New Connecticut,* why the closest approach to *Manfred* was Ellery Channing's *Eliot*. How is it, too, that most of what the Transcendentalists wrote about themselves lacks both the fervor and the immediacy of such classics of spiritual self-analysis as *Grace Abounding* or the *Journal* of George Fox? And why, in an age of intense national self-consciousness, didn't they take more of a literary interest in themselves as Americans, or at least New Englanders?

To answer these questions fully would carry us far afield. Just as a start, we would need to make a complete juxtaposition of Transcendentalist aesthetics, religion, and social attitudes with those of the English romantics on the one hand and the rest of the New England intellectual establishment from the Mathers to the Adamses on the other. But an adequate conception of literary self-consciousness in Transcendentalist writings, for our purposes, can be derived from picturing the Transcendentalists primarily as inheritors of the tradition of spiritual self-examination. Their lives were too interior for the third sort of approach; none were public figures, few were much interested in politics or society except sporadically. Nor, as we have seen, were they greatly interested, like the English romantics, in the literary ordering of experience, except as a reflection of a prior ordering in nature and the life of the writer. Here again, the Transcendentalists differed from the English romantics in taking the notions of the latter more literally—in this case, the cult of sincerity.[14] Their main motive for introspection was self-improvement, in which respect they were the heirs of the Puritans.

The most obvious literary sign of this link is the diary. "In the tradition of New England," Perry Miller has said with little exaggeration, "it was respectable—nay, even imperative—that youths compose diaries."[15] In Edward T. Channing's rhetoric course at Harvard, one of the old standbys for paper topics was "The Advantages of Keeping a Journal." Henry Thoreau dutifully (and prophetically) noted three. In ascending order of importance they were: (1) "preservation of our scattered thoughts"; (2) self-expression; and inevitably (3) self-improvement.[16] Whatever the direct influence of such environmental conditioning, every major Transcendentalist kept a diary and/or commonplace book—Emerson, Alcott, Thoreau, Fuller, Parker, and Charles King Newcomb being the most significant

[14] For an interesting parallel case, see Patricia M. Ball, *The Central Self* (London: Athlone Press, 1968), pp. 152–165, which argues that the Victorians extended the idea of sincerity far beyond what the Romantics had in mind.

[15] Introduction to *Consciousness in Concord* (Boston: Houghton Mifflin, 1958), p. 46.

[16] F. B. Sanborn, *The Life of Henry David Thoreau* (Boston: Houghton Mifflin 1917), pp. 73–74, prints the essay.

writers in this vein. Like their forefathers, they approached journal-writing as a solemn task. "In thy journals let there never be a jest!" wrote Thoreau (*JT*, III, 222), and indeed there aren't many—certainly much fewer than in his essays.

Journalizing was a more complex and difficult affair for the Transcendentalists than for their ancestors, however. The latter undeniably fretted more about the state of their souls, but they were sustained by a common and fairly clear-cut notion of the process of conversion and sanctification and the rhetoric with which to describe it. They did not have to ask who they were and what value of an individual was, but simply how they stood in relation to the state of grace—which was a big question, to be sure, but a much more clearly defined one. It is instructive to compare Transcendentalist journalizing with the spiritual diary of a latter-day Puritan who was their near contemporary, the Reverend Edward Payson of Portland, Maine (1783–1827), a saint well known in Orthodox circles of the day.

Feb. 8 [1806]. There is no vice, of which I do not see the seeds in myself, and which would bear fruit, did not grace prevent. Notwithstanding this, I am perpetually pulling the mote out of my brother's eye.

Feb. 9. Was much favored in prayer, and still more in reading the Bible. Every word seemed to come home with power. Of late, I have none of those rapturous feelings, which used to be so transporting; but I enjoy a more calm and equable degree of comfort; and, though slowly, yet surely, find myself advancing.

. . . . .

Feb. 16. Very dull and lifeless in the morning. Made a resolution to restrain my temper, and the next moment broke it. Felt more lively at meeting. In the afternoon and evening, was remarkably favored. I felt such an overwhelming sense of God's amazing goodness, and my own unworthiness, as I never had before. . . .

Feb. 19. What a poor, weak, unstable creature I am, when Christ is absent! Read Baxter's Saints' Rest; but, though it is very affectingly written, I was totally unmoved by it.

Payson was, understandably, regarded by his audience as morbid but exhilaratingly pious.[17] The record of his emotional ups and downs gives an impression of hypersensitivity but also of unremitting steadfastness that is unapproached in Transcendentalist writing, except by the later journals of Thoreau. Most Transcendentalist diaries are comparatively varied and miscellaneous in subject and style. They lack momentum; they are more interesting in patches than in their progressive unfolding.

Payson should not, of course, be taken as typical of all Puritan diarists; but he does epitomize the qualities which most differentiate traditional spiritual autobiography from what the Transcendentalists wrote. He was one of the last figures in the New England intellectual establishment to be able to maintain, in all its purity and naiveté, the conventional Calvinist self-image or persona of "the chief of sinners," to use Bunyan's phrase. The exact character of this persona varies from Bunyan's self-flagellations to William Cowper's mild abjectness to Jonathan Edwards' mystical adoration, but the type is recognizable. By 1830, however, this way of proceeding had begun to seem quaint and artificial, even to Calvinist readers. In explanation of the masochistic tone of another minister's diary, a reviewer in *The Spirit of the Pilgrims* emphasized that "a "self-examiner, with pen in hand, is a very different creature from a self-examiner empty-handed." [18] The Reverend Henry Martyn castigated himself so unwontedly, the reviewer speculates, because he knew that his diary might some day be published! Surely some of Cotton Mather's audience must have felt the same thing a century before; the interesting feature of the review is that the suspicion is publicly aired in a conservative sectarian journal.

The Transcendentalists, who felt this sort of skepticism very

[17] Asa Cummings, *A Memoir of the Rev. Edward Payson, D.D.*, 5th ed. (Boston: Crocker and Brewster, 1832), p. 49–50, iv–v.

[18] Review of *A Memoir of the Rev. Henry Martyn*, *Spirit of the Pilgrims,* 4 (1831), 430.

keenly, distrusted not only the old rhetorical and doctrinal formulas, but also the very idea of a structured spiritual development. They did have a general conception of life as a process of spiritual improvement or self-culture, which they saw as being helped along by cultivation of morality and self-discipline, but what really excited them was not process or method but spiritual experience per se, the significant moment, the intuitive perception. Even some of those who paid most attention to empirical method, like Parker and Thoreau, were quick to point out the uselessness of that method in matters of faith or spiritual experience. This perhaps explains why none of the Transcendentalists, except for Brownson, ever wrote anything like a conversion narrative—that sort of fiction was simply too plot-oriented for their tastes. (On the other hand, their inability to reduce their own spiritual lives to order may be one reason why they were addicted to writing memoirs of each other.)

Speaking more generally, one might say that the shift in spiritual orientation made the element of self-consciousness in Transcendentalist writing more complex, more literary, and less intimate than in traditional spiritual autobiography. First and most obviously, the sense of self in Transcendentalist writing is more complex because its field of inquiry is not centered in a supernatural frame of reference. "Well, & what do you project?" Emerson asks in his journal. "Nothing less than to look at every object in its relation to Myself" (*JMN*, IV, 272). Of course this objective is not exhaustively carried out, but one does see the Transcendentalists moving in this direction, from an I-Thou relationship with Spirit to an I-Nature relationship; and to the extent that they do, their inner lives become more diffuse. Spiritual health now seems to consist in perceiving the divinity in as many different shapes as possible, not in regular encounters in one's prayer closet. Every circumstance, every emotional nuance was potentially of spiritual import. In a sense the same was true for the Puritans, but the

Transcendentalists differed in at least two ways. First, they came closer to believing that all phenomena were of equal relevance (one recalls Emerson's insistence that a gnat is as good a metaphor for God as a Lord of Hosts); second, and more important, the Transcendentalists felt actively compelled to seek out and perceive significance in phenomena. The sense of spiritual torpor which gave rise to much of the guilt-feeling in Payson and other Puritan self-examiners has its counterpart in Transcendentalist confessions of failure of perception. "Set ten men to write their journal for one day, and nine of them will leave out their thought, or proper result,—that is, their net experience,—and lose themselves in misreporting the supposed experience of other people" (*W*, VIII, 308). This remark of Emerson's is a new sort of complaint for the spiritual diarist: Edward Payson had his troubles but at least he did not have to question whether what he was recording was original with him.

Equally significant are Transcendentalist confessions of inability to synthesize or articulate their perceptions. "Thoughts of different dates will not cohere," Thoreau noted (*JT*, III, 288). Like Emerson, whose mixed feelings about his own incoherence have already been shown, Thoreau could only take refuge in the fact that Nature herself "strews her nuts and flowers broadcast, and never collects them into heaps" (I, 200). The pages of the most voluminous journalizer of the group, Alcott, are filled with similar confessions of inadequacy. At times he is smug: "No important thought, emotion, or purpose, has transpired within me, that has not been noted therein," he says of his diary for the first half of 1839. But by the end of the year he discovers that though "I have written out myself more fully during this, than any previous year of my life," "my chronicle gives me little satisfaction. I do not yet copy the best passages of my spiritual being. I have not yet mastered the art of drawing. . . . I am a spectre moving in Infinitude, devoid of flesh & blood." [19]

[19] Alcott, "Diary from January to July 1839," p. 948, MS 59M–308 (12); "Diary for 1839 from July to December," p. 502, MS 59M–308 (13), Houghton Library, Harvard University.

As the foregoing examples show, the journals of Emerson, Thoreau, and Alcott—like much of Transcendentalist writing —aspire to an encyclopedic quality, to take in the whole range of human experience, which inevitably they fail to do. They are defeated by their own commitment to spontaneity, to recording their impressions moment by moment. One is left in each case with the image of a somewhat nebulous, unformed soul. The same is true also of Theodore Parker's diary, whose most common motif is "I know not what will come of it," [20] and the surviving fragments of Margaret Fuller's journal in the *Memoirs of Margaret Fuller Ossoli*. In the journals of Ellery Channing and Charles King Newcomb, the sense of frustration erupts into self-loathing. Both feel the awkwardness of writing about themselves; both are plagued by the awareness of the superficiality of their records. "Indefinite I was born—indefinite I shall die," wails Channing.[21]

The sorts of complaints we have just been hearing point to a much more literary interest in journalizing than had traditionally been the case. Witness Alcott's desire to master "the art of drawing." Although their immediate purpose for writing diaries was to preserve their memorable experiences and explain themselves to themselves, all except for Parker had the long-range hope of using this material for literary purposes. Alcott, for

[20] Parker's is the only major Transcendentalist journal which is yet unpublished, except in very brief excerpts. It consists of some twenty-two volumes, covering the period 1835 to 1860, all but one of which are housed in the Library of Congress, the Andover-Harvard Theological Library, or the Massachusetts Historical Society. (For a list of Parker's journals and where each is located, see Herbert Hudson, "Recent Interpretations of Parker: An Evaluation of the Literature Since 1936," *Proceedings of the Unitarian Historical Society*, 13 [1960], 38). Parker journalized irregularly, interspersing notes from his reading, sermon outlines, and autobiographical tidbits. The result is not of great literary interest, but does shed considerable light on Parker and Transcendentalism generally, as do Parker's unpublished letters.

[21] Ms. Journal, "Out-of-door Life," p. 9, bMS Am 800.6, Houghton Library.

example, praised "the habit of journalizing" as "a life-long lesson taken in the art of composition, an informal schooling for
authorship." [22] Thoreau declared quite frankly his intent "to
set down such choice experiences that my own writings may
inspire me and at last I may make wholes of parts" (*JT*, III,
217). Emerson saw his journal as a "Savings Bank" (*JMN*, IV,
250). Hence one often finds the Transcendentalist journalizers
applying a considerable degree of craftsmanship to copying
and recopying, revising, indexing, excerpting "gems" and trans-
ferring them to other notebooks. In Alcott's journal especially
are frequent entries of this sort: "I write Diary all day," "Copy
Diary," "I write Diary all day again," etc. (*JA*, p. 305–306). The
characteristic Transcendentalist pattern of composition, established by Emerson and imitated with varying degrees of success
by Alcott, Thoreau, and Channing, was of course a threefold
process of revision from journal to lecture to essay.

  The literary pretensions of the Transcendentalist diarists help
to explain why their journals are less intimate than those of
their forbears. Certainly Payson lays bare his heart a great deal
more extensively than Emerson and Thoreau. As Alcott said
of Emerson, Transcendentalist journals might better be called
"commonplace books," if one extends that term to apply not
only to passages culled from other authors but choice insights
of the writer's own. Emerson's journals, as Alcott noted, "are
full of elegant sketches of life and nature. . . . He does not
record the history of his facts, but idealizes whatsoever he observes and writes his thought in this general form. He works like
an artist from his sketches and models" (*JA*, p. 126). Again the
metaphor of the journalizer as artist. We must be careful of
stereotyping here: Alcott's own journals, despite his literary
aspirations, differ from Emerson's in including a great amount
of biographical and autobiographical trivia—which is what
makes them the single richest storehouse of Transcendentalist
gossip ever written. In this respect, Alcott and Emerson stand

  [22] Bronson Alcott, *Table-Talk* (Boston: Roberts, 1877), p. 12.

almost at opposite poles among Transcendentalist journalizers and dramatize the considerable variety which did in fact exist among them. Nevertheless Alcott too is clearly more interested in memorializing his ideas, his significant perceptions, than he is in painting a full-length, flesh-and-blood portrait of himself like a Boswell or a Rousseau.

The interest is not to be explained only or even primarily in terms of the diarist's literary objectives, of course. The basic reason for it is religious. In traditional religious confessional the entity of the self (one aspect of it, that is) is necessarily more particularized than in Transcendentalist writing, because the main subject of interest is the dealings of God with a particular so-and-so, whereas for the Transcendentalist the primary subject is the relation of mankind, of which so-and-so is a representative, to the rest of the universe. On the face of it, to argue in this manner that the Transcendentalists were *less* interested in the self than the Puritans seems quite paradoxical, given the fact that the former proclaimed the potential divinity of the individual and the latter were neo-Calvinists. The solution seems to lie, first, in the Transcendentalists' distrust of supernaturalism: for instance, particular providences and the doctrine of election. As democrats in the spiritual realm they did not believe in a special relationship between an individual and a personal God, or if they did (and Parker, Fuller and Alcott in old age are cases in point) they felt it most important to stress the universality of such an experience. Similarly they were less likely to interpret phenomena in the visible universe as having explicit reference to themselves and their community.

In the second place, because of their more liberal religious views the Transcendentalists were also less liable to experience the overwhelming soul-struggles which make traditional confessions from Augustine to Bunyan to Payson seem such "personal" documents. They do of course confess to feelings of spiritual malaise, but for the most part they exhibit a basic serenity or optimism about their spiritual state which keeps their vision focused on the design of the universe rather than their own alienation from it.

In concluding this discussion of Transcendentalist literary self-consciousness, we might briefly look beyond the genre of spiritual self-examination and take note of how, in general, the Transcendentalists fit into the trend toward increasing self-consciousness in western literature as a whole during the nineteenth century. For it was the century between roughly 1750 and 1850 that saw the emergence of biography, autobiography, fictional characterization, and lyric poetry in the modern senses.

Authorities on the subject of autobiographical writing agree that the most distinctive feature of the modern period is its emphasis on the self in all its psychological complexity. For John N. Morris there is a direct link between spiritual self-examination and this modern attitude: essentially " 'self' is the modern word for 'soul.' " Morris regards Wordsworth and John Stuart Mill, for example, as repeating in a secular context "the religious melancholy and conversions set down in the autobiographies of earlier heroes of religion." [23] Of course there is a difference in kind between the paradigmatic quality of the confessant's spiritual development and the sense of the unfolding of a unique self in such writers as Rousseau and Mill. Wayne Shumaker has a provocative explanation for this on philosophical grounds:

Until a mechanistic or naturalistic universe came to be posited, it was impossible that autobiography should attempt to *account for* the personal uniqueness of its subject. . . . But when determinism began increasingly, and, among authors, almost regularly, to be postulated of human life, as well as of nonhuman nature, autobiographers—many of whom, like Darwin, Huxley, Galton, Bray, Mill, Spencer, and Wallace, were either scientists or scientific philosophers—began to feel it their duty not only to describe how the in-

[23] *Versions of the Self,* pp. 6, 5.

dividual life was lived, but also to explain why it was necessarily lived so and not otherwise.[24]

This hypothesis is clearly oversimple (for example, there is a kind of determinism operative in Calvinist thought), but it is useful as a way of pointing up the nature and limits of Transcendentalist self-consciousness and, I think, of the romantic movement in general. The Transcendentalists started with the conception of the individual as unique and the intention of formulating their own special views of the world empirically by accumulating significant perceptions; but they were resolved not to rest in the conception of a deterministic universe and a spiritually isolated individual which eighteenth-century thought seemed to impose upon them and which to later generations seemed inevitable. Their interest quickly shifted, therefore, from phenomena which evidenced personal uniqueness to that which evidenced the divinity or the universality of the individual. All the writers we are about to examine are deeply interested in converting the "I" from a fallible personality into an authoritative voice. Emerson prophesies; Thoreau creates a semiautobiographical hero; Very identifies himself with the Trinity; Whitman projects himself as a mythic figure. We must now see how these strategies work in detail.

[24] *English Autobiography,* pp. 89–90.

11 Emerson and Thoreau: Soul versus Self

When comparing Emerson and Thoreau one inevitably wants to see the two men as representing the complementary sides of Transcendental individualism. Thoreau was self-reliant; Emerson was God-reliant. Emerson was diffident, Thoreau pugnacious. Emerson's essays seem comparatively diaphanous and impersonal; Thoreau's are concrete and crotchety. Roughly speaking, Thoreau seems to epitomize the colorful, abrasive, renegade side of the movement, along with Parker, Brownson, Ellery Channing, and perhaps Margaret Fuller; Emerson seems rather to speak for the more genteel, refined, contemplative side, along with most of the Transcendentalist ministers and Bronson Alcott.

Since the main basis for these stereotypical images of Thoreau and Emerson is their literary presence, a comparative study of the use of the speaking voice in their prose would seem to be the most direct way of getting beyond the usual generalizations to a fuller sense of what "Emerson" and "Thoreau" really are like, as literary figures.

Almost nothing has been written about the persona in Emerson's essays, because it has been almost universally assumed that there is none. Emerson's abstractness, his frequent ex cathedra disparagements of egoism, and his reputation for personal reticence and aloofness have led his readers to accept without cavil the verdict of his son: that autobiographical "incidents are gen-

eralized and personality merged in a type" (*W*, XII, 470–471n).
To be sure, it has been shown that Emerson's literary style is
sufficiently idiosyncratic to give a personal stamp to all he wrote.
Both originality with language is not the same thing as individuality of character. However strongly one responds to Emerson
the writer as a subtle intellect or original artist, it is quite
another thing to think of his writings as personal disclosures. I
suspect that we tend to question his individualism in life so
much more quickly than Thoreau's partly because we assume
that with respect to his literary persona Emerson *is* a generalized
abstraction and wished to be taken as such. He may give us
idealized self-portraits, like the Scholar or the Poet, but not direct self-revelation; he may allude to personal experience, but
only for the sake of illustration.[1]

But is the traditional view wholly faithful to the facts? Perhaps the best way to begin the inquiry is to consider Emerson's
method of transposing thoughts and experiences from life to
diary to lecture to essay. Among the thousands upon thousands
of instances, the majority do seem to follow his declared purpose
of winnowing away the circumstantial from the universal, to

[1] Very little has been written about any aspect of the Emersonian persona. Among Emerson's contemporaries, Brownson was alone in feeling
that his essays "often remind us of Montaigne, especially in the little
personal allusions, which the author introduces with inimitable grace,
delicacy, and effect" ("Emerson's *Essays*," *Boston Quarterly Review*, 4
[1841], 308). The only sustained modern discussion of the speaker in the
essays, so far as I know, is Jonathan Bishop's provocative chapter on
"Tone," in *Emerson on the Soul* (Cambridge: Harvard University Press,
1964), pp. 128–143, though even it is devoted to exploring Emerson's tonal
richness and variety rather than the persona itself. Another part of
Bishop's study which stimulated my discussion, again in a different direction, is his reading of the first chapter of *Nature* (pp. 10–15). For an interesting study using quantitative methods to identify personality traits of
Emerson and Thoreau through their work, see Albert Gilman and Roger
Brown, "Personality and Style in Concord," *Transcendentalism and Its
Legacy*, ed. Myron Simon and Thornton H. Parsons (Ann Arbor: Uni-
versity of Michigan Press, 1966), pp. 87–122.

the point that one often cannot tell without the aid of the Journals that the passage derives from an actual experience. Take for example this sentence from *Nature:* "In the tranquil landscape, and especially in the distant line of the horizon, man beholds somewhat as beautiful as his own nature" (*W*, I, 10). This *could* be a purely cerebral improvisation, especially the figure of the horizon as symbolic of the circumference of the soul. As it happens, the sentence derives from a particular experience. The journal for August 12, 1836, reads: "I went to Walden Pond this evening a little before sunset, and in the tranquil landscape I behold somewhat as beautiful as my own nature" (*JMN*, V, 189). But in revising, Emerson eliminates local detail, adds intellectual complexity (the horizon metaphor), and turns a personal experience into a general proposition. Indeed the result is even more abstract than it needs to be—the rest of the paragraph in which it is placed is first-person. Altogether it would seem that in transposing Emerson's mind was not on the experience itself but on the subtle formulation into which he was able to convert it. And so the passage gains in literary charm but at the cost of some immediacy.

But if we look at the rest of the paragraph to which the sentence serves as the conclusion, we get a different impression. Its high points are two instances of inspiration through nature, both reported by a persona: the metamorphosis into transparent eyeball, and the sensation of joy upon crossing the common. The second experience is more generalized, taking place merely "in the woods," anytime, anywhere; Emerson tries to recreate the sense of the infinite mainly through rhetorical flourish. The first is localized—on "a bare common, in snow puddles, at twilight, under a clouded sky"—and relies more upon the imagery for its impact. Both passages happen to be reworkings of journal antecedents; and interestingly, in the journal versions there is no appreciable difference between the two, in rhetorical level. For purposes of publication, Emerson inflated the second and made the first more homely. Passage two originated with a feeling "as I walked in the woods" on March 19, 1835 (*JMN*, V, 18);

in revising, Emerson softened the sense of specificity and added such ornmentation as the symbolic eyeball, which is not in the Journal. But the original version of the other passage reads simply "I rejoice in Time. I do not cross the common without a wild poetic delight notwithstanding the prose of my demeanour" (*JMN*, IV, 355). This is less personal, less anecdotal than the corresponding sentence in *Nature*. Contrary to what one might expect from Emerson's strictures about the use of the subjective in art, he revised this passage so as to increase the illusion of autobiography.

Indeed, the whole chapter seems designed to do the same thing. Richard Francis observes that it functions in the structure of *Nature* as a counterweight to Emerson's preliminary definitions, as "a highly personal statement about how we perceive what has just been defined." [2] The message it seems to convey is: reader, whatever we conclude from the formal analysis of nature that will follow, the original relation to the universe exists, for I have experienced it. Perhaps the chapter is called "Nature" for that reason: because the experiences there described epitomize the philosophy of the whole book.

Emerson does not make this point overbearingly. On the contrary, he takes some pains to make his speaker represent our experiences too. For instance, the chapter begins:

To go into solitude, a man needs to retire as much from his chamber as from society. I am not solitary whilst I read and write, though nobody is with me. But if a man would be alone, let him look at the stars. [*W*, I, 7]

By alternating here between "I" and "a man," and by making "I" the subject of a proposition we can easily accept, Emerson

---

[2] "The Architectonics of Emerson's *Nature*," *American Quarterly*, 19 (1967), 44; rpt. in Merton M. Sealts, Jr., and Alfred R. Ferguson, *Emerson's "Nature": Origin, Growth, Meaning* (New York: Dodd, 1969), p. 168. I am indebted to this book also for its index of journal and lecture passages used in *Nature*.

persuades us that his first person is universal. The "I" could easily be changed to "one." In this sense, Emerson is quite within the limits of his theory of subjectivity. But the part that the theory leaves out, or underplays, is that the first person adds a special tone to the context. Not autobiography, exactly, but still the sense of a personal witness. The fact that the "I" represents himself here as a solitary writer adds to the impression that the author is speaking in his own person. And when we catch Emerson occasionally transposing from journal to essay circumstantial facts which are completely extrinsic to his message— "The charming landscape which I saw this morning" (*W*, I, 8); "Not less excellent . . . was the charm, last evening, of a January sunset" (*W*, I, 17) it becomes clear that he must have consciously striven for such coloring. This impression is reinforced as one notes, now and then, additional cases where an essay passage is made more personal than its original. For instance, the "reminiscences" of the devil's child in "Self-Reliance" (*W*, II, 50), the Orthodox preacher in "Compensation" (*W*, II, 94–95), and the "certain poet" in "The Poet" (W, III, 22) all seem to be fabrications.[3]

The chapter just discussed, then, is not an isolated case. The personal element recurs throughout Emerson's prose, on the average of about eight to ten passages an essay, but sometimes much more often. In addition to *Nature,* perhaps the most significant instances are "Self-Reliance," "Friendship," "Experience," "New England Reformers," "Montaigne," "Worship," "Illusions," *English Traits,* and Emerson's contribution to the *Memoirs of Margaret Fuller Ossoli.* In all these works, the personal element is exploited far more than Emerson's reputation for impersonality would suggest.

This element, however, is not a single entity but a composite

[3] For the first two examples, cf. *JMN,* 48–49, and *JMN,* VII, 182–183, respectively. That the encounter reported in "The Poet" is a fabrication is clear from the previous draft of the passage in the unpublished lecture, "Genius," Houghton Library, Harvard University.

of two rather different first-person forms, each of which has its own effect, though they appear side by side. We have seen them both in action already. One is the voice of private feeling or opinion, as in "What right have I to write on Prudence, whereof I have little?" (*W*, II, 221); "I confess to an extreme tenderness of nature on this point" (*W*, II, 195); "I do not find the religions of men at this moment very creditable to them" (*W*, VI, 207). The speaker in all these cases is aware of himself as separate from his audience, aware of possible disagreements or misunderstandings, which make it necessary for him to confess or pontificate.

The other persona lacks this self-consciousness. It is exemplary or representative; it asks you to take what is said not as opinion but as axiom: for instance, "I am not solitary whilst I read and write"; "I am made immortal by apprehending my possession of incorruptible goods" (*W*, IV, 22); "I am always environed by myself" (*W*, III, 98). This is the "I" which in its more ambitious moments we think of as "transcendental," as in "I can even with a mountainous aspiring say, *I am God*" (*JMN*, V, 336). Its pervasiveness in Emerson's writing, that is, has a partly doctrinal basis, in the idea that the individual can speak for the universal. Emerson himself clarifies the strategy in a rare bit of self-exegesis: "A great man is coming to eat at my house. I do not wish to please him; I wish that he should wish to please me. I will stand here for humanity, and though I would make it kind, I would make it true" (*W*, II, 60). As in the journal passage just quoted, here we have the two voices side by side—the private voice explaining what the exemplary voice proclaims. The latter is the Emersonian counterpart to Whitman's speaker in "Song of Myself." In each case, the author's defense against the charge of egoism is that he is speaking according to the informing spirit, rather than as an individual.

Doubtless it was the exemplary persona for which Emerson was really contending, in his criticism, as the proper use of the subjective. And his preference for what was universal in a man's work, as against what was merely personal, increased as he aged. In *Nature* the poet is pictured as a hero who subdues the world to the service of his imagination (*W*, I, 51–54); in "The Poet" he has become a mere medium (though a glorious one) for recording the poetry which "was all written before time was" (*W*, III, 8).[4] Upon turning from Emerson's criticism to his own style, however, one finds a precisely opposite trend. The voice of private opinion is used more and more; the essays become more anecdotal; the speaker seems increasingly ready to speak off the top of his head; one sees more and more fillers like "Here is a lesson which I brought along with me in boyhood from the Latin School" (*W*, VI, 195).

Perhaps *Representative Men* marks the beginning of this trend, to the extent that it could be subtitled "my favorite people"—though Emerson is still a long way from the cozy, crotchety old scholar that one finds in "Books." One step closer is his contribution to the Ossoli *Memoirs*. Here Emerson goes into a surprising amount of detail about how Margaret affected him—how she impressed him upon first acquaintance, how she reacted to him, and how their friendship developed.[5] Finally, in *English Traits*, the man Emerson emerges for the first time as a unifying figure in his own writing. The main subject is of course the people and things Emerson saw, but we also learn in detail how he fared on his voyage (*W*, V, 25–33), how he got one-up on his English friends (287–288), and how "I made the acquaintance of DeQuincey, of Lord Jeffrey," and a host of other notables (294). On the whole, *English Traits* contains far less personal trivia than most travel books, but for Emerson it is

[4] This is not to imply that the difference between the two positions is absolute (v. Stephen Whicher, *Freedom and Fate* [New York: Barnes and Noble, 1961], pp. 136–140).

[5] Helen McMaster notes perceptively of the *Memoirs* that "the part contributed by Emerson is valuable as a study in self-revelation, scarcely to be matched in his private *Journals*" ("Margaret Fuller as a Literary Critic," *University of Buffalo Studies*, 7 [1928], 38).

quite gossipy. The essays are never quite the same again. His later works mark a return to the general-idea essay format, but with a shade of difference which is well illustrated by the following passages on the same theme, from "Manners" and "Behavior," respectively.

I dislike a low sympathy of each with his neighbor's needs. Must we have a good understanding with one another's palates? as foolish people who have lived long together know when each wants salt or sugar. I pray my companion, if he wishes for bread, to ask me for bread, and if he wishes for sassafras or arsenic, to ask me for them, and not to hold out his plate as if I knew already. [*W*, III, 137–138]

Every hour will show a duty as paramount as that of my whim just now, and yet I will write it,—that there is one topic peremptorily forbidden to all well-bred, to all rational mortals, namely, their distempers. If you have not slept, or if you have slept, or if you have headache, or sciatica, or leprosy, or thunderstroke, I beseech you by all angels to hold your peace, and not pollute the morning, to which all the housemates bring serene and pleasant thoughts, by corruption and groans. [*W*, VI, 196]

In both passages the private voice is speaking; and the burden is much the same—the speaker is requesting us, with some impatience and sarcasm, to maintain a little decorum. But the second tirade exposes the speaker more. The persona in "Manners" knows where he is going; he is confident of his authority over the reader; his language is crisp and peremptory. The other man is a bit fuddled. He is not sure, in the first sentence, whether his thought is worth saying. In the second, he becomes long-winded —the comic hyperbole takes much longer to unwind than in the last sentence of the first excerpt—so that the "beseeching" suggests impotence, where the "I pray" in the other passage comes as a command. Altogether, the Emerson of "Behavior" seems rather like a garrulous, scolding grandfather, who runs on even as he is aware that he may be ignored. Thus the posture is more revealing: in "Manners" we are being given orders by someone whom we don't quite know; in "Behavior" the speaker exposes more than he intended.

Of equal importance with this development is what happens to the exemplary persona during the course of Emerson's career. It is used frequently and to good effect through *Essays, Second Series,* but after that it largely disappears. "In my daily work I incline to repeat my old steps. . . . But some Petrarch or Ariosto, filled with the new wine of his imagination . . . smites and arouses me with his shrill tones, breaks up my whole chain of habits, and I open my eye on my own possibilities" (*W,* II, 312–313). So Emerson writes in "Circles." In "Illusions," a similar thought becomes, "I, who have all my life heard any number of orations and debates, read poems and miscellaneous books, conversed with many geniuses, am still the victim of any new page" (*W,* VI, 316). The *intent* of both passages is precisely the same—to illustrate the power of the poet. But in the second, the "I" is given a biography, so that the statement comes out less like testimonial than soliloquy. Equally common is for the exemplary persona to give way to an impersonal construction. "I can see my own vices without heat in the distant persons of Solomon, Alcibiades, and Catiline" (*W,* II, 5) becomes "every man in moments of deeper thought is apprised that he is repeating the experiences of the people in the streets of Thebes or Byzantium" (*W,* VII, 174).

Neither of these examples should be too surprising. It is understandable that the exemplary persona should wane as the private one increases, since there is an inverse relation between the particular and the cosmic. Again, the more conscious one is of himself as a limited, private person, the less likely he will be to identify with Alcibiades. Both of these shifts, furthermore, are consistent with Emerson's general drift towards conservatism. Just as it became progressively harder for him to affirm the soul's ability to conquer the Not-me, so, in his rhetoric, it became harder for him to represent his persona as universal and more normal for him to take the position of observer.

It would seem, then, that the basis of Emerson's repudiation of false subjectivity in his criticism, namely his sense of individual limitation, was the very thing which led him increasingly into it in his later writing. "Experience," for example, has a more confessional air than "Self-Reliance," even as it takes a lower estate of man, because the speaker admits to a greater disparity between self and Self than he had supposed. The self-revealingness in his memoir of Margaret Fuller, likewise, stems also from his deliberately standing at one remove from the mystery of her character and taking it a tone of benevolent perplexity:

Our moods were very different; and I remember, that, at the very time when I, slow and cold, had come fully to admire her genius, and was congratulating myself on the solid good understanding that subsisted between us, I was surprised with hearing it taxed by her with superficiality and halfness. She stigmatized our friendship as commercial. It seemed, her magnanimity was not met, but I prized her only for the thoughts and pictures she brought me. . . .

But as I did not understand the discontent then,—of course, I cannot now. [*Ossoli*, I, 288]

As this excerpt shows, the later Emerson has a talent for turning his own admissions of "inadequacy" to his own advantage, and with good comic-ironic effect. The unmistakable impression created here is that Margaret's overtures were gauche, while the author was infinitely forbearing. Emerson is even capable of the same urbanity in speaking about so tender a subject as the failure of inspiration: "I envy the abstraction of some scholars I have known, who could sit on a curbstone in State Street, put up their back, and solve their problem. I have more womanly eyes. All the conditions must be right for my success, slight as that is. What untunes is as bad as what cripples or stuns me" (*W*, VIII, 288–289). Here again the apparent claims of envy and self-deprecation in some measure give way to the impression that the scholars in State Street are rather crude and hasty, whereas Emerson is exquisitely sensitive.

The persona in Emerson's later prose—modest but knowing, comparatively anecdotal, witty, and even droll—would
seem to some extent to answer the complaint that the man hid
himself behind his ideas. At the same time, admirers of the early
Emerson will find the later version comparatively tame and eva-
sive. The factors which account for this reaction range far
beyond the one under consideration here, but the use of the personal element does, I think, enter in. First, the exemplary persona, despite its generalized nature, does have a distinctive
character of its own, and a far more vigorous one than the
dominant voice of the later essays. It believes in its own universality; it has a tremendous imaginative reach, as in "I am
God in nature; I am a weed by the wall" (*W*, II, 307), or "I am
always insincere, as always knowing there are other moods" (*W*,
III, 247). It is a hard-headed and uncompromising character.
When it appears it often gives the sense of great emotional stake
and commitment, as in this passage from "Friendship": "I
ought to be equal to every relation. It makes no difference how
many friends I have and what content I can find in conversing
with each, if there be one to whom I am not equal. If I have
shrunk unequal from one contest, the joy I find in all the rest
becomes mean and cowardly" (*W*, II, 200). This would sound
impressive even if Emerson took it all back in the next paragraph (as he partly does). In substance, the passage is only one
half of a rather nebulous equivocation about what to expect
from friendship, but the mode of statement here gives it the
force of a personal credo.

Secondly, the private voice, in early Emerson, reinforces this
tone, and gives it more concreteness. As we saw in comparing
"Manners" and "Behavior," the private voice changes not just
in frequency but in character too. Several times in the early
essays, for example, it appears in the form of what might be
called "disclaimers"—points when Emerson steps unexpectedly
outside his train of thought and makes, momentarily, as if to
throw it all aside. As in *Nature:* "But I own there is something

ungrateful in expanding too curiously the particulars of . . .
idealism" (*W,* I, 59). Or in "History": "Is there somewhat over-
weening in this claim? Then I reject all I have written." (*W,*
II, 39). Or—best known—in "Circles": "Let me remind the
reader that I am only an experimenter . . . , an endless seeker
with no Past at my back" (*W,* II, 318). I find no such audacity
in the later essays. But it is quite characteristic of early Emerson,
and it adds to the impression of a flesh-and-blood author who is
prepared to back up with actions his most intransigent words
about self-reliance.

Thinking partly of passages like the one last quoted, Jonathan
Bishop calls the Emersonian speaker an "experimental self." [6]
That seems to me admirably precise, provided that we recognize an ambivalence in the word "experimental." The usual
speaker in the early essays is experimental chiefly in the nineteenth-century usage of the word as a religious term, meaning
"experiential," having to do with religious experience. For in
the early essays, the speaker is primarily an experiencer of the
holy, ready to take on the protean manifestations of the soul in
nature: to make himself equal to every relation, and to deny
them all too, if the spirit demands. The later speaker, by contrast, is eminently an observer, experimental in the sense of
testing out all possibilities but embracing none. The distinction
is not hard and fast—nothing is in Emerson—but the shift of
emphasis is clear enough. Perhaps it is symbolized by the difference between the first chapter of *Nature* and the introduction
to "Illusions," a rather long-winded account of an expedition to
Mammoth Cave. In the first, nature is expressed as possibility
by one who invites us to participate in his experience; in the
second, possibility is shown as frustration by a talkative racon-
teur. Each tone has its own appeal, but the first is truer to the
original notion of self-reliance, which stresses the potential
authoritativeness of intuition, as opposed to its potential inaccuracy.

[6] Bishop, p. 130.

Altogether, then Emerson's attitude toward subjectivity in writing was fundamentally sound according to his own doctrine. The Emersonian speaker is most himself when his pronouncements come cross also as universal laws. But Emerson might also have noted in his criticism that the enunciation of these laws depends, for full effect, upon the sense of an experiencer. "Though I prize my friends, I cannot afford to talk with them and study their visions, lest I lose my own" (*W*, II, 215). How much more telling this is in the first person than in the third, or the second. Emerson must have known that also, or he would not have used a persona as often as he did, or retained as much circumstantial detail, or fabricated an occasional anecdote. Why then did his criticism short-shrift these devices? Probably for the same reason that he disparaged talent, as opposed to genius, notwithstanding his own attention to craftsmanship and his dislike of its neglect in others: he took the matter for granted. In his method of composition, the private experience was a given; it is where he started; the universal dimension was what he sought to attain. Just as he saw the danger of structural eccentricity in composing by collation of journal snippets, he saw that to base his essays on his daily experience might betray him into solipsism. And on both counts he grew more sensitive as he aged, because on both counts his fears were borne out.

If Thoreau is today considered the most memorable character among the Transcendentalists, it is because his writings evoke most strongly the sense of a man behind the book. Whereas Emerson's impulse was to convert his private perceptions into general maxims, Thoreau remained conscious, even if only as a limitation, "that it is, after all, always the first person that is speaking" (*Wa*, p. 3). Partly, no doubt, because of his less certain position in both social and literary circles, Thoreau was from the start more aware than Emerson of living in a land remote from other men, and more likely to exploit this sense of his separateness in his writing. He establishes himself as a more distinct character in his own books, telling far more about himself and almost never using an exemplary "I."

Given the amount of critical attention Thoreau's writing has recently attracted, one might suppose that his use of the persona had been thoroughly discussed, but in fact it falls in between the two main concerns of modern scholarship. Biographical researchers have primarily been concerned with the man behind the style, not with Thoreau as he appears in his books but as he "really was." Such readers have generally tended to look for significant discrepancies between literary and biographical fact and to create a portrait of Thoreau which will seem different or more complicated from the one his verbal image suggests. Thus we have the "hidden Thoreau," Thoreau the nature mystic, Thoreau the sensitive aesthete, Thoreau the frustrated provincial, and—not to be neglected—Thoreau the (relatively) normal person. Literary analysis of Thoreau's work, on the other hand, have shown but a limited interest in his use of the persona. From Matthiessen to Anderson the main theme of this body of criticism has been Thoreau's literary use of nature, and particularly the symbolism of *Walden*.[7]

To the extent that Thoreau's works are designed to replicate a universe in miniature, this approach is certainly a fruitful one, but it tends to distract attention too much from the hero of

[7] There are exceptions, however, notably Joseph Moldenhauer, "Paradox in *Walden*," in *The Recognition of Henry David Thoreau*, ed. Wendell Glick (Ann Arbor: University of Michigan Press, 1969), pp. 351–365; and Charles Anderson, *The Magic Circle of Walden* (New York: Holt, Rinehart & Winston, 1968), pp. 47–56. Some discussions of the relationship between Thoreau's life and book which I have also found interesting and/or helpful in preparing this chapter are Paul Schwaber, "Thoreau's Development in 'Walden,' " *Criticism*, 5 (1963), 64–77; Thoms Woodson, "The Two Beginnings of *Walden:* A Distinction of Styles," *ELH*, 35 (1968), 440–473; Joel Porte, "Emerson, Thoreau and the Double Consciousness," *New England Quarterly*, 41 (1968), 40–50; and Lauriat Lane, Jr., "*Walden*, the Second Year," *Studies in Romanticism*, 8 (1969), 183–192.

the story. To most readers, I suspect, the metaphorical unity of
Walden is really less interesting than the succession of exploits
of its crusty, resourceful, unpredictable narrator: Thoreau
hoeing beans, Thoreau nearly devouring a woodchuck, Thoreau throwing his limestone paperweight out the window, and
so forth.[8] To take a more direct look than usual at this memorable literary character may help to give perspective both to the
impressive body of formalist criticism on Thoreau and to the
provocative portraits of recent Thoreau biography.

For a basic sense of Thoreau's literary presence, a good place
to start, as in Emerson's case, is the level of cliché. The Lowell-
Holmes caricature of Thoreau as a cranky social dropout who
nibbled his asparagus at the wrong end would not have per-
sisted as it did had it not been suggested beforehand by his
friends and himself to boot. "There was somewhat military in
his nature," Emerson noted in his "eulogy" of Thoreau, "as if
he did not feel himself except in opposition. He wanted a
fallacy to expose, a blunder to pillory, I may say required a
little sense of victory, a roll of the drum, to call his powers into
full exercise. . . . It seemed as if his first instinct on hearing a
proposition was to convert it" (*W*, X, 455–456). Throughout
Emerson's address, Thoreau is portrayed as a "born protestant,"
"hermit and stoic" (452, 456), albeit with an admixture of
humane qualities. Emerson's journal shows that he did not start
to view his friend in such formidable terms until their falling
out in the 1850s,[9] but even in the early years of their relationship he shows a certain wariness about "my brave Henry"
(*JMN*, VII, 201);[10] and what is more, Thoreau himself, both
in his journals and his public prose and verse, continually
talks about himself and the experiment of life in general in

[8] One of the most charming evidences of this response is E. B. White's
homage/parody of Thoreau, "Walden," in *One Man's Meat* (New York:
Harper & Row, 1939).

[9] E.g., *JE*, VIII, 375, 397, 415, 467; IX, 15–16, 34, 45.

[10] E.g., *JMN*, VII, 144, VIII, 118, 375.

terms of battle, heroics, discipline, denial, and a cluster of loosely related terms. Writing is like fighting: "The writer must direct his sentences as carefully and leisurely as the marksman his rifle" (*JT*, III, 231). Friendship is opposition; Alice Ford's unwelcome proposal of marriage comes as an attack: "I really had anticipated no such foe as this," he writes Emerson.[11]

It is interesting that this note of militancy sounds especially strong at the beginning and end of Thoreau's literary career, in his earliest attempts at literary self-description, in the early journals and "The Service," and in his three speeches in behalf of John Brown. As a young man, he constantly depicts life in a romanticized version of the metaphor of Christian warfare, or spiritual struggle: "we do all stand in the front ranks of the battle every moment of our lives" (*JT*, I, 96). The good man is the brave man. His bravery, however, "deals not so much in resolute action, as healthy and assured rest"; his armor is his virtue; his enemy is falsehood; his bravest deed is a perfect life; the music to which he marches is the measure of the soul.[12] In John Brown, Thoreau thought he saw, for the first and only time in his life, a man who embodied those ideals engaging in a literally heroic act, a man who also happened to be a New England farmer, a Puritan in the true sense, an ex-surveyor, a man of "Spartan habits," and "above all" a "Transcendentalist" (*Wr*, IV, 413). If we view Thoreau's career from a sufficient distance, it becomes very tempting to sum it up as a quest for the heroic life realized vicariously in the person of John Brown.[13]

To reduce the Concord saunterer to such a formula would of

[11] *The Correspondence of Henry David Thoreau*, ed. Walter Harding and Carl Bode (New York: New York University Press, 1958), p. 191.

[12] *The Service*, ed. F. B. Sanborn; rpt. in Kenneth W. Cameron, *The Transcendentalists and Minerva* [Hartford: Transcendental Books, 1958]), III, 959 ff.

[13] Other figures and situations also inspired Thoreau to military romanticizing. The motif appears in "Wendell Phillips before the Concord Lyceum" and *A Yankee in Canada*, among other instances.

course be simplistic. After all, his youthful tone of "operatic
heroism," as Perry Miller calls it,[14] dwindles into a leitmotif
after the early 1840s, and the John Brown speeches, along with
several other homilies in the same vein, contrast rather sharply
in tone with his travelogues. Thoreau seems to show himself
more truly when he leaves the Concord jailhouse to go huckle-
berrying, or when he ends his diatribe against "Slavery in
Massachusetts" with the hopeful emblem of the water lily,
purity springing from slime. He did indeed aspire to heroism,
but not of the militant sort, for the most part. His precise brand
of virtù is suggested by a second platitude, the idea that Thoreau acted out Emerson's theories. Neither half of this proposition is strictly true. Emerson actually did more of the acting;
he was more of a public figure, much more of a genuine threat
to the establishment (in, say, the Divinity School Address) than
Thoreau ever was. Thoreau was more of a contemplative than a
man of action, and in his philosophy he was much more than
Emerson's disciple. But the basic relationship is undeniable: as
both men realized, Thoreau's main ambition was to realize the
ideal of self-reliance at all levels, in the context of nature.
What is more to the point of his literary practice, Thoreau
liked to dramatize his experiences as adventures on a grand
scale, as we have seen. Sauntering was like going to the Holy
Land; Fairhaven was his Lake of the Woods, St. Anne's his
Ultima Thule (*JT*, II, 374). Such comparisons, which abound
in Thoreau's writing, are sometimes made tongue-in-cheek and
sometimes not; but Thoreau was always dead serious about the
significance of the quest, if not the quester: "Though man's
life is trivial and handselled, Nature is holy and heroic" (*JT*,
II, 384). This basic reverence for nature and the pursuit of
nature, combined with the compulsion to render an account of
that pursuit, gives Thoreau's writing an epic (sometimes mock-
epic) quality.[15] *Walden* in particular can be read as the hero's

[14] *Consciousness in Concord* (Boston: Houghton Mifflin, 1958), p. 197.
[15] As to Thoreau's compulsion to render account, Ellery Channing reports how "on his return from one of his Maine journeys, he told the story

attempt to realize a heroic life-style. More than in Thoreau's other books, where the persona plays a relatively passive role of mediator and reporter for the most part, the speaker in *Walden* becomes the main character in an action of his own making. Thoreau's masterpiece is thus the closest the Transcendentalists came to creating a major work of prose fiction.

Some of these fictive devices have been pointed out in detail by previous commentators.[16] Thoreau compresses the events of two years into one, using the cycle of the seasons as a plot line. The principle of complementary chapters is another organizing principle. Thoreau ends deliberately on a note of qualified optimism, adding the somewhat ambiguous "Conclusion" to the triumphant "Spring" ending of the first version of the book, but without including such journal passages as:

But why I changed? why I left the woods? I do not think that I can tell. I have often wished myself back. I do not know any better how I ever came to go there. [*JT*, III, 214]

In addition to recounting what he himself did, Thoreau also created a series of dramatic encounters, between "himself" and the railroad, Alec Therien, John Field, "The Poet," and sundry other people and animals—all of which, one might say, also serve to reflect and exemplify the book-long dialogue between speaker and audience.

---

at great length (though it was already written in his note-book) with the important details, not only to his family, but to his friends, with the utmost alacrity and pleasure,—yet as if he were discharging a sacred duty, —then wrote it out carefully in his Journal, and next as carefully corrected it for its issue to the public" (*Thoreau the Poet-Naturalist*, ed. F. B. Sanborn [Boston: Goodspeed, 1902], pp. 9–10). A provocative study of Thoreau's epic qualities is Raymond Adams, "Thoreau's Mock-Heroics and the American Natural History Writers," *Studies in Philology*, 52 (1955), 86–97. Adams concentrates on epic analogies in *Walden* and *A Week;* for a representative discussion of similar tactics in Thoreau's shorter works, see James Morse Marshall, "The Heroic Adventure in 'A Winter Walk,'" *Emerson Society Quarterly*, No. 56 (1968), 16–23.

[16] See note 7 and Chapter 7, note 27, above.

Then there is the characterization of the speaker himself.
Thoreau here follows the practice, also used in *Cape Cod, A
Yankee in Canada,* "Life without Principle," and other works,
of placing the persona solidly before the reader at the outset,
insisting in effect that what follows is a personal experience
rather than an objective report. In fact it is not quite either,
inasmuch as the narrator is "a deliberately created verbal personality" and certain facts are altered to suit Thoreau's conception of his role.[17] The hero of *Walden* could "send home each
nail with a single blow of the hammer" (*Wa,* p. 245) when
lathing; the real Thoreau left hundreds of bent nails in his
cellar hole.[18] The real Thoreau left his cabin for three weeks
the first fall "on account of plastering" (*JT,* I, 387). Like
Thoreau himself, the hero strolled to town "every day or two"
(*Wa,* p. 167), but no mention is made of going home to his
family; his habit is to "make an irruption into some houses"
and "escape to the woods" again (169). The real Thoreau
"bivouacked" at *Walden,* Ellery Channing said;[19] the hero
withdraws "within the great ocean of solitude" (144), with a
"horizon bounded by woods all to myself," as isolated "as on
the prairies" (130). The hero tells us with an air of vatic superiority, that "I left the woods for as good a reason as I went
there" (323); the real Thoreau was unsure why.

It is not necessary to go on multiplying illustrations of a
point which I am scarcely the first to notice: that the reader
of *Walden* sees Thoreau as more resolute, competent, and
pioneering than he actually was. The critics who have said the
best things about this self-stylization, Joseph Moldenhauer and
Charles Anderson, see it in terms of Frye's idea of the archetypal pattern of comic confrontation between the narrator as
eiron and society at large (sometimes including the reader) as

[17] Moldenhauer, p. 356.

[18] Walter Harding, *The Days of Henry Thoreau* (New York: Knopf,
1965), p. 182.

[19] Channing, p. 24.

alazon. As Anderson explains, the *eiron* is "the witty and virtuous character whose actions are directed ultimately toward the establishment of an ideal order; the *alazons* are the hecklers and imposters, those who stand in the way of this fulfilment." [20] Throughout *Walden,* according to this view, the eiron seeks to overcome the alazon by using the resources of wit, invective, shape-shifting and, above all, paradox. The coincidence of his semivictory at the end with the coming of spring fulfils another of Frye's prerequisites for the comic mythos.

The foregoing interpretation is indeed an admirable way of describing the comic and satiric elements in *Walden,* in addition to being a most appealing portrait of Thoreau's persona in an age like ours, which is an age of irony. The interpretation has the limitations, however, of picturing the narrator too exclusively as conducting a rhetorical tour de force and of overemphasizing the comic side of his histrionics.[21] A more satisfactory analogy in some respects, if one is to apply classical terminology to Thoreau, is the epic. Certainly this seems to have been closer to the spirit in which the venture was originally conceived. Ethel Seybold rightly calls it a "Homeric experiment." [22] The published excerpts of the Walden journal, which contain the germ of the book, frequently describe the experience in Homeric terms. Thoreau's house reminds him of "the halls of Olympus" (*JT,* I, 361); it is "my Ithaca" and he himself is "a fellow-wanderer and survivor of Ulysses" (363); the pine tree before his door is "perfect as [Nature's] Grecian art" (363); he is visited by Paphlagonian and Lestrigonian men (365–366); he feels surrounded by Elysian fields (375).

[20] Anderson, p. 54.

[21] In fairness to Anderson and Moldenhauer: their interpretations range far beyond the one point in question, though when they discuss Thoreau's speaker per se they concentrate on the approach described.

[22] *Thoreau: The Quest and the Classics* (New Haven: Yale University Press, 1951), pp. 48–63. See also Raymond Adams, "Thoreau's Mock Heroics."

In *Walden* itself, as in many of Thoreau's excursions, this larger dimension is continually introduced through a more eclectic network of allusions to travel, history, and myth, and through a variety of ritualistic patterns from the seasonal cycle to Thoreau's daily bath.[23] The transfer of the shanty to the shore of Walden is like the removal of the gods of Troy (*Wa*, p. 44); Thoreau moves in on Independence Day (45); the mosquito's hum sounds like "Homer's requiem" (89); he gives his visitors the same welcome that Samoset gave the pilgrims (154); he cuts down his weeds as Achilles slew Hector (161–162). Though such comparisons are often made lightly, the prevailing tone is serious; as Thoreau says of economy, the subject admits of levity but cannot be so dispensed with. *Walden* bears out Emerson's praise of Thoreau's gift for referring "every minute fact to cosmical laws" (*W*, X, 479). That is indeed one of the primary attributes of the narrator. He wants to (1) grasp every fact within his ken and (2) see or sense its eternal significance. The culmination of this process of perception is of course the description of the sand bank in "Spring," which is shown both naturalistically and as it illustrates "the principle of all the operations of Nature" (*Wa*, p. 308).

Our sense of the narrator's "character," however, is perhaps established not so much by such remarkable passages as this, as by the habitual attention of his mind to small things and their implications: refusing the gift of a mat because "it is best to avoid the beginnings of evil" (67), perceiving as he cleans house how "much more interesting most familiar objects look out of doors" (113), measuring the undulation of the ice and speculating about the possible undulation of the earth (293). These details, and many more like them, collectively establish the vitality and penetration of the narrator's inquiring mind.

[23] For discussion of rituals in *Walden*, see Reginald Cook, "Ancient Rites at *Walden*," *Emerson Society Quarterly*, No. 39 (1965), 52–56; rpt. *Twentieth Century Interpretations of Walden*, ed. Richard Ruland (Englewood Cliffs, N.J.: Prentice-Hall, 1968), pp. 93–100.

Some exception to my picture of *Walden*'s hero as engaged in a search for the spiritual significance of natural fact might be taken by those readers who rightly point out that the ratio of observation to speculation increases during the latter part of the book, betokening (or so the argument runs) a spiritual advance on the speaker's part: he becomes somewhat de-intellectualized, more spontaneously immersed in nature.[24] If this view is correct, it is ironic that the latter part of the book (from "House-Warming" on) was largely added after the writing of the journal account and the first version of the book, since both of these are more personal, spontaneous documents than *Walden* itself. The fact is that mere descriptiveness or natural detail in a writer like Thoreau has nothing to do with the depth or immediacy of his personal responses to nature. If anything the relationship is not proportional but inverse. It was precisely during those years when he perfected the art of natural description, the last decade of his life, that Thoreau became acutely conscious of a loss of poetic sensibility and rapport with nature. His inclusion of so much extra descriptive detail in the successive drafts of *Walden* is one sign of this. The reason why it does not seem to bore the majority of serious readers who are not naturalists, in contrast to some of Thoreau's other descriptive writings, is probably that one feels the latent presence of a larger dimension. In "The Pond in Winter," for example, one senses that eventually all Thoreau's soundings are going to produce some meaningful results. As it turns out, his discovery amounts to the fulfilment of the statement of purpose at the end of "Where I Lived and What I Lived for," where the narrator urges the reader to join him in a quest for the "hard bottom" of reality (98). "There is a solid bottom every where," he is able to reaffirm from personal experience in the "Conclusion" (330).

As this last example suggests, however, *Walden* undeniably

[24] See especially Schwaber; and William Reger, "Beyond Metaphor," *Criticism*, 12 (1970), 333–344.

follows a pattern of initiation into nature. Though the narrator does not begin exactly as a tyro, having previously served
in such capacities as "self-appointed inspector of snow storms
and rain storms" (18), one gets the sense of his continually
acquiring new expertise, as he passes through a succession of
new enterprises—"ordeals," one critic calls them, again linking
the process to epic [25]—from house-building to bean-hoeing to
surveying the geography of the area. The fact that he builds his
house in two stages, improves his method of farming the second
year, refines his description of the pond in his second chapter
on the subject, and gives a comprehensive account of the animals and previous settlements in the vicinity after a series of
casual references, all conspire to give the impression of a growing acquaintance with the territory. It would be a mistake to
say that his character actually *changes*. *Walden* is not that kind
of book; the narrative is encased in a rhetorical appeal to the
reader. The narrative part is a validation of the speaker's claims
to authority rather than a report of how a formerly desperate
man found a new life through nature, although the latter interpretation may be inferred from Thoreau's biography.[26] The hero
of *Walden* is no less competent in the business of ground-
breaking than in his perceptions of the coming of spring.

At the same time, the suggestion is planted by such clues as
the memory of being taken to the pond as a four-year-old
(*Wa*, p. 155) that the Walden experience is in some sense the
proper culmination of the life of narrator and author. The
journal version is most explicit; the childhood experience, says

[25] Cook, pp. 94–95.

[26] My thinking on the distinction between narrative and rhetorical approaches has been clarified by Sheldon Sacks, *Fiction and the Shape of
Belief* (Berkeley: University of California Press, 1967), pp. 1–69. Sacks uses
the term "apologue" to distinguish from predominantly plot-oriented
prose fiction that type of narrative whose primary purpose is to demonstrate a theme, e.g., Johnson's *Rassellas*. Sacks categorizes too rigidly for
my taste, but he supplies a useful way of distinguishing between fictions
like *Walden* and the genre of the novel.

Thoreau, "for a long time made the drapery of my dreams. That sweet solitude my spirit seemed so early to require that I might have room to entertain my thronging guests, and that speaking silence that my ears might distinguish the significant sounds. Somehow or other it at once gave the preference to this recess among the pines . . . as if it had found its proper nursery" (*JT*, I, 380–381).

This passage may help explain Thoreau's fondness for talking about his experience in mythological terms, and why his first set of allusions was classical. Walden was a return to his own spiritual origins, to the morning of his life, just as ancient Greece was the morning of his race. For Thoreau and his contemporaries, Greece and Homer *meant* Spartan, spontaneous, childlike, natural, heroic. "That is the glory of Greece," he exclaims in his journal, "that we are reminded of her only when in our best estate, our elysian days, when our senses are young and healthy again" (*JT*, III, 319). Other ancient civilizations lacked this precise appeal. As he put it elsewhere: "The Greeks were boys in the sunshine, the Romans were men in the field, the Persians women in the house, the Egyptians old men in the dark" (*JT*, I, 165).

Thoreau's feeling of personal attachment to Walden, in the book itself, is expressed obliquely for the most part. Passages like the speaker's poetic identification with the pond in "The Ponds" are exceptional. Usually, his devotion is presented in the form of glowing descriptions and lingering attention to detail, as if his love for Walden were too pure to dwell upon what it meant to him. One particular way in which this love affair is dramatized is through personification. On the one hand, Thoreau tends to denigrate society at large as unfit to associate with; on the other, he peoples his natural solitude with imaginary companions. His one moment of loneliness, for example, is relieved by the sense of "sweet and beneficent society in Nature, in the very pattering of the [rain] drops" (*Wa*, p. 132). A more important though less obtrusive way in which the speaker points up his relation to nature is in his manipulations of the sense of time. He interweaves particular perceptions and events with habitual or generalized action, uses both the past and the present tense to describe Walden events, and shifts backwards and forwards chronologically to include events both before and after the fact.

The chapter on "Sounds" is an instructive example. It begins as if to discuss a present philosophical concern: "But while we are confined to books . . . we are in danger of forgetting the language which all things and events speak without metaphor" (111). From here it proceeds to a summary of the speaker's routine at Walden:

I did not read books the first summer; I hoed beans. Nay, I often did better than this. There were times when I could not afford to sacrifice the bloom of the present moment to any work, whether of the head or hands. . . . Sometimes, in a summer morning, having taken my accustomed bath, I sat in my sunny doorway from sunrise till noon, rapt in a revery, amidst the pines and hickories and sumachs, in undisturbed solitude and stillness. [111]

The action described here is habitual—not events which were done only once, but which were repeated over and over until they achieved a timeless quality, which is reinforced by the use of this passage as an exemplum illustrating the general remarks with which the chapter begins. The passage becomes somewhat more specific, though, as it proceeds. As Thoreau continues in this vein, it seems intermittently as if he were describing a particular action taking place now, as in his description of house-cleaning: "It was worth the while to see the sun shine on these things, and hear the free wind blow on them; so much more interesting most familiar objects look out of doors than in the house. A bird sits on the next bough, life-everlasting grows under the table, and blackberry vines run round its legs" (113). It is as if the general truth of what the speaker has observed through long practice entitles him to describe the action as if it is taking place now and always. A paragraph later, he slips entirely into the present tense: "As I sit at my window this summer afternoon, hawks are circling about my clearing; . . . the sedge is bending under the weight of the reed-birds flitting hither and thither; and for the last half hour I have heard the rattle of railroad cars" (114). The next section of the chapter is written mainly in the present—with some significant exceptions which deserve a more extensive analysis than can be given here. After he has dispensed with the railroad, however, the speaker returns to description of habitual action for the rest of the chapter.

Through such manipulations as these, Thoreau manages to describe experience which has taken place in the past, to call attention to its regular or routine aspects, and yet to give the sense that it is simultaneously unique and present. One does not have to read the journal to see that Walden has been for Thoreau the object of a lifetime of contemplation; one is not asked to take the speaker's declaration that he is now "a sojourner in civilized life again" to mean that he is no longer present at the pond. Walden is that which always has given and always will give body to the speaker's thoughts and beliefs—the place he habitually turns for illustration of those thoughts, the place which in large part originally inspired those thoughts.

Knowing this, however, we must be wary of overemphasizing the role of the unifying consciousness on *Walden*. The book is a tribute to the pond rather than the memoirs of Thoreau per se. It is significant that Thoreau revised *Walden* in such a way as to make his own role somewhat less prominent than it is in the original version. Comparing the first and last stages of chapters 1 through 8, which are the most complete in the original, one sees that the most typical alterations are additions in allusions, literary anecdotes, illustrations, and general discussion. For example, ten of the eleven indented quotations from Thoreau's reading were added, while he reduced the amount of his own verse; he greatly lengthened his discussions

of clothing and food, added to the ones on shelter and philanthropy, and devised a new one on furniture. These changes
show the Transcendentalist propensity for universalizing one's
own experience. The immediate and final reasons for writing
the book, according to the speaker, are public and not private:
to satisfy the curiosity of his neighbors and to say something
which may speak to the condition of his audience, especially
"poor students." Of course we know Thoreau's purposes were
more complicated than that and included the desire to make his
life into a poem, as well as more conventional literary ambitions;
but it remains that his experiences at Walden are explicitly
presented for whatever exemplary value they may contain.
Though he does issue several disclaimers to the effect that no
one should follow his example because everybody is different,
when he warms to his subject his confessions turn into an
apologia for his mode of life. A case in point is his remarks on
philanthropy. Thoreau begins at least pseudo-modestly, by
trusting that since there are so many do-gooders, "one at least
may be spared to other and less humane pursuits" (73), but ends
by admonishing his readers, unless they are very rich, to be free
as the cypress (79). Thoreau surely is not trying to get everyone
to build his own cabin in the woods, but he is using his
example as a way of commending self-development and self-
reliance, and particular views of reading, nature, society, solitude, work, and play.

To the extent that life at Walden becomes a test case of
self-reliance, then, the speaker becomes an exemplar rather than
a protagonist and the book as a whole an apologue rather than
an epic, or comedy, or novel, or autobiography, or whatever
other generic analogy one wants to adduce. But Thoreau still
differs from Emerson in the way he represents the Transcendental self as a particular person. Emerson undermines himself when he makes his speaker more personal in his later essays,
whereas Thoreau seems to succeed almost in proportion to the
degree to which his writing becomes personal. Thoreau's per-

sona is more interesting as a man: he is an actor and doer as well as a seer; Emerson's "I" is more interesting as a consciousness or tone of voice.

The range of both speakers seems somewhat inhibited, however, by contrast to those of the personae of the writers we are about to consider. Very and Whitman combine the instinct for self-dramatization with an extreme mystical bent, which enables them to experiment more radically than either Emerson or Thoreau with the literary persona both as character and as cosmic symbol.

12 Transcendental Egoism
in Very and Whitman

Jones Very and Walt Whitman would certainly have disliked
sharing a chapter with each other, even though one of the Very
family's cats, "an enormous grey woolly" animal, was named
after Walt.[1] Very's austere pietism and Whitman's metropolitan
expansiveness do not mix. But they resemble each other in the
lengths to which they go in experimenting poetically with the
idea of the self. Emerson invented the equation which all such
experiments assume, $i = I$ (or self $=$ Self, soul $=$ Soul), but
modestly refrained from exploiting it in his own person, except in a limited way. Thoreau presented a version of himself
as a representative man, but did not press his claims to prophetic status beyond a point. Whitman and Very, however,
both regarded themselves as charismatic figures called to be
spokesmen, through their poetry, of the divine word. Not that
this was the only view they had of themselves: in Very's case,
it lasted with full intensity only for a brief period; in Whitman's, it alternated with more modest images of himself as lyrist
and language experimenter. Partly because of these complicat-
ing factors, one of the salient features of the poetry of both is
a fascinating interplay of voices. Now the poet speaks from
one side of his mind, now from another; now he speaks in his
own person, now he is prophet or God.

[1] William Irving Bartlett, *Jones Very: Emerson's "Brave Saint"* (Durham, N.C.: Duke University Press, 1942), p. 122 (hereafter abbreviated B).

312

In their development of the possibilities of the poetic speaker's role, Very and Whitman suggest Tennyson and Browning's contemporaneous achievements in the dramatic monologue. The four poets share in common the impulse to project themselves imaginatively into as many forms of experience as possible. The main difference is that the Victorians maintain a certain ironic distance from their poetic masks, while Very and Whitman express lyric empathy with theirs. This latter characteristic can be traced back to the idea of cosmic unity-in-diversity discussed in Part III, above. According to this principle, the individual may stand before all the monuments of the past, as Emerson puts it, and tell himself, " 'Under this mask did my Proteus nature hide itself' " (*W*, II, 5). There is no identity in nature or history which the inspired soul may not assume. Hence one finds Emerson in his poetry speaking in the person of Alphonso of Castile, Mithridates, Montaigne, Merlin, Saadi, Brahma, Nature, a nun, and other identities.

But as Jonathan Bishop points out, often Emerson's "projected identities are playful, even capricious." [2] Emerson writes in an increasing awareness of the insufficiency of the individual perception and therefore the inevitability of role-playing when one assumes a given stance or identity. In his later writing, accordingly, the figure of Proteus stands no longer for unity-in-variety but for the elusiveness of truth and the illusoriness of appearances. But while Emerson himself thus becomes something of a Victorian, detaching himself from the identities he momentarily assumes, his successors take their "I" more seriously and attempt to orient their creative worlds around it. Thus the poetic stance of Very and Whitman is truer to the original Transcendentalist idea of self, and it is in their writings rather than in Emerson's or Thoreau's that one sees the literary possibilities of this idea exploited to the fullest.

[2] *Emerson on the Soul* (Cambridge: Harvard University Press, 1964), p. 130.

Jones Very was temperamentally much less urbane and more intense than Emerson, and far less inclined to view man's relation to God and nature in impersonal terms.[3] For Emerson, God was a "sublime It"; Very, as a self-professed Channing Unitarian, experienced God as a father and was therefore much more likely to write about spiritual experience in familiar terms.[4] As for Very's attitude toward nature, he seems to have held that nature is a stumbling block for man in his fallen or unenlightened condition (a notion which Emerson would have rejected as a calvinistic anachronism), but that regenerated man is restored to Adam's position of mastery over the things of nature:[5]

> For he who with his maker walks aright
> Shall be their Lord as Adam was before.[6]

This sentiment seems identical with Emerson's position in *Nature,* but in fact there is an implicit difference. For Very is deeply committed to the idea of man's relationship to nature as a kind of personal mastery (though he would reject this way of putting it), while Emerson sticks rather closely to an impersonal view of this relationship as spirit answering to spirit.

[3] The best discussion of the Very-Emerson relationship is Edwin Gittleman, *Jones Very: The Effective Years* (New York: Columbia University Press, 1967), passim. Earlier treatments are Carlos Baker ("Emerson and Jones Very," *New England Quarterly,* 7 [1934], 90–99) and Yvor Winters "Jones Very and R. W. Emerson: Aspects of New England Mysticism," in *Maule's Curse* [Norfolk, Conn.: New Directions, 1938], pp. 125–146). For critical comments on Very the most helpful works are Gittleman and Bartlett, though more needs to be written.

[4] For Channing's theology on this point, see Robert L. Patterson, *The Philosophy of William Ellery Channing* (New York: Bookman, 1952), pp. 63–92.

[5] Very's idea of nature is discussed in Anthony Herbold, "Nature as Concept and Technique in the Poetry of Jones Very," *New England Quarterly,* 40 (1967), 244–259.

[6] Jones Very, *Poems and Essays,* ed. James Freeman Clarke (Boston: Houghton Mifflin, 1886), p. 91 (hereafter abbreviated C).

Superficially, this claim will seem paradoxical, since Emerson frequently expresses an admiration of the great man who dominates his environment, whereas Very's extreme pietism keeps him from such hero worship. But that same pietism made Very more aware of spiritual grandeur as a personal feeling.

A comparison of the essays each man wrote about Shakespeare will give a better sense of this difference between them. To a large extent they are interested in Shakespeare for the same reasons: his creative range or negative capability, the way in which he seems to illustrate the idea of the creative process as inspired and spontaneous, and the alarming discrepancy between his genius and his "immorality." The difference is that Emerson is content to know nothing of the "real" Shakespeare. He sees it rather as a virtue that "Shakespeare is the only biographer of Shakespeare" (*W*, IV, 208). Very, on the other hand, is intensely concerned with reconstructing and typing Shakespeare's mind. Even his negative capability Very insists on seeing as a mark of personality: "In this activity of mind, then, in this childlike superiority to the objects by which it was attracted, we find Shakespeare," although Very goes on to concede that "this condition of mind might perhaps be designated as an impersonal one, so strongly is it always possessed by that which is before it, as to seem for the time to have no other individuality" (C, 38–39).

The standard by which Very finally judges Shakespeare is also instructive. He sees Shakespeare as a spiritual child, as representing "that primaeval state of innocence from which we have fallen" (39), but by the same token having the moral limitations of a child. In the sense that a child's mind spontaneously and amorally reflects everything in its environment, Shakespeare represented both the pure and the impure. "In Wordsworth and Milton, on the contrary, we see the struggle of the child to become the perfect man in Christ Jesus" (46), which is a higher aspiration. This intermediate stage of development is something of a declension also, in that the poet loses his power of total empathy and becomes trapped in self-consciousness, "but when the war of self which these and other bards have so nobly maintained shall have ceased, and the will of the Father shall be done on earth as it is in heaven . . . then shall the poet again find himself speaking with many tongues. . . . Each soul shall show in its varied action the beauty and grandeur of Nature; and shall live forever a teacher of the words it hears from the Father" (47). This formulation contains an interesting and characteristic mixture of the ideas of self-abasement and self-glorification. Very had more of both than Emerson, insisting on the necessity both of absolute submission to the will of God and the infallible authority of him who had done so, as Very believed himself to have done.

Very's peculiar brand of intoxication with the self comes out most strikingly in the last of three unpublished letters "To the Unborn," evidently designed as a preface to the 1839 *Essays and Poems* but rejected by Emerson.[7] These letters (on "Birth," "Prayer," and "Miracles"), called "Epistles" after St. Paul but written in the style of St. John, are in effect three mini-sermons on redemption. Each of his three subjects Very interprets metaphorically in the transcendental or post-Unitarian manner discussed in Chapter 4, above. Real birth is the new birth; true prayer is the total action of the reborn man; the true miracle is the unity of the self with God which awaits the reborn. To dramatize this last idea, Very abruptly drops his role as preacher and speaks with the tone of God himself. Just as Jesus told his hearers "I am the Resurrection and the Life," Very says:

So say *I* to you to whom as the unborn I stand in a similar position. *I* am your Resurrection and life, believe in *Me* that speaks and you though unborn, shall be born. . . . "He that receives

[7] Gittleman, pp. 326, 336. The three epistles, as well as other unpublished writings of Very are in an appendix to Harry Lawrence Jones, "Symbolism in the Mystical Poetry of Jones Very," Ph.D. dissertation, Catholic University of America, 1967. Original manuscripts are in Wellesley College Library, Wellesley, Massachusetts.

you," said he to his disciples, receives *Me* and he that receives *Me* receives Him that sent *Me*. These *Me*'s and *I*'s are the *I*'s and *Me*'s of the persons in the different worlds or states of which I have spoken and which because they are used are confounded by you and you are led to think that the person who speaks is like yourself.

For the moment his unborn audience will fail to recognize the speaker's divine authority, but they surely will perceive it when they themselves are reborn to his estate: "Now you *make* me what I am to you; then you shall see me as *I am;* for you yourself will be made like unto me." [8] What Very has done is to push the Unitarian view of Jesus as representative man, as extended by the Transcendentalist idea of God's potential immanence, to its uttermost limits, and dare to assert that he too has His authority. This Very had been doing in the flesh for some time, to the confusion of his friends and neighbors; "The Epistle on Miracles" simply represents his nearest attempt to explain himself deliberately in writing.

Like Emerson, Very was a poet before he was a mystic, and his vision necessarily expressed itself more compellingly (at least to an unbeliever) in poetry than in prose, because it was profoundly metaphorical. When he looked at nature he saw emblems; when he looked at the self he saw God; when he looked at society he saw parables of spiritual death, or the potential for regeneration. It is no wonder that when his talent dwindled he became an occasional poet, because it seems always to have been instinctive with him to convert the external stimuli of the moment into tropes: biblical phrases, natural images, popular sayings, and the like.[9] But his most distinctive hallmark as a poet is the reinterpretation of scripture and the creation from the perspective of one who has merged with God.

On one level, the speaker travels at will through a circuit of identities. He assumes the role of any or all the prophets: John the Baptist, Isaiah, Noah, Moses. Adamlike he dreams:

[8] Jones, pp. 158, 160.
[9] See for example, C, pp. 248, 259, 265, 269, 272.

> I saw the spot where our first parents dwelt,
> And yet it wore to me no face of change.   [C, 76]

The speaker here is not the old Adam but the new man in Christ, himself a kind of deity. Elsewhere he becomes God the Father:

> I am the First and Last declare my Word
>
> There is no voice but it is born of Me
> I am there is no other God beside
> Before Me all that live shall bow the knee   [B, 173]
>
> Wouldst thou behold my features cleanse thy heart   [B, 172]

or Christ the son:

> This is the rock where I my church will build   [B, 154]
>
> Come then partake the feast for you prepared
> I have come down to bid you welcome there   [B, 156]
>
> Why come you out to me with clubs and staves,
> That you on every side have fenced me so   [B, 197]

or the Holy Ghost:

> I come the rushing wind that shook the place
> Where those once sat who spake with tongues of fire
> Oer thee to shed the freely given grace   [B, 163]

It is surely no accident that all but one of the seven sonnets just excerpted remained unpublished during the nineteenth century, as they are among the most daring Very ever wrote.[10] Most of the fifty or so in which the speaker impersonates the

---

[10] A less extravagant reading is possible, however, if one thinks of these poems as addresses from above to the humble poet. Gittleman, pp. 312 ff, takes this approach, and it is supported by the line following the excerpt last quoted: "And bid them speak while I thy verse inspire." The fact remains that the poems are written as if spoken by the deity.

deity do not live up to their extraordinary beginnings and become vitiated by filler lines and overuse of biblical phraseology,
but in conception they are a remarkable group of poems. (In-
cidentally, Emerson was wrong in insisting that the Spirit be
grammatical. These poems read best without punctuation, just
as Bartlett printed them from the manuscript.)

Very's prophetic speaker does not always ventriloquize
through the mask of deity or biblical figure, by any means. He
has an identity of his own, albeit of a somewhat generalized sort.
One often finds him having millennial visions of "The White
Horse" (C, 108), "The New Jerusalem" (B, 199), the resurrection of the dead (C, 107), and the like; decrying "The Unfaith-
ful Servants" (C, 120), "The Glutton" (C, 129), and other ava-
tars of sin, even to the point of presenting himself as the
scourge of God (B, 168); comforting the people with words of
encouragement (C, 101); petitioning God to use him as an instrument (C, 103) or aid mankind Himself (C, 120). The most
interesting poems of this group, because they come closest to
breaking the Old Testament stereotype Very usually sets for
himself, are those in which the prophet attempts to establish
some sort of human relationship with his audience in addition
to his official capacity.

> My brother, I am hungry,—give me food
> Such as my Father gives me at his board;
> He has for many years been to thee good,
> Thou canst a morsel then to me afford;
>
> . . . . .
> I ask the love the Father has for thee,
> That thou should'st give it back to me again;
> This shall my soul from pangs of hunger free,
> And on my parched spirit fall like rain;
> Then thou wilt prove a brother to my need,
> For in the cross of Christ thou too canst bleed.   [C, 94]

A poem like this makes it clear that the speaker has a personal
investment in his mission. He is not merely re-enacting the role
of Jesus for the benefit of the unborn (although the poem is

based on the gospel maxim that what is done for the least of
mankind is done for the Lord); he himself, the poem suggests,
has a genuine need for reciprocal communication with the
neighbor he has come to admonish, as indeed Very seems to
have had in life.

Frequently, indeed, the speaker does not appear at all in the
role of deity or prophet, but as a single person, in a variety of
mental states. The most common of these is a prayerful attitude, either of praise or petition to God. In "The Prisoner," he
is "a slave to mine own choice" (C, 141), who looks forward
only distantly to his transfiguration; in "The Presence" (C, 83)
he is the solitary worshiper suffused with a sense of the protect-
ing spirit. In another group of poems he presents himself as a
soul seeking to emulate Christ, anticipating a similar crucifixion, either for his own salvation ("That I through Christ the
victory may win" [B, 199]) or, less often, to serve as a model for
the rest of mankind. Another series of poems portrays the
speaker in contemplation of or active relationship with nature;
in still another, smaller group, but more interesting as far as
self-dramatization is concerned, the speaker pictures himself in
an unstable relationship with others. Significantly, the speaker
does not attain intimacy with those to whom he speaks to the
extent that he does with God and nature. Usually he sees himself as rejected or rejecting; at most, he issues us invitations to
come with him on a "ramble" through the fields (C, 119) or to
join him in his spiritual quest (C, 137).

The alternation between divine, prophetic, and human
voices from poem to poem to have a provocatively disorienting
effect on the reader, who sometimes becomes unsure just who is
speaking. For example, the poems in which God apparently
speaks have been interpreted as dialogues between God and
the poet, rather than as monologues in which the poet assumes
the role of God. On the other hand, a poem which seems to
begin on the human level may turn out to be a divine communication.

> I knock, but knock in vain; there is no call
> Comes from within to bid Me enter there.   [C, 146]

Not until one comes to "Me" is it clear that this is the complaint of Christ, not of the frustrated soul. Again, the opening of "To-Day"—"I live but in the present; where art thou?"— might seem to express the confusion of a superficial mind, but it turns out to be the call of the omnipresent God to the distant sinner, who is "far away and canst not hear" (C, 173). In a few poems, it is finally impossible to resolve the speaker into a single voice. "Terror," for example, seems to begin with a prophet or onlooker witnessing the apocalypse:

> There is no safety! fear has seized the proud;
> The swift run to and fro but cannot fly;
> Within the streets I hear no voices loud,
> They pass along with low, continuous cry.

Yet at the end of the poem God himself emerges as the speaker:

> Repent! why do ye still uncertain stand,
> The kingdom of My Son is nigh at hand.   [C, 110]

But to take God as the speaker throughout would be to deny the note of awe in the tone at the outset.

Very's use of the speaker is altogether sufficiently versatile and subtle as to suggest conscious manipulation of the persona for literary effect, despite his professed disinterest in revision and his friends' claims that he "composed without a thought of literary form." [11] For example, his two haunting sonnets on the I-Thou relationship, "Yourself" and "Thy Neighbor," read like exercises in wit. Here is the latter:

> I am thy other self; what thou wilt be
> When thou art I, the one thou seest now;
> In finding thy true self thou wilt find me,
> The springing blade where now thou dost but plow;

[11] William P. Andrews, Introduction, *Poems by Jones Very* (Boston: Houghton Mifflin, 1883), p. vii.

I am thy neighbor, a new house I've built
Which thou as yet hast never entered in;
I come to call thee; come in when thou wilt,
The feast is always waiting to begin;
Thou shouldst love me, as thou dost thyself;
For I am but another self beside;
To show thee him thou lov'st in better health,
What thou wouldst be when thou to him hast died;
Then visit me, I make thee many a call;
Nor live I near to thee alone but all.   [C, 117]

Who speaks here? Is it the local prophet, or Christ speaking
through him, or does one first of all imagine one's own neighbor speaking, and then see Christ standing behind him? The
three types of persona intermingle here; the invitation is essentially to the heavenly banquet, but it has overtones of a New
England dinner. In a faint way, Very anticipates Whitman in
saying that you will find "myself" everywhere: in the speaker-
countryman who has come to call on the farmer-reader; in
yourself; even under your bootsoles, in "the springing blade."
These multiple suggestions show Very's considerable gift for
swerving away from outright didacticism in the direction of
wit and emotional complexity. Not that the content of the
poem is hard to grasp; it all opens up quite easily as soon as
one perceives the biblical associations of self-neighbor-Jesus.
The complexity consists in the dislocating effect of having a
poet, or rather a poem, express this idea in its own person; and
in the laconic way in which it is expressed, so that the poem
seems halfway in between an exhortation and a riddle.

In view of what we know about Very's moral seriousness, it
is quite unlikely that he intended to exploit the element of
ambiguity in his personae for its own sake, or that he published
his poetry under the pseudonym of "I" for literary effect. When
Sophia Peabody and her brother expressed "our enjoyment of
his sonnets," for example, Very replied that "unless we thought
them beautiful because we also heard the Voice in reading

them, they would be of no avail." [12] The strong probability is
that Very was simply intoxicated by the mystical relationships
between self and Self, oneself and oneSelf, so that in certain
situations it was instinctive for him to elaborate these relationships poetically in what seems to us a very modern way. In any
case, Very almost never fails to create an arresting effect when
he writes of the disparity between the temporal and spiritual
aspects of the I and the I-Thou relation, particularly in those
poems which begin with an ostensibly mundane speaker making what would be an outrageous statement if interpreted in
less prophetic terms:

> 'Tis to yourself I speak; you cannot know
> Him whom I call in speaking such an one,
> For thou beneath the earth liest buried low,
> Which he alone as living walks upon   [C, 116]

> I have no Brother,—they who meet me now
> Offer a hand with their own wills defiled   [C, 87]

> I weigh out my love with nicest care   [B, 198]

> I do not need thy food, but thou dost mine   [B, 201]

As these lines suggest, Very's specialty as a poet, just as in life,
was self-righteousness, justified (in his mind, anyhow) by the
spiritual authority with which he felt himself to be invested.
The incongruity of a Harvard tutor speaking as the Messiah
was a practical stumbling block to his mission among the Revs.
Charles Wentworth Upham, John Brazer and other Salem
worthies, but a poetic asset in the long run.

In his excellent study of Very, Edwin Gittleman suggests that
Very intended in the late 1830s to publish his poems in an arrangement whereby the spiritual cycle outlined in the "Letters
to the Unborn" "would be unfolded in systematic fashion," but

---

[12] Quoted in Rose Hawthorne Lathrop, *Memories of Hawthorne* (Boston: Houghton Mifflin, 1897), p. 24.

that Emerson refused. However well thought out Very's scheme actually was, Gittleman is quite right in pointing out that his holy sonnets, "if arranged without regard for the exact order of composition . . . comprise the only form of epic Very thought still possible in the modern world," a drama of unfolding spiritual consciousness.[13] Very's friend W. P. Andrews, in his edition of Very's poetry, tried to give a sense of what this order might be by organizing the selections into a sequence of categories: "The Call," "The New Birth," "The Message," "Nature," "Song and Praise," and "The Beginning and the End." In Gittleman's somewhat more apocalyptic interpretation, the hypothetical sequence would have been "organized in terms of the promise of the Second Coming," depicting "the prelude and consequences of this manifestation of deity on earth." [14] These conjectures attest to the impression of organic relationship among the poems of this period which anyone who reads them all through is bound to feel. They do invite rearrangement into a sequence, and the sequential approach seems also to be validated by Very's prophecies of imminent millennium during his period of illumination. Actually to reorder Very's work in this manner, however, is to impute to him a degree of calculation which clashes somewhat with one's impression of him as a visionary, and to make his work seem more contrived and less spontaneous. Very may well have had such a poetic plan in mind, judging from his attempts to evangelize his friends. But had he carried it out, his poetry would seem a great deal less transcendental than it now is. The rich interplay of voices and moods which the very confusion of Clarke's edition (bad as it is) preserves would have been regularized and toned down, and the prophetic voice would begin to sound like that of the pitchman.

Carried to its logical conclusion, the idea of the self as God means that the "I" is capable of the same infinite variety as

[13] Gittleman, pp. 336, 312.   [14] Andrews; Gittleman, p. 323.

nature and that every thought and act is (at least potentially) significant and holy. The Transcendentalists realized this, but the thought disturbed them. The Transcendentalist ministers from the conservative Clarke to the radical Parker shrank back from cosmic egoism; Emerson and Thoreau and even Very entertained it only under strict conditions. They made a sharp distinction between higher and lower natures and reserved their praise for the first; even Emerson's tributes to instinct and Thoreau's to wildness are based on the assumption that the primitive impulse is essentially chaste. Secondly, though the Transcendentalists delighted in the multiplicity of nature, in seeing Spirit manifest itself in a variety of forms, they preferred to think of the self as essentially unitary, not liable to change, except in the direction of greater purification. Thus Emerson comes very close in "Experience" to the modern idea of a disintegrated self when he describes personality as a succession of moods, but he regards this successiveness as a tragic thing and falls back with relief upon the vision of a Spirit which underlies all such change. The personae of Thoreau and Very have even less tolerance for the chaos of experience. One sees them constantly trying to order their perceptions and maintain their integrity against a hostile and philistine audience. "They were all in some particulars much alike," Whitman said of Emerson, Alcott, and Thoreau. "They all had the same manner—a sort of aloofness: as though they meant me to see they were willing to come only so far: that coming an inch beyond that would mean disaster to us all." [15]

Whitman ventured further. His earlier poetry in particular exploits the literary potential of the Transcendental "I" to its fullest. He was prepared to celebrate a much greater range of human experience, the body as well as the soul; his gift for empathy was unsurpassable; and he was enough of an exhibitionist to make "myself" a much more dominant figure than

[15] Quoted in Horace Traubel, *With Walt Whitman in Camden* (New York: Mitchell Kennerley, 1914), III, 403.

the New Englanders would have thought to do. One may draw
dim analogues between Whitman, Thoreau, Very and the idea
of a romantic epic of the self; but only in *Leaves of Grass* (and
particularly "Song of Myself") is anything like the feeling of
epic scope really attained.[16] In this respect, Whitman's book
stands as both the culmination and the epitaph of literary
Transcendentalism. A short review of both these aspects here
may also serve as a postscript to this survey of the Transcendentalist persona.

Whether or not Emerson was really Whitman's "master," as
he averred in 1856, is an unanswerable question.[17] In any event,
Whitman can be seen as extending all the creative possibilities
of the self which have been discussed so far: its socially representative or democratic aspects; its double or multiple nature;
and the mysteriousness of that multiplicity. "Myself" in Whitman's poetry becomes, by turns, a demiurge or Oversoul; an
epitome of America; a proteus of vicarious shapes and moods;
the book or poem itself; and lastly, you, the reader.[18] As a re-

[16] For application of the idea of the epic to *Leaves of Grass*, see Roy
Harvey Pearce, *The Continuity of American Poetry* (Princeton: Princeton
University Press, 1961), pp. 69–83; Charles R. Metzger, "Walt Whitman's
Philosophical Epic," *Walt Whitman Review*, 15 (1969), 91–96; and James
E. Miller Jr., *A Critical Guide to Leaves of Grass* (Chicago: Chicago Uni-
versity Press, 1966), pp. 256–261.

[17] The definitive discussion of this point I take to be Roger Asselineau,
The Evolution of Walt Whitman: The Creation of a Personality, trans.
Asselineau and R. P. Adams (Cambridge: Harvard University Press), pp.
52–55.

[18] Helpful previous discussions of Whitman's use of personae are
Philip Y. Coleman, "Walt Whitman's Ambiguities of 'I,' " in *Studies in
American Literature in Honor of Robert Dunn Faner,* ed. Robert Partlow
(Carbondale, Ill.: Southern Illinois University Press, 1969), pp. 40–59;
Donna L. Henseler, "The Voice of the Grass Poem 'I': Whitman's 'Song of
Myself,' " *Walt Whitman Review*, 15 (1969), 26–32; and Bruce R. Mc-
Elderry, Jr., "Personae in Whitman (1855–1860)," *American Transcen-
dental Quarterly*, No. 12 (1971), 25–32. My thinking on this subject has
also been clarified by Edwin Haviland Miller, *Walt Whitman's Poetry:*

sult, Whitman's speaker comes much closer than the Transcendentalists' to encompassing the whole range of human consciousness. He is not ashamed of his body; he is not so insistent on identifying himself with his best moments; he is willing, indeed eager, to show himself loafing, dreaming, doubting, hungering, masturbating, dying. When it comes to presenting the self in its universal aspects, moreover, Whitman does not merely assert this claim in theory, but has the persona act it out, by imaginatively projecting into a series of identities or situations. In this way, the principle of spiritual metamorphosis which the Transcendentalists celebrated in the activity of nature is at last fully dramatized on the human level. Thus Whitman's speaker seems more pretentious than the Transcendentalists', but the element of moral elitism is largely absent. Unlike the speakers of Very and Thoreau, who think of themselves in the company of heroes and prophets, Whitman's persona embraces even the "cotton-field drudge" and the "cleaner of privies" (l. 1003). One feels too that the speaker genuinely wants this experience of human contact, despite his weakness for factitious rhetoric.

Whitman's powers of empathy also give him a greater awareness of the ineffability and unpredictableness of the self: "I hear and behold God in every object, yet understand God not in the least" (l. 1281). And why should he bother to figure it all out? "To elaborate is no avail, learn'd and unlearn'd feel that it is so" (l. 47). The grass may be any number of things, and all is well; the speaker may be in New York one moment and Montana the next, without knowing how he got there, and it is well; he is "amused, complacent, compassionating, idle, unitary" (l. 76) or "hankering, gross, mystical nude" (l. 389) and it is no real contradiction, but rather a sign of healthful fecundity.

A Psychological Journey (Boston: Houghton Mifflin, 1968), though I dissent from some of Miller's psychological interpretations; and Howard J. Waskow, *Whitman: Explorations in Form* (Chicago: University of Chicago Press, 1966).

As we saw in Chapter 6, however, the willingness to incorporate the whole of experience into one's self-conception involves certain risks, to which Whitman repeatedly succumbs. Indiscriminateness, for example. When Whitman's empathy becomes fatuous or mechanical, one cries out with D. H. Lawrence, "Oh Walter, Walter, what have you done with it? What have you done with yourself? With your own individual self? For it sounds as if it had all leaked out of you, leaked into the universe." [19] The problem is not merely one of self-parody. Whitman was also aware of the potentially self-destructive consequences of empathy. It can lead to sickness and shame and even death. In "Song of Myself" the speaker is betrayed by his sense of touch into temporary insanity; in "Calamus" he is the victim of his adhesiveness; in "The Wound-Dresser" he presents himself as haunted, years later, by the young men he attended. Partly, perhaps, because of the spiritual exhaustion of being torn apart so many times, Whitman's gift for empathy dwindled as he aged, as was also true of the Transcendentalists. Beginning even before 1860, a sense of weariness begins to creep in. The poet assumes less often the role of multiform cosmic force, more often the role of observer. If he dons a mask in a given poem, it tends to be a single and limited one: Columbus, a dying redwood tree, a November bough, a sailor embarking on the ultimate voyage. Death is of course the linking motif in these examples, just as the thought of death pervades all of Whitman's good poetry and much of the rest after "Out of the Cradle." In different ways, he turns the fact of death to his advantage: by welcoming it, like a mother or protector, by celebrating the persistence of spirit, by looking forward to the continuance of his fame, by seeing himself as a martyr to the Civil War. All the same, *Leaves of Grass* is ultimately a tragic poem compared to the work of Emerson, Thoreau, and Very, in the sense that

[19] *Studies in Classic American Literature* (New York: Doubleday, 1951), p. 177.

one sees the godlike hero decline and die. Whitman winds up like the "lonely old grubber" of Allen Ginsberg's poem,

> Soon to be lost for aye in the darkness—loth, O so loth to depart!
> Garrulous to the very last.
> ["After the Supper and Talk," ll. 11–12]

In such passages as this, *Leaves of Grass* undercuts the Transcendental conception of self and epitomizes in its unfolding the demise of American romanticism. Youthful bravado inevitably sinks into humility as the godlike element in the self shrinks into the more respectable "spark of the divine" and the Oversoul acquires a gray beard and a throne.

To the extent that Whitman and the Transcendentalists took seriously the cosmic dimension of their self-dramatizations they ring less true to a modern reader than, say, Ellery Channing's poetic expressions of self-doubt, or the lyrics of Emily Dickinson. Channing was saved from Transcendental naiveté, as we have seen, by the awareness that he was personally unsuited for the self-reliant life. Dickinson, a parallel product of the heritage of self-examination, also shows what seems to us an authenticity —at the cost of her happiness—in being unable either to accept or break away from an inherited religious framework (Orthodox, in her case, not liberal). Like Whitman, she is an experimenter in the first-person, moving through a series of masks: the little girl, the queen, the rebel, the sufferer, the corpse. But one senses in her, as in Channing, a greater awareness of the pose as pose. She admits defeat too often; her moods do not complement each other in the same way as Whitman's—partly because her poems are not run together into sustained visions, as Whitman's often are. She is, in short, more appealingly baffled and lost, in the modern way.

Nevertheless, the Transcendentalist conception of self, however delusory, did lead to some important poetic discoveries,

which through Whitman's example have had a permanent impact on literary history. First, it provided a way of talking about
the unity-in-diversity of American society. Second and more
far-reaching, it made possible the introduction of stream-of-
consciousness techniques into western poetry. The psychological
basis of this technique is precisely the Transcendentalist idea
of self, stripped of its metaphysical basis: the idea that identity
consists of one's perceptions of the universe moment by moment. As Emerson saw, if one denies the assumption of a unifying, essential soul, personality disintegrates into chaos. Because
they rested on this assumption, the Transcendentalists put their
trust in the "method" of moment-by-moment inspiration as the
most "natural" path for the intellect. Whitman's contribution,
in turn, was to use this method more uncompromisingly than
the Transcendentalists did except in their journals, and to
apply it more directly to the self, and thereby to indulge and
express the chaos of experience that Emerson came to fear. The
somewhat ironic result was that Transcendentalism's last and
greatest celebration of the heroic possibilities of the self also
foreshadowed those twentieth-century classics in which the self
is shown as finally baffled and lost in its labyrinths of perception. Today the self remains in the same divided condition that
Emerson describes at the beginning of "The American Scholar."

Index

Individual works (listed under authors) are indexed only if they are discussed as literary entities. Works mentioned only in passing or used merely to furnish passages for illustration are not listed.

LITERARY TRANSCENDENTALISM
Style and Vision in the American Renaissance
LAWRENCE BUELL

"Unquestionably the most significant volume on Thoreau, Emersor and their circle to appear since F. O. Matthiessen's monument; *American Renaissance.* . . . It is obviously based on a tremendousl wide reading in and about the field, yet it is much more than a rehas of things already said. It is a breath of fresh air in the scholarshi of the period, a book that does not hesitate to demolish accepte theories and evaluations and propose new ones. Not all of Buell' ideas may win acceptance, but they should result in a much neede rethinking about the achievements of one of our greatest groups o American writers. An essential book for all who are concerned wit them."—*Library Journal*

"In his introduction Professor Buell states that it is his purpose 'through a combination of intellectual history, critical explication and genre study' to 'outline the nature and evolution of th Transcendentalists' characteristic literary aims and approaches, an the ways in which these express the authors' underlying principle or vision." The book accomplishes this purpose admirably and con tributes significantly to our understanding of the literary productior of the Transcendental movement."—*Virginia Quarterly Review*

CORNELL PAPERBACKS ⊕ CORNELL UNIVERSITY PRESS